Collins · *do brilliantly!*



# Revision**Guide**

# GCSE Modern World History

Christopher Culpin

Series editor: Jayne de Courcy

# Contents and Revision Planner

# About This Book

Exams are about much more than just repeating memorised facts, so we have planned this book to make your revision as **active and effective** as possible.

**How?**

- by breaking down the content into manageable chunks (Revision Sessions)
- by testing your understanding at every step of the way (Check Yourself Questions)
- by providing extra information to help you aim for the very top grade (A* Extras)
- by listing the most likely exam questions for each topic (Question Spotters)
- by giving you invaluable advice from an examiner about exam technique (Exam Practice)

REVISION SESSION 1

## Revision Sessions

- Each topic is divided into a number of **short revision sessions**. You should be able to read through each of these in no more than 30 minutes. That is the maximum amount of time that you should spend on revising without taking a short break.
- Ask your teacher for a copy of your own exam board's **GCSE Modern World History syllabus**. Tick off on the Contents list each of the revision sessions that you need to cover. It will probably be most of them.

## ? Check Yourself Questions

- At the end of each revision session there are some Check Yourself Questions. By trying these questions, you will immediately find out whether you have understood and remembered what you have read in the revision session. **Answers** are at the back of the book, along with **extra hints and guidance**.
- If you manage to answer all the Check Yourself Questions for a session correctly, then you can confidently tick off this topic in the box provided in the Contents list. If not, you will need to tick the 'Revise again' box to remind yourself to return to this topic later in your revision programme.

## A* EXTRA

These boxes occur in each revision session. They contain some **extra information** which you need to learn if you are aiming to achieve the **very top grade**. If you have the chance to use these additional facts in your exam, it could make the difference between a good answer and a very good answer.

## QUESTION SPOTTER

It's obviously important to revise the facts, but it's also helpful to know how you might need to **use** this information in your exam.

The author, who has been involved with examining for many years, knows the sorts of questions that are most likely to be asked on each topic. He has put together these Question Spotter boxes so that they can help you to **focus your revision.**

# Exam Practice

- This unit gives you **invaluable guidance on how to answer exam questions well**.
- The author focuses on **each type of exam question** you are likely to meet and gives you detailed guidance on **how to tackle it successfully**.
- There are also a number of **typical exam questions** for you to try answering. Model answers are given at the back of the book for you to check your own answers against. There are also examiner's hints highlighting **how to achieve full marks**.
- Working through this chapter will give you an excellent grounding in exam technique. If you feel you want further exam practice, look at ***Exam Practice GCSE Modern World History***, also published by Collins Educational.

# About your Modern World History course

## Skills required

Modern World History specifications require students to do these three things:

**1 'Recall, select, organise and deploy knowledge of the specifications content...**

In other words, you have to know the History you have studied very well. You have to be able to remember names, dates, places and people, and use this knowledge in the right place in the exam. This book is written as clearly as possible, with lots of maps, pictures and questions to help you get to grips with the facts you must know.

**... to communicate it through description, analysis and explanation of: the events, people, changes and issues studied; the key features and characteristics of the periods, societies or situations studied.'**

You will be asked to explain why things happened the way they did, what the results were, how successful someone or something was, or why they failed. This book emphasises these sorts of questions. There are lists of causes and results, and clear summaries of key events.

**2 'Use historical sources critically in their context, by comprehending, analysing, evaluating and interpreting them;**

**3 Comprehend, analyse and evaluate, in relation to the historical context, how and why historical events, people, situations and changes have been interpreted and represented in different ways.'**

The *Check Yourself* section in each revision session and the exam questions, answers and *examiner's comments* in the exam practice unit will teach you how to deal with all the types of historical sources used in exams: photographs, cartoons, letters, reports, statistics, newspapers and the writings of other historians. They show you how interpretations and representations are built up and evaluated.

**4.9** *Nazi poster of an 'ideal' family*

## Topics covered

All three English GCSE Exam Boards and the Welsh Joint Examinations Council offer Modern World History specifications. All their exams ask students to do the things listed above. The only differences are in the topics you can study with each. Some boards have every topic as an option. Check with your teacher which topics you need to study and revise and then mark them off on the Contents list. This book covers all the popular topics from all of these specifications. It is unlikely that you need to use all of the book, although you may find it useful to read the topics you are not taking in order to pick up further hints on technique.

## Exam papers

GCSE History exams usually consist of two papers of about 1 to 2 hours each. There is normally a choice of questions. All students take both papers and answer from the same questions. Marks for both papers, plus coursework marks, are added together and an overall grade awarded. There are no tiered papers or limited grade papers as in most other subjects.

REVISION SESSION 1

# The Liberal Reforms

## What was Britain like in 1906?

Britain in 1906 was the richest country in the world. Income from **land**, **industry** and **trade** across the enormous British Empire brought some people huge wealth.

- You were rich with an income of over £10,000 a year (see 1.1).
- The **middle classes** lived comfortably on about £400–£600 a year.
- **Lower middle-class families** – people like teachers, police sergeants, clerks and shopkeepers – could live in a well-furnished house and hire a servant on an income of £150 a year.
- Most people earned far less than this. In fact, large numbers of people lived in **poverty** (see 1.2).

**QUESTION SPOTTER**

Typical exam questions on this topic:

- How many differences can you find between the lives of the two families in 1.1 and 1.2?
- How reliable are these two sources for finding out about the lifestyles of people in Britain in the early 20th century?
- How useful are 1.1 and 1.2 for finding out about Britain in 1906?

**1.1** *Tea on the lawn at Knole House, Sevenoaks, Kent, in 1899*

**1.2** *Poor family in London*

## A* EXTRA

The figures in 1.3 give more precise statistical detail on the class divisions, supporting an answer to a question on Britain in 1906.

**1.3** *Class divisions in Britain in 1906*

| Class | Income | Percentage of population | Percentage of national wealth |
|---|---|---|---|
| Upper | At least £100,000 a year | 1% | 55% |
| Upper middle | At least £400 a year | 2% | 25% |
| Lower middle | At least £150 a year | 8% | 11% |
| Skilled working | At least £1.50 a week | 56% | 8% |
| Casual workers and farm labourers | Less than £1.05 a week | 33% | 1% |

## QUESTION SPOTTER

Typical exam questions on this topic:

- Who was worried about poverty in Britain before the First World War?
- What kinds of people were in poverty?
- Why is the work of Seebohm Rowntree important?

## Why were the Liberal Reforms passed?

The Liberal government of 1906–1914 passed a whole series of laws to deal with poverty. Why did they do this?

### INFORMATION

In the first few years of the 20th century, a number of surveys were published which provided accurate information about poverty; they also caused some surprises.

- **Charles Booth** was a wealthy shipowner who could not believe there were so many in poverty. He began a huge survey of London's poor, published 1889–1903. He found that as many as 38% of London's population lived on wages which were only just enough to live on, or less.
- **Seebohm Rowntree** carried out a big survey of working-class people in York, published in 1901. He realised it was important to decide what level of income was just enough to live on. Anyone below that could be defined as **'living in poverty'**. Rowntree calculated that a family of 2 parents and 3 children needed £1.08½p a week to live on. By his definition, 10% of the population were in poverty all the time, and another 18% were below it for some part of their lives.
- Rowntree described a life cycle in which working people hovered just above or below the **poverty line** all their lives:

  1 A young unmarried person could live on the low wages.

  2 Marrying and having children pushed people below the poverty line.

  3 When the children began to earn, and left home, the worker passed above the poverty line, but could easily fall below it if illness or unemployment struck.

  4 Finally, old age brought poverty through loss of work or lower earnings.

### DEFENCE

- Government and army leaders were worried about the physical health of the British people. When recruiting for the **Boer War** (1899–1902), they were shocked to find that so many young men were too small, too under-nourished or too ill to be taken into the army. How was Britain going to fight its wars in future?

### THE LABOUR PARTY

- The Liberal Party had always tried to speak for working men (women did not have the vote). There were several working-class **Members of Parliament (MPs)**, by 1906, who were in the Liberal Party. They called themselves 'Lib-Labs'.
- In 1900, some **socialists** and some trade unions set up a new party to represent working people. It took the name 'The Labour Party' and won 29 seats in the 1906 election.
  1. They were keen to point out that the other parties had failed to deal with poverty.
  2. They called for higher wages and higher taxes on the rich to help the poor.
- Although the Labour Party was only a small group in 1906, the Liberals were worried that they would lose working-class votes to them. They had to show that they cared about poverty too.

### OTHER COUNTRIES

- Other countries (e.g. Germany) had set up schemes to help people in poverty and workers on low wages a few years earlier.

## THE LIBERAL REFORMS

CHILDREN

1906 School meals started

1907 School medicals introduced, to check on the health of all children

1908 'The Children's Charter': children in trouble with the law to be treated differently from adults.

OLD PEOPLE

1909 Old age pensions introduced for people over 70: 25p a week for a single person, 37.5p for a married couple, if their income was less than 60p a week.

WORKING PEOPLE

1908 Compulsory 8-hour day for miners

1909 Trade Boards Act controlled working hours for 'sweated labour'
Labour Exchanges

1910 Shop Act guaranteed half a day a week off for shop workers.

**Illness and unemployment: The National Insurance Act, 1911**

PART 1: ILLNESS
Every worker earning under £160 a year (about £3 a week) paid 4 pence (2p) into an insurance scheme. The employer added 3 pence ($1^1/_2$p) and the government 2 pence (1p). The worker thus got 9 pence worth of insurance for 4 pence.
If he was too ill to work, he could claim 50p a week for up to 26 weeks.

PART 2: UNEMPLOYMENT
This scheme covered 2 million workers in 7 trades. The worker, the employer and the government each paid 2 pence (1p) a week. If he became unemployed, the worker could claim 35p a week for up to 15 weeks.

### A* EXTRA

Many Liberals believed people had to choose whether to look after themselves, and not rely on the government to help them. But younger Liberals, like David Lloyd George and Winston Churchill, pointed out that the poor people revealed by Booth and Rowntree had no freedom to choose. The government should intervene to provide basic security in their lives.

## How successful were the Liberal Reforms?

- The amounts paid to workers in times of illness or unemployment were small, not enough to live on. The system was intended only as a 'lifebelt'.
- The payments lasted only for 26 weeks (illness) or 15 weeks (unemployment). It was a 'lifebelt' to help a man over a temporary crisis. After the First World War, especially in the 1930s, **economic depression** hit many British industries. Some men were out of work for years on end and the system the Liberals set up was no help to them.
- The system was based on the stereotype of a working man being the breadwinner for his family. This was the norm at this time, but became less typical as the 20th century went on.
- There was no health coverage for other members of the family, who were often in dire need of better health care, especially women.
- Despite the four criticisms above, it was a start. Many people call it the beginning of the **'welfare state'**.

## Passing the National Insurance Act

- The schemes outlined above would obviously cost a lot of money. In 1909 Lloyd George, the Chancellor of the Exchequer, prepared what he called a **'war budget'** – to wage war on poverty. The rich would have to pay more tax.
- The **House of Lords**, where the **Conservatives** had a majority, threw out the budget. So the Liberals called an election, which they won. The new king, George V, threatened to create lots more new Liberal peers if the House of Lords threw out the budget again. This time they backed down and the budget was agreed. The 1911 National Insurance Act was eventually passed.
- The Liberals passed a **Parliament Act in 1911** so that this long crisis could not happen again:
  1. The House of Lords could not reject a money bill, such as the budget.
  2. The House of Lords could only delay a bill for 2 years, not reject it completely.
  3. MPs should be paid a salary, so ordinary people could afford to enter Parliament.

### QUESTION SPOTTER

Typical exam questions on this topic:

- How did the Liberal Government of 1906 try to help: children? old people? unemployed?
- The Liberal schemes for the unemployed set up in 1911 were insurance schemes. How did they work?
- What were the benefits and drawbacks of the 1911 Liberal Reforms?

## CHECK YOURSELF QUESTIONS

**Q1** Why was Rowntree's survey of poverty important?

**Q2** What help did the Liberal Reforms offer to sick, or unemployed, workers?

*Answers are on page 182.*

REVISION SESSION 2

# Women and the vote

## What was life like for women in Victorian Britain?

There was great inequality of the sexes in 19th-century Britain. Men were held to be superior in all things.

- It was widely believed that women were too weak to study and incapable of making decisions.
- **Women did not vote** or receive more than a basic education.
- They were not expected to work, and many jobs were completely closed to them.
- A woman's property and possessions became her husband's on marriage.
- The ideal Victorian woman stayed at home and raised children. This was not possible for working-class women, who often had to work, but in worse jobs for less pay.

By the late 19th century, things were changing.

- Some women were getting educated and qualifying for important jobs:
  1. **Elizabeth Garrett Anderson** became the first woman doctor in Britain in 1865.
  2. There were women teachers (though paid less: £127 a year for a man, £92 a year for a woman).
- **New inventions**, like the telephone and the typewriter, brought **new job opportunities.**
- Women gained the right to vote in local elections.

But the big decision – the right to vote in Parliamentary elections – was still closed to women.

## Who were the suffragists and suffragettes?

Women had been campaigning for the right to vote (**suffrage**) from the 1860s. They could see that all their other concerns – fairer divorce laws, better health care for women, a fair education, etc. – depended on having a say in the place where big decisions were made, in Parliament. This meant trying to persuade the all-male Parliament to change – not an easy task.

In 1897 the **National Union of Women's Suffrage Societies (NUWSS)** was set up.

- It was led by **Millicent Fawcett**, Elizabeth Garrett Anderson's sister.
- They were called **suffragists** and campaigned peacefully: writing letters, holding meetings, lobbying MPs (see 1.4).
- Members were mainly middle class, except in Lancashire, where women cotton-mill workers had a long tradition of independence.

■ There were over 500 branches of the NUWSS, all over the country.

But still women did not have the vote.

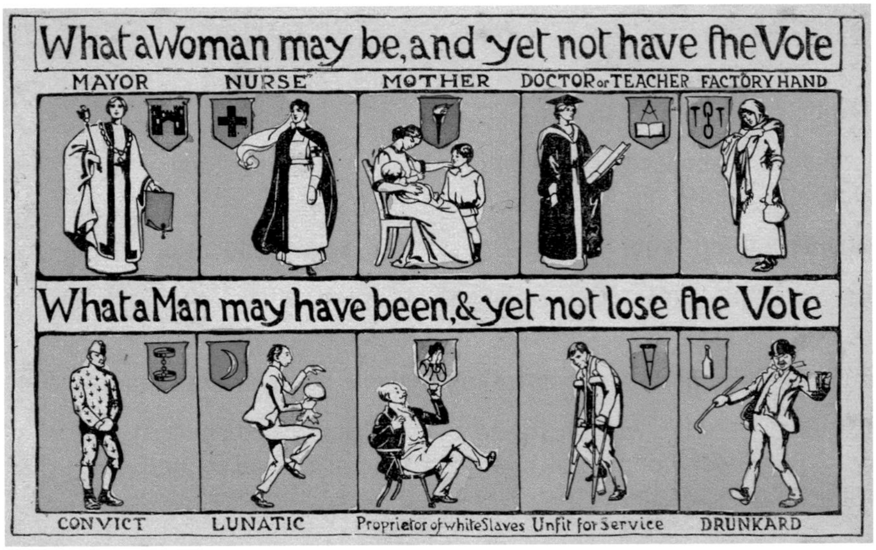


**1.4** *Suffragist propaganda postcard*

Frustrated with the lack of success of the NUWSS, **Mrs Emmeline Pankhurst** and her daughters, Christabel and Sylvia, formed the **Women's Social and Political Union (WSPU)** in 1903. They were called **suffragettes.** They thought the NUWSS was too polite. As the NUWSS was being ignored, the WSPU decided to step up the campaign. They used more forceful tactics, including breaking the law.

**1.5** *Mrs Pankhurst being arrested after chaining herself to the railings outside Buckingham Palace, February 1907.*

Suffragettes deliberately tried to get arrested and thus gain publicity (see 1.5). They:

- interrupted political meetings, shouting 'Votes for women!'
- smashed shop windows
- set light to letter-boxes
- dug up (all-male) golf courses
- one suffragette, Emily Davison, tried to grab the king's horse at the Derby in 1913 and was killed.

When they were arrested, suffragettes went on hunger strike. Prison officials fed them by force – a very painful and disgusting experience. In 1913, the government passed the **'Cat and Mouse' Act**, which allowed them to release suffragettes who were ill and then re-arrest them when they had recovered.

## Why was there opposition to votes for women?

The suffragettes received lots more publicity than the suffragists, but still women did not get the vote. Why?

- Some men still had old, 19th-century attitudes that women were not fit to vote.
- Some men were angered, rather than won over, by the suffragettes' violence.
- Only about **60% of men had the vote** at this time – less well-off men could not vote.
- The Labour Party and some Liberals wanted *all* men, as well as *all* women, to have the right to vote.

**Asquith, the leader of the Liberals**, was unwilling to give the vote to women on the same restricted basis as men. He feared, probably rightly, that better-off women would be likely to vote for the Conservatives. Nor was he prepared to consider votes for all men and all women. He was also unwilling to be seen to give in to violence.

So, as war broke out in August 1914, women still did not have the vote.

**QUESTION SPOTTER**

Typical exam questions on this topic:
- Why did the suffragettes campaign in the way they did?
- Why did the suffragettes fail to win votes for women before 1914?

## Check Yourself Questions

**Q1** What kinds of actions did suffragettes carry out?

**Q2** What was the difference between the suffragists and the suffragettes?

*Answers are on page 182.*

REVISION SESSION 1

# The beginning of the war

> **A* EXTRA**
>
> Most people expected a short, fast-moving war because the last big European war – the Franco-Prussian war – had been over in a few months in 1870. A better lesson would have been the drawn-out slugging of the American Civil War (1861–65) or the Boer War in South Africa (1899–1902).

## A long war

- Although the First World War actually broke out on **3 August 1914**, the people of Europe had been expecting a war for some time. Young men rushed to join their country's armies.
- Everyone expected a short war – all over by Christmas. In fact, the war went on for over four years (**August 1914 to November 1918**). Nine million people were killed. Many millions more were mutilated, orphaned or widowed.
- The heaviest fighting and the greatest loss of life was on the **Western Front**. The Western Front is the line of trenches marked on 2.2. It is called Western because there was also an Eastern Front (see p14). Soldiers dug into trenches on the Western Front from which they hardly moved for most of the war.

## What was the Schlieffen Plan?

- Germany had enemies on two sides: Russia to the east and France to the west. It looked as though Germany would have to split its powerful army into two.

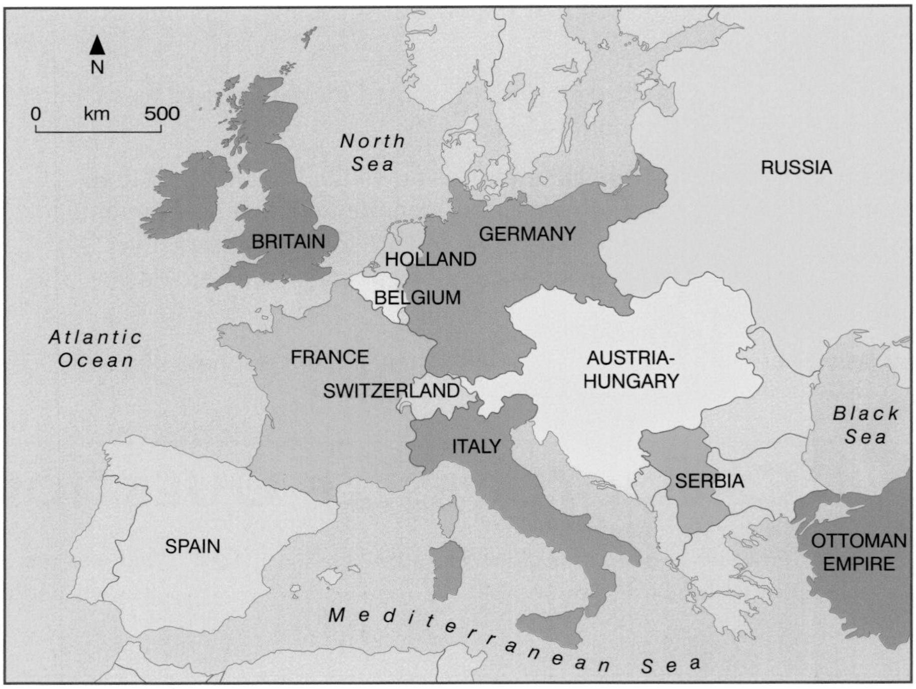


**2.1** *Europe in 1914*

- **General von Schlieffen** had worked out a plan (see the two large arrows on 2.2) – as long ago as 1895. He calculated that:

1 As Russia was a vast country and poorly organised, the Russian army would be slow to get ready.

2 The German left would keep the main French army busy.

3 The German right would invade France through Belgium, cross northern France and capture Paris (the French capital). France would be defeated in 3 weeks and the German forces would then turn to deal with Russia.

4 Britain had a treaty dating back to 1839 promising to protect Belgium. Germany guessed that Britain would not fight for 'a scrap of paper' – as the **Kaiser** called it.

## Why did the Schlieffen Plan fail?

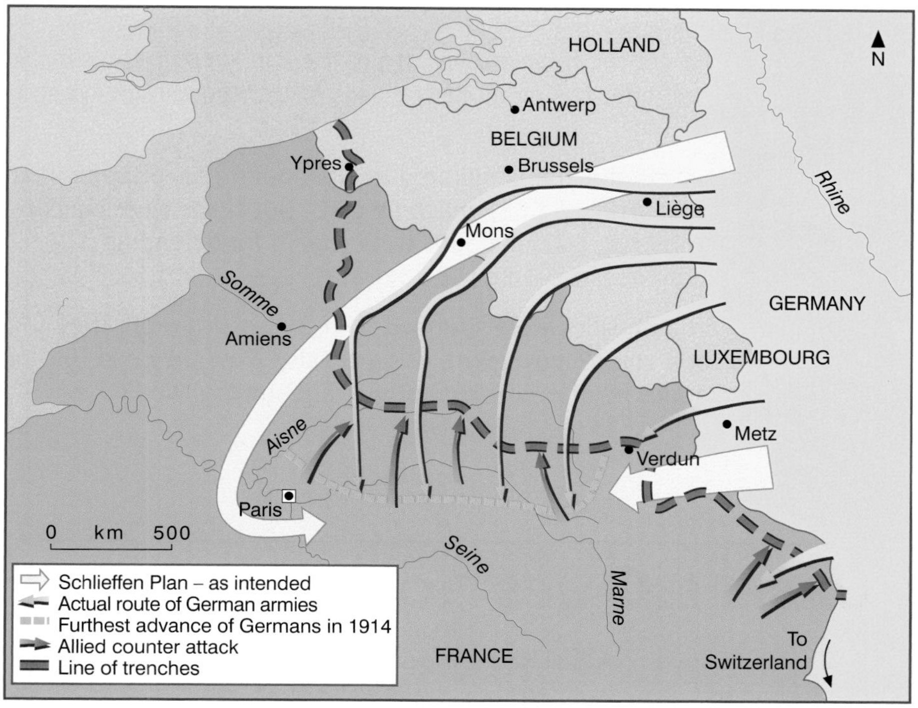


**2.2** *The beginning of the war*

- The Belgians put up more resistance than Germany had expected.
- Britain declared war on 4 August and sent the **British Expeditionary Force (BEF)** to France – 160,000 men. Although the Kaiser called them 'a contemptibly little army', the BEF helped to force the German advance to the east of Paris, not the west as planned (2.2).
- Russia was quicker than expected at mobilising its army and invaded Germany. 10,000 German soldiers had to be moved to the **Eastern Front**.
- After 3 weeks the German army was only 30 km from Paris, but exhausted.

**QUESTION SPOTTER**

Typical exam questions on this topic:
- What problems faced Germany in waging a war in 1914?
- How was the Schlieffen Plan supposed to help Germany wage a successful war in 1914?
- What happened when the Schlieffen Plan was put into action in 1914 which prevented it from succeeding?

## A* EXTRA

The war would last as long as the balance between the two sides remained roughly equal. Once the Schlieffen Plan had failed, Germany was likely to lose, but it would take years for a real imbalance between the two sides to develop.

## The Battle of the Marne and the trenches

- In early September 1914, the Allies **counter-attacked** at the Battle of the Marne. The taxis of Paris were used to take men into battle.
- The Germans were forced to retreat to a line of trenches they had prepared. Some more German soldiers were rushed north to try to get round the **Allied lines**. By November both sides had dug into trenches which stretched from the sea to the Swiss Alps (2.2).

## Why wasn't it a short war?

- Both sides had enormous armies, but they were more or less evenly balanced. By 1918 the total numbers of millions of men **mobilised** in the war was:

| Central Powers | | Allies | |
|---|---|---|---|
| Germany | 13.25 | France | 8.2 |
| Austria-Hungary | 9 | Russia | 13 |
| | | Britain & British Empire | 9.5 |

- Both sides could get the huge armies into battle and keep up the supply of food and ammunition using modern means of transport: railways and motor lorries.
- Both sides had factories that could produce vast quantities of **powerful modern weapons**: artillery, rifles, machine guns. But these were mainly defensive weapons, e.g. machine guns were superb for defending a position, but could not be used on the move.
- The generals on both sides were stumped by this new situation. They had planned for a war of movement, using cavalry. Now they had to develop new tactics for this new kind of warfare and this would take time.

## QUESTION SPOTTER

Typical exam questions on this topic:

- Why was the First World War a trench war?
- What impact would a trench war have on the economies of those countries taking part?

## CHECK YOURSELF QUESTIONS

**Q1** Use the two big arrows on 2.2 to describe how the Schlieffen Plan was supposed to work.

**Q2** Use the smaller arrows on 2.2 to describe what actually happened in 1914.

**Q3** Use these points to explain why the war was not 'over by Christmas':

**a** balance of forces
**b** weapons
**c** tactics.

*Answers are on page 182.*

# Stalemate on the Western Front

By the end of 1914, the two huge armies were dug into their trenches on the Western Front. There they stayed until mid-1918. Neither side could break through the enemy lines. There was **stalemate**. (Stalemate is a word used in chess. It means that whatever move either player makes, no one can win.)

## Why were the armies in trenches?

The way a war is fought is decided by the weapons used.

- **Machine-guns** were operated by two men. They could fire eight bullets a second and so were deadly in breaking up attacks. You were only safe below ground level in a **trench** (see 2.4).
- **Artillery** (heavy guns) pounded enemy lines, destroying the landscape (see 2.3). Even in a trench you were not safe against a direct hit from the enemy artillery.

**2.3** *Landscape on the Western Front in 1917*

## What was life in the trenches like?

Diagram 2.4 shows what a trench was like. Soldiers took turns in the trenches, spending three or four days in the front line. This was followed by time in support trenches, or resting.

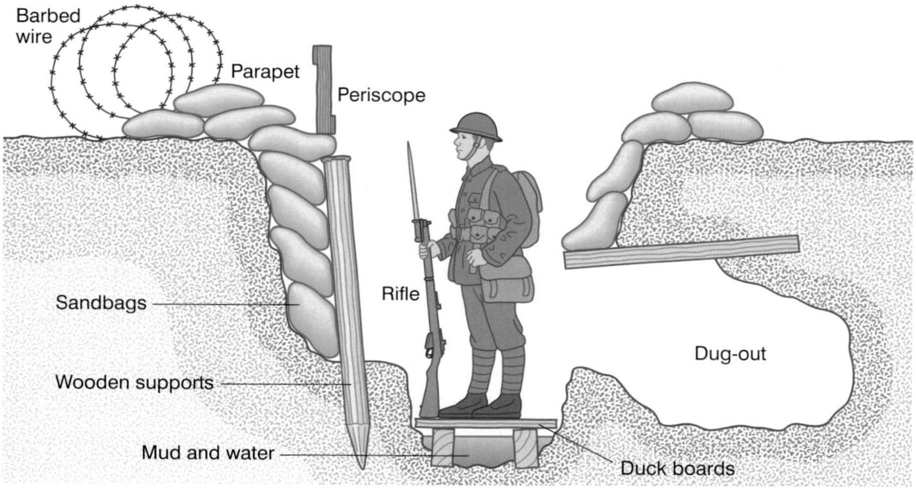


**2.4** *Diagram of a trench*

## QUESTION SPOTTER

Typical exam questions on this topic:

- Why was there stalemate on the Western Front from late 1914 to 1918?
- Describe how an attack was launched from the trenches.
- Describe the living conditions of soldiers in trenches on the Western Front.

- In the trenches, the day started just before dawn - the most likely time for an enemy attack. Soldiers waited, with their rifles at the ready.
- After this, some soldiers stayed on sentry duty while others rested or did necessary jobs. There was another alert at dusk. At night, patrols would go out over **'No Man's Land'** to spy on the enemy.
- Apart from the dangers from artillery fire and **'snipers'** (marksmen who shot at anything that moved), life in the trenches was unpleasant in other ways:

1 They were infested with lice and rats.

2 They were often waterlogged.

3 This led to a painful condition called 'trench feet', in which the soldiers' permanently wet feet swelled and rotted.

4 Food was poor and monotonous.

## How did they try to break the stalemate?

The generals tried to find ways of breaking through the enemy lines.

### ARTILLERY BARRAGES

- Generals on both sides thought that if they could get enough heavy guns, with enough shells, to keep pounding the enemy line, they would break through. Pressure was put on industry at home. Factories frantically turned to making guns and shells. However, as the British discovered at the Battle of the Somme in 1916 (see p13), it was possible for the enemy to survive tremendous **artillery barrages** by digging into deep bunkers. The barrage also gave the enemy warning that an attack was about to start.

### OVER THE TOP

- For most of the war the only way the generals thought enemy trenches could be captured was by sending men **'over the top'** (of the trench). They would run towards the enemy lines, carrying rifle, kit and trench-digging tools. Generals hoped that enough men would survive the charge to capture the enemy trench. As you would expect, this led to millions of deaths. As the war went on, the generals demanded more and more men to send 'over the top'.

### GAS

- Both sides used **poison gas** – chlorine or mustard gas – to try to clear the enemy line of soldiers. It was not very reliable so it was not used much in the later part of the war.

### TANKS

- These are an example of the new technology invented during the war. **Tanks** were first used in 1916. They carried machine-guns and moved across No Man's Land at around 2 miles per hour, crushing barbed wire barriers. However, many broke down. As they were also used on their own, they were not very successful. They were also unable to cross trenches. Only late in the war did commanders learn how to use them more successfully.

## A* EXTRA

If soldiers advancing across 'No Man's Land' did capture part of an enemy trench, it was very hard to follow up. The group of successful soldiers had to be supplied, across 'No Man's Land'. Enemy counter-attacks were often successful. This helps to explain the small territorial gains made from enormous attacks involving huge loss of life.

## What were the key battles?

### VERDUN, 1916

- Verdun was a massive French fortress (see 2.5). The German commander calculated that if he attacked Verdun, the French would defend it to the last man. If two Frenchmen died for every German, France would be 'bled white' and have to surrender.

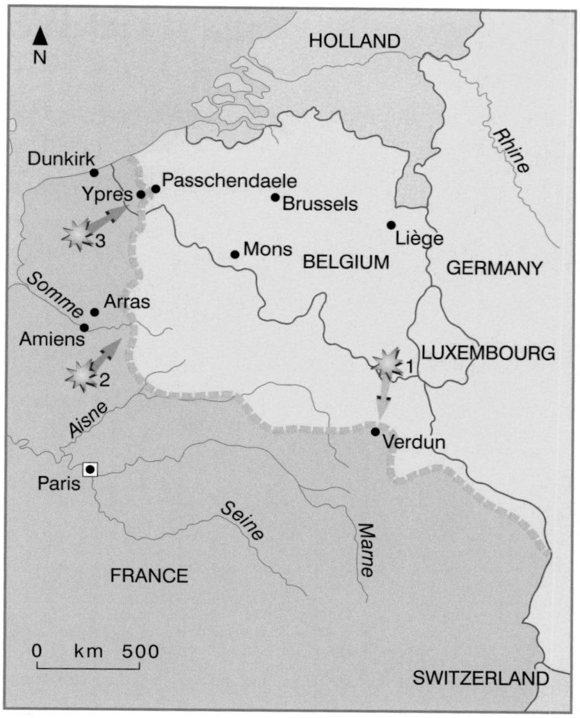


- The German bombardment of Verdun began in February 1916. There were enormous casualties on both sides: 315,000 French and 282,000 German soldiers had been killed by August 1916.

### THE SOMME, 1916

- To relieve pressure on Verdun, the French asked the British commander, **General Douglas Haig**, to attack further along the line. Haig ordered a 5-day artillery barrage then, on 1 July 1916, 100,000 British soldiers went 'over the top'. They had been told they would be able to walk into the German trenches.
- Unfortunately, the massive barrage had failed to destroy the German barbed wire entanglements. Haig was also unaware that the Germans had spent the last two years digging deep bunkers, so they survived the artillery barrage.
- By the end of the first day, 20,000 British soldiers were dead. By the time the battle was called off, in November, total British losses were 420,000 and German losses were almost as many.

### YPRES (often called Passchendaele), 1917

- This battle began in July but the British advance was soon bogged down in deep mud. By November, 265,000 men had been killed for a gain of about 8 kilometres.

### QUESTION SPOTTER

Typical exam questions on this topic:

- How did the commanders try to break out of the stalemate conditions on the Western Front?
- Explain why the British attacked along the Somme in June 1916 and why casualties were so great.

## CHECK YOURSELF QUESTIONS

**Q1** Describe three things you can see in the photograph 2.3.

**Q2** Compare the photograph 2.3 and the diagram of a trench (2.4). Which do you think tells you more about life on the Western Front?

**Q3** Make a list of all the reasons you can think of to explain why the numbers killed on the Western Front were so large.

*Answers are on page 183.*

# The war on other fronts

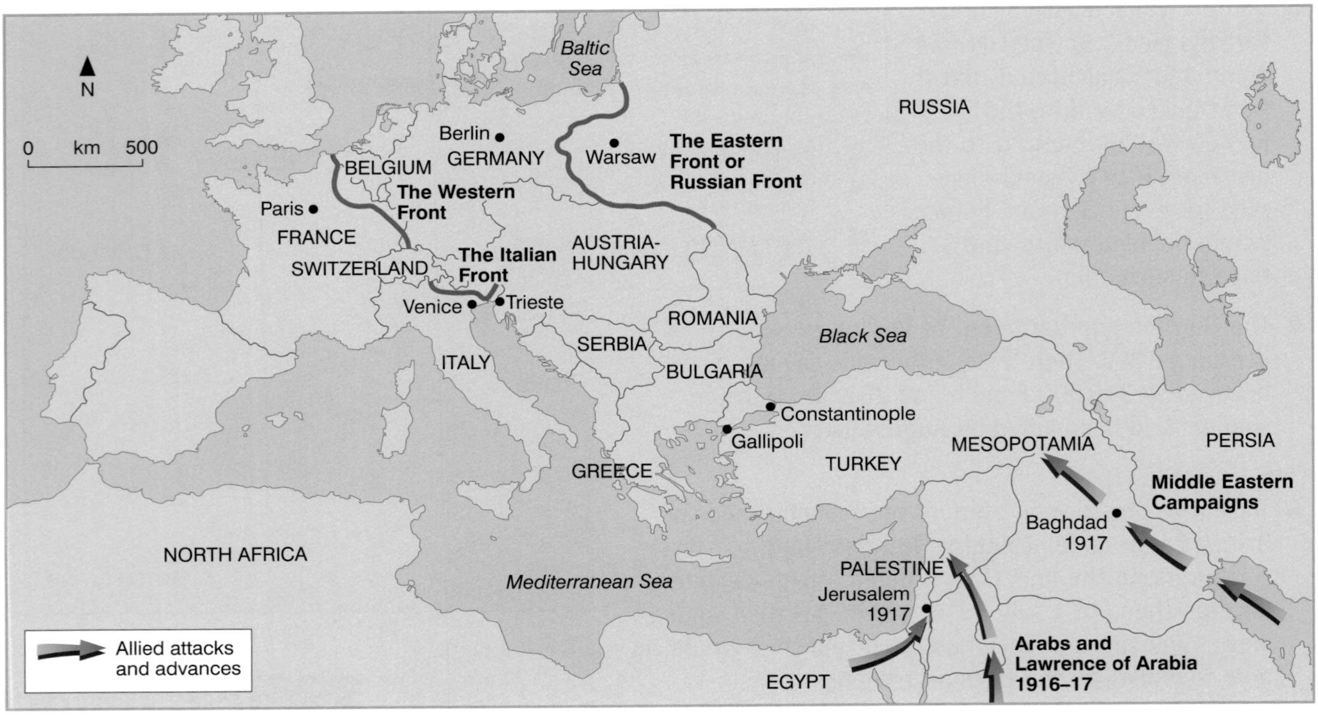


**2.6** *Other fronts in the First World War*

## The Eastern Front

- The Russian army attacked Germany in August 1914 but was soon defeated in two battles - **Tannenberg** and the **Masurian Lakes** – in September.
- The war on the Eastern Front never became bogged down in trenches. There was more space and more movement.
- Russia did quite well against **Austria-Hungary**. Germany sent troops to support its ally and drove the Russians back. Russian soldiers fought bravely, but suffered from poor leadership, poor transport, lack of weapons and few medical supplies.
- There was a successful Russian counter-attack in 1916, the **Brusilov offensive**.
- However, this could not be followed up. By winter 1916, German forces were 400 kilometres into Russia. Russia was in chaos and the country on the verge of revolution.
- As long as Russia was fighting on the Eastern Front, Germany had to fight on two fronts at once and could not put all its efforts into the Western Front.

### GALLIPOLI

- The British government looked for a way of breaking out of the stalemate on the Western Front. **Winston Churchill** suggested an attack on **Turkey**, Germany's ally, at Gallipoli. He said this would:

1 Knock Turkey out of the war.

2 Open up a supply route to Britain's hard-pressed ally, Russia.

3 Open up another front by advancing through the **Balkans** to attack Austria-Hungary.

- In March 1915, British and French warships attacked but suffered heavy losses from Turkish guns and mines.
- In April, British, French and **ANZAC** (Australia and New Zealand Army Corps) soldiers were landed. The Turks resisted hard, helped by German advisers.
- The Allies were unable to get beyond the beach. There they stayed, unable to advance inland, suffering from extreme heat in summer and extreme cold in winter, until they were taken off in December 1915.

### THE MIDDLE EAST

- Turkish forces with German advisers threatened British oil supplies in **Persia** (now called Iran). Combined forces of 600,000 British, ANZAC and Indian troops drove the Turks out of **Palestine** and **Iraq** from 1916-1918. In Palestine, they were helped by Arab guerrilla forces led by T. E. Lawrence (Lawrence of Arabia).
- The tough resistance of the Turks meant that the war in the Middle East took time and lots of men to win. There was never a breakthrough, which might have affected the rest of the war.

## The war at sea

- The British navy was the most powerful in the world, but the large, modern German fleet was the Kaiser's pride and joy.
- Victory would come to the side that could survive, and fight, longest. European countries could not feed themselves: they had to have supplies from overseas. The British navy therefore blockaded Germany, preventing vital food and war supplies from getting in. It was boring but vitally important to victory in the end.
- Germany retaliated with submarine (**U-boat**) attacks on Britain's supply ships. A new weapon, the **torpedo**, made these very successful. In 1915 the liner 'Lusitania' was sunk, with the loss of 1,198 passengers, including 128 American citizens. It looked as if the USA might come into the war against Germany and the U-boat war was called off.
- There was only one big naval battle: in 1916 at **Jutland**. Fourteen British and 11 German ships were sunk, but both fleets returned to port where they stayed for the rest of the war.
- In 1917, suffering from the blockade and desperate to break the stalemate, Germany began unrestricted U-boat warfare again. In March and April 1917, 600 British ships were sunk.
- Only the introduction of the **convoy system** (grouping large numbers of ships together and giving them an armed escort) prevented a serious crisis.

**QUESTION SPOTTER**

Typical exam questions on this topic:

- Explain why the Allies carried out the Gallipoli campaign.
- Why were there so few naval battles in the war?
- What was the importance of the naval blockade for the Allied victory?

> **A* EXTRA**
>
> Italy stayed out of the war at first. Then it declared war on Austria-Hungary in 1915. Germany sent support to Austria-Hungary and Italy was defeated at the battle of Caporetto in 1917.

## The war in the air

- German **zeppelins** (airships) bombed British cities (see 2.7). As defences improved, more and more of them were shot down.
- **Aeroplanes** were a new invention (the first powered flight was only in 1903). The first aeroplanes used in the war were basic. They were used to observe and photograph enemy trenches and troop movements.
- Pilots began to take weapons up with them and have **'dogfights'** (one-to-one combats). Soon aeroplanes were being designed with mounted machine-guns. The only popular heroes of the war were pilots, like Baron von Richthofen of Germany and Albert Ball of Britain.
- By the end of the war, enormous developments had taken place. Britain began the war with 37 aeroplanes and ended it with 20,000. The **Royal Air Force** was founded in 1918. Aeroplanes did not affect the course of the war, but they were bigger, faster and better made by the end. A new age of warfare was about to begin.

**2.7** *A zeppelin*

## CHECK YOURSELF QUESTIONS

**Q1** Why would the Allies be worried if Russia was defeated?

**Q2** Why was the British naval blockade 'boring but vitally important'?

**Q3** Why did the British and German fleets avoid a pitched battle for most of the war?

*Answers are on page 183.*

# REVISION SESSION 4 The Home Front: the government

## How were the forces recruited?

For many years, Britain had relied on its powerful navy for defence and kept only a small army. When it became clear that this was going to be a long land war, the Minister for War, **Lord Kitchener**, began to build up the British Army (see 2.8).

- At first the government relied on persuading men to **volunteer**. There was a massive recruitment campaign, with posters and recruiting offices in every town. A million men had joined up by early 1915, sooner than Kitchener expected.
- However, by 1916, **conscription** had to be introduced:
  1. The army needed more and more men as the casualties on the Western Front grew.
  2. Volunteering was seen as unfair.
  3. Volunteering left some factories and mines short of skilled workers. Better planning was needed.
- In January 1916, all unmarried men between 18 and 40 were called up. In May 1916, this was extended to married men.
- Some people refused to be called up. They were called **conscientious objectors** (COs or 'conchies') because they objected to the war on grounds of conscience (their beliefs). Each CO had to appear before a tribunal to state his case. Many of these tribunals were hostile to COs and 6,500 were put into the army anyway. In the army, they were treated harshly.

## What other measures were taken by government?

### DEFENCE OF THE REALM ACT

- This Act (known as DORA), was passed on 8 August 1914, just after the war began. It gave the government sweeping powers:
  1. To take over businesses, factories and land. The government used this power at once to take over the important coalmining industry.
  2. To censor what the public was told about the war.

### PROPAGANDA

- The British government used **propaganda** for several reasons:
  1. To persuade men to join the army (up to 1916) (see 2.9).
  2. To keep up the morale of people at home. This was important: everyone was involved in the war effort (see p20). One way of doing this was to make people hate the Germans (see 2.10).
  3. To persuade people to do what the government needed, such as getting women to work in munitions factories (see 2.11).

**2.8** *Recruiting poster*

### A* EXTRA

Conscientious objectors were mainly pacifists, who believed that all war was wrong. Some were also socialists, who believed that this was a capitalists' war and workers ought not to fight each other. Later on during the First World War, the British Army realised that enlisting COs was wasting their time, so they put them in prison instead. After the war, COs lost the right to vote for 5 years.

### QUESTION SPOTTER

Typical exam questions on this topic:

- How did the government try to persuade young men to join the armed forces?
- How did the government use propaganda during the war?

**2.9, 2.10, 2.11** *First World War posters*

NEWS

- DORA was used to restrict news of the war. Only victories and stories of heroism were published. No journalists were allowed near the Front. The numbers killed in battle were only released over several months, so the impact was weakened.
- The Battle of the Somme in 1916 was a turning-point. Casualties were so huge that it was impossible to hide the figures.
- The government made a film about the battle, much of it taken at the Front. Millions of people flocked to cinemas to see it. The film was realistic and included shots of dead soldiers. Some cinema-goers were deeply shocked, but many felt that the truth was better than lies.

## How did the government react to the situation?

In the first wave of patriotism everyone supported the Liberal government, led by **Asquith**.

- By 1915, generals were blaming the government for not supplying them with enough shells to win the war. Asquith reacted by forming a **coalition government** (i.e. he included leaders from all parties in his Cabinet). **Lloyd George**, a Liberal, was made Minister for Munitions to try to solve the 'shell shortage'.
- In December 1916, Lloyd George pushed Asquith out and became Prime Minister himself.
- It was clear by 1915 that if Britain was to have both a large army and the industry to keep it going for a long war, there would not be enough male workers. The government began to persuade women to take jobs in industry previously closed to them (see 2.11). They met resistance from trade unions who were worried that women would do the same jobs as men for less pay. Lloyd George promised the unions that women would be paid the same as men, but that their jobs were only temporary – until

**A* EXTRA**

Lloyd George split the Liberal Party by pushing Asquith out. The Liberal Party never recovered from the split. The Labour Party, on the other hand, increased its support. Arthur Henderson, the leader, was a minister in the wartime coalition and trade unionists worked in close partnership with the government. Labour got 2 million more votes in 1918 than they had before the war.

the men returned from the war. He also employed thousands of women in the government's own **munitions** (weapons) **factories**. (For more on women's roles in the war, see p20.)

- By 1917, unrestricted U-boat warfare (see p22) was creating a serious **shortage of food**. The government response was:

1 **Women's Land Army** formed, February 1917.

2 2.5 million acres of land taken over by the government under DORA, to grow food.

3 November 1917: early voluntary rationing schemes failed. Food prices rose, queues formed, foodshops closed early when they ran out. There were strikes in some areas as the lack of **rationing** seemed to favour the rich.

4 February 1918: rationing of sugar, butter, meat and beer in London. Extended to rest of Britain in April.

## CHECK YOURSELF QUESTIONS

**Q1** Look at the 3 posters opposite. How does each get its message across?

**Q2** **a** What attitudes did people at home in Britain have to the war at the beginning?

**b** How did these change during the war?

**Q3** DORA gave the government special wartime powers. Pick out some examples of these powers from pp14–19.

*Answers are on page 184.*

# The Home Front: the people

## Why was this known as a 'total war'?

Previous wars had involved only the fighters or those unlucky enough to be nearby. Everyone else could get on with their lives as normal. The First World War was Britain's first total war. This means a war in which everyone in the country is involved, whether they like it or not.

- Britain was no longer a safe island haven. East-coast towns were shelled by German battleships in December 1914. **Air-raids** on British cities started in January 1915.
- **1,500 civilians were killed** by enemy action in the war.
- The soldiers depended on industry at home to supply them with weapons and ammunition. Factory workers were therefore as important as soldiers in this war.
- Almost everyone lost a relative, killed in the war, or knew someone who had.
- Food shortages eventually led to rationing which affected everybody.

## What was Britain like in 1914?

- Women did not have **equality** with men. They were not expected to work, but to stay at home and look after their families. For working-class women this was not possible, but many jobs were closed to them, leaving only low-paid work. Women did not have the vote, despite the efforts of the suffragettes in the years before the war.
- There was a huge difference between the lives of the **rich** and the **poor**. The well-off ran the country. They owned land and businesses. They had houses in London, the country and abroad. They had lots of servants. Although there was a growing **middle class** and increasing numbers of better-off workers, there were millions of poor, earning under £1 a week. They suffered from low standards of housing, health and education. Only about 75% of men had the vote.

## How did women get involved in the war effort?

- From the beginning, women supported the war as keenly as the men. They encouraged recruitment. They collected books and clothing for the troops. Many became nurses in the **VAD** (Voluntary Aid Detachments).
- When, in 1915, the government called on women to volunteer to work in industry, many responded. Once the opposition of male employers and trade unionists had been overcome (see p18), they took on all kinds of jobs. They worked on the land, in transport, as nurses, in factories and in offices. They worked in government munitions factories, amid the dangers of explosives and chemical poisoning. Table 2.12 shows the most important changes:

**A* EXTRA**

From 1917 women also joined the forces: 57,000 joined the Women's Auxiliary Army Corps, 3,000 the Women's Royal Naval Service and 32,000 the Women's Royal Air Force. They were in the forces, with military uniforms, and learnt to march, but the work they were given was mainly in the kitchens and offices.

**2.12** *Women's employment in Britain, 1914 and 1918*

| | 1914 | 1918 |
|---|---|---|
| Munitions | 212,000 | 947,000 |
| Transport | 18,000 | 117,000 |
| Business | 505,000 | 935,000 |
| Agriculture | 190,000 | 228,000 |
| Government and teaching | 262,000 | 460,000 |
| Hotels and catering | 181,000 | 220,000 |
| Industry | 2,179,000 | 2,971,000 |
| Servants | 1,658,000 | 1,250,000 |
| Self-employed | 430,000 | 470,000 |
| Nursing and secretarial | 542,000 | 652,000 |

In all, there were over **2 million more women working** in 1918 than in 1914.

## What was Britain like in 1918?

### MEN AND WOMEN

- When the men came back from the war, nearly all women gave up their jobs, willingly or unwillingly. There were actually fewer women working in 1920 than in 1914.
- Men were forced to recognise that women could do virtually any job as well as they could. The door never quite closed again.
- Even if they had to give up their job, women had gained confidence. Family relationships were never quite the same again.
- In 1918, about **60% of women over 30 got the vote**. In 1928, all women got the vote.

### RICH AND POOR

- After the sacrifices the soldiers had made in the war, there was a feeling that the country had to pay more attention to everyone's needs.
- Lloyd George promised 'a country fit for heroes to live in'. All men were given the vote in 1918. A start was made on improving housing and education, although many of these hopes were shelved by the **economic depression** of the 1920s and 1930s.
- The old **upper classes** began to lose their hold on power. The bullets had struck down young aristocrats as well as young workers. Old titles began to die out for lack of heirs. It became hard to get people to work as servants.

### A* EXTRA

Britain was financially ruined by the war. The National Debt (the money the country owes) had risen by 1,200%. Britain owed the USA £1,000 million.

Some old industries – coal, steel, shipbuilding, textiles – had done well on government contracts during the war. They now had to wind down, struggling to find customers in a new and competitive world. Some new industries were given a boost by the war: electric goods, aeroplanes and motor lorries.

### QUESTION SPOTTER

Typical exam questions on this topic:

- What does 'total war' mean?
- How did the war change the lives of civilians?
- How did the war change women's lives?
- Were the British people permanently affected by the war?

## CHECK YOURSELF QUESTIONS

**Q1** Using 2.12, make 3 statements about how the war changed the position of women at work.

**Q2** Why did the war open up more jobs for women?

**Q3** What changes did the war make to attitudes in Britain concerning

**a** gender roles?

**b** class differences?

*Answers are on page 184.*

REVISION SESSION 6

# The ending of the war

The **USA** entered the war on the Allied side in April 1917. Although it was some months before US troops fought on the Western Front, the might of US industry and the promise of more men were a great boost to the Allies.

> **A* EXTRA**
>
> US President Woodrow Wilson did not just throw in his lot with the Allies. If the USA was going to enter the war, they would do so in order to create a better world after it was over. In January 1918, Woodrow Wilson listed 14 Points for a fair and lasting peace as the war aims of the USA. (For more on the 14 Points, see p26.)

## Why did the USA enter the war?

- Germany returned to U-boat warfare in early 1917. This angered the Americans as it led to the loss of American lives and goods. (Note that the sinking of the 'Lusitania' in 1915 [see p15] did not bring the USA into the war immediately. Germany abandoned unrestricted U-boat warfare for a while. **US President Woodrow Wilson** won the 1916 presidential election on the promise of keeping the USA out of the war.)
- Germany made secret suggestions to Mexico to declare war on the USA. British intelligence found out about this and made sure Woodrow Wilson was told.

## What impact did other events have?

RUSSIAN REVOLUTION, 1917 (see unit 5 for a full account)

- The Russian Revolution of March 1917 threw out the Tsar and set up a democratic **Provisional Government**. They decided to continue the war.
- However, the revolution of November 1917 brought **Lenin and the Bolsheviks** to power. They made peace with Germany at the **Treaty of Brest-Litovsk** in March 1918.

THE GERMAN SPRING REVOLUTION, 1918 (also called the Ludendorff Offensive)

- By early 1918 Germany was desperate. The naval blockade (see p15) had brought severe food shortages, affecting everyone – soldiers and civilians. Many of their best soldiers had been killed. Morale was low. The entry of the USA was the last straw.
- However, peace on the Eastern Front gave the Germans one last chance. Soldiers were moved to the west. New tactics were worked out. The attack began in March and was at first successful in breaking the stalemate.

  1 **General Ludendorff**, the German commander, used heavy guns and gas attacks to start with.

  2 Then small groups of well-armed, well-trained, fast-moving soldiers – called '**storm troops**' – broke through at many points in the Allied line. For the first time in over 3 years, they saw open country in front of them.

  3 But it did not lead to victory:

  - They had no overall plan: where did they go once they had broken through?
  - The Allies retreated and re-grouped.

- The Germans were short of supplies and could not keep up the effort. They had no reserves. As they advanced further, their supply-lines became longer.
- German soldiers had been told the Allies were just as hungry as they were. When they reached Allied food and wine stores, they were amazed and stopped to loot.

### THE ALLIED COUNTER-ATTACK

- In August 1918, the Allies counter-attacked. They had plenty of food, supplies and soldiers. They had learnt how to use accurate artillery, gas, tanks and aircraft. The demoralised German army began to retreat. They could not hold their lines. Their commanders asked for a ceasefire (**armistice**) and the war ended on 11 November 1918.

## Why did Germany lose the war?

- Once the Schlieffen Plan had failed, Germany had to fight a war on two fronts. They could not keep this up over a long period, with limited population and resources. The peace of 1918 with Russia came too late.
- The naval blockade prevented supplies getting through to German industry and food getting through to the German people. By 1918, their morale was almost broken.
- The entry of the Americans was decisive. By mid-1918, American troops and supplies made a difference. Even before that the knowledge that they were coming helped the Allies to hang on.
- By 1918, the Allied commanders had learnt how to break the stalemate of trench warfare, particularly by using tanks. The German army did not have an effective tank.

**QUESTION SPOTTER**

Typical exam questions on this topic:

- Why did the Allies win the First World War?
- Was the entry of the USA in April 1917 the main reason for the defeat of Germany?

## CHECK YOURSELF QUESTIONS

**Q1** Why was US entry into the war so helpful to the Allies?

**Q2** Why was Germany's spring 1918 offensive their 'last chance'?

**Q3** Was it obvious by the end of 1917 that the Allies would win the war?

**a** Start by listing the events which support the idea that things looked good for them by the end of 1917. Then list anything which pointed in the other direction.

**b** Then write your own opinion in answer to the question in one sentence.

**c** Now write an essay answer, using the following sentences to start each paragraph:

'By the end of 1917 the USA had joined the war on the Allied side. This was good news because...'

'However, the prospects for the next year were not all good. Russia...'

'In conclusion, I think that at the end of 1917 it was/was not obvious that the Allies would win the war. I think this because...'

*Answers are on page 185.*

REVISION SESSION 1

# The problems faced in 1919

Many people have criticised the treaties at the end of the First World War, both at the time and since. For several reasons, it was hard for the peacemakers to do a good job.

## What was the situation in Europe in 1919?

- In large parts of Europe people were suffering from near-starvation because of the Allied naval blockade of Germany, which continued while the **Versailles Conference** was going on. Then a flu epidemic, in 1919, caused over a million deaths.
- Many countries were in chaos. In Germany, the **Kaiser** had **abdicated** and fled to Holland. A new government had taken over, but was having difficulty controlling the country.
- Spurred on by the Russian Revolution of 1917, there were Communist uprisings in Berlin and Munich. Communists had seized power in Budapest. There were **nationalist risings** all over eastern Europe. It looked as if changes would be made whatever the peacemakers decided.
- Many people in the Allied countries were angry and wanted revenge:
  1. Over 9 million had been killed.
  2. Their economies were in ruins.
  3. The areas of **France** and **Belgium** that had been fought over were devastated (see 3.1). Houses, villages, whole towns were destroyed.
  4. They believed Germany had been to blame for starting the war and so should be made to pay for it.

**3.1** *The desolate landscape of 1918*

- The desire for revenge was all the stronger when people saw the harsh terms of the **Treaty of Brest–Litovsk** between Germany and Russia, signed in 1918. Germany had made Russia give up huge amounts of land (see unit 5, p75).

## Who met at Versailles in 1919?

- **The Allies** met at Versailles, just outside Paris. Holding the Conference in the country most deeply affected by the war influenced the peacemakers. Although 32 nations took part, none of the defeated countries – **Germany**, **Austria–Hungary**, **Turkey** or Bulgaria – were represented.
- **Russia** was also left out because it had a Communist government and because it had broken its alliance with the Allies by making its own peace. In fact, the terms of the most important Treaty affecting Germany were worked out by the representatives of Britain, France and the USA (see 3.2).

**3.2** *The 3 leaders at Versailles: Lloyd George (left), Clemenceau (middle), Woodrow Wilson (right)*

### BRITAIN: LLOYD GEORGE

- Lloyd George won a sweeping election victory in Britain in 1918. Many successful candidates had promised to punish Germany. Lloyd George listened to these views, but he felt that severe terms would probably only lead to another war as Germany looked for revenge. He wanted Germany back on its feet quickly, in order to restore trade with Britain, which would help British industry. He also wanted to increase the **British Empire** by taking some of Germany's overseas colonies.

### FRANCE: CLEMENCEAU

- Clemenceau was 29 when Germany had invaded France in 1870 and 73 when Germany did it again in 1914. He wanted to cripple Germany so that it could never happen again, by imposing a huge fine and by permanently disarming it.

### USA: WOODROW WILSON

- The USA had obviously suffered less death and destruction than its European allies. Wilson put forward idealistic reasons for coming into the war. In a speech in January 1918, he laid down **14 Points** for a better world after the war:

**QUESTION SPOTTER**

Typical exam questions on this topic:
- What were the aims of the peacemakers at the Treaty of Versailles?
- What differences were there between their aims?

## A* EXTRA

Wilson believed that the war had been caused by national frustration at being ruled by people of a different nationality. He did not know much about eastern Europe or understand the tangle of nationalities in some areas. Complete self-determination was impossible: there would always be some people living as a minority under different rulers.

### The 14 Points

1 No secret treaties: all diplomacy should be open.
2 Freedom of the seas in peace and war.
3 **Free trade** between all countries: no customs barriers.
4 **Disarmament** by all nations.
5 The wishes of people in colonies should be listened to when deciding their future.
6 German forces to leave Russia.
7 Belgium should be independent.
8 Alsace–Lorraine, taken by Germany in 1871, to be returned to France.
9 Italy's frontier with Austria to be changed to avoid further disputes.
10 **Self-determination** for the peoples of eastern Europe. This meant that the nationalities living in each area should rule themselves.
11 Serbia should have access to the sea.
12 Self-determination for the peoples of the Turkish Empire.
13 Poland should become an independent country, with access to the sea.
14 An international organisation should be set up to settle disputes between countries, called the **League of Nations**.

Woodrow Wilson's allies were far from happy about the 14 Points when he announced them, but they were eager to get the USA into the war. **Disagreements** began to emerge between the three leaders at the Conference:

- Clemenceau felt that Wilson was being far too soft on Germany and did not understand how much France had suffered and lost.
- Lloyd George could not agree with Wilson over point 2. The British blockade of Germany had contributed to the Allied victory.
- Clemenceau felt Lloyd George was prepared to be lenient with Germany in Europe only to be greedy for Germany's colonies.

## CHECK YOURSELF QUESTIONS

**Q1** Look at Woodrow Wilson's 14 Points. Put them into groups:

**a** those which dealt with certain named bits of territory

**b** those which laid down ideas for deciding what should happen to certain groups

**c** those which laid out plans for a better way of running the world and keeping peace in the future.

**Q2** Why did the people of Britain want revenge on Germany?

**Q3** Why didn't Lloyd George entirely support this wish?

*Answers are on page 185.*

# REVISION SESSION 2 The terms of the treaties

The Treaty of Versailles is often used as the name for all the peace treaties at the end of the First World War. In fact, there were 5 treaties. The Treaty of Versailles was the most important. It was signed in June 1919 and dealt with Germany.

## What was in the Treaty of Versailles?

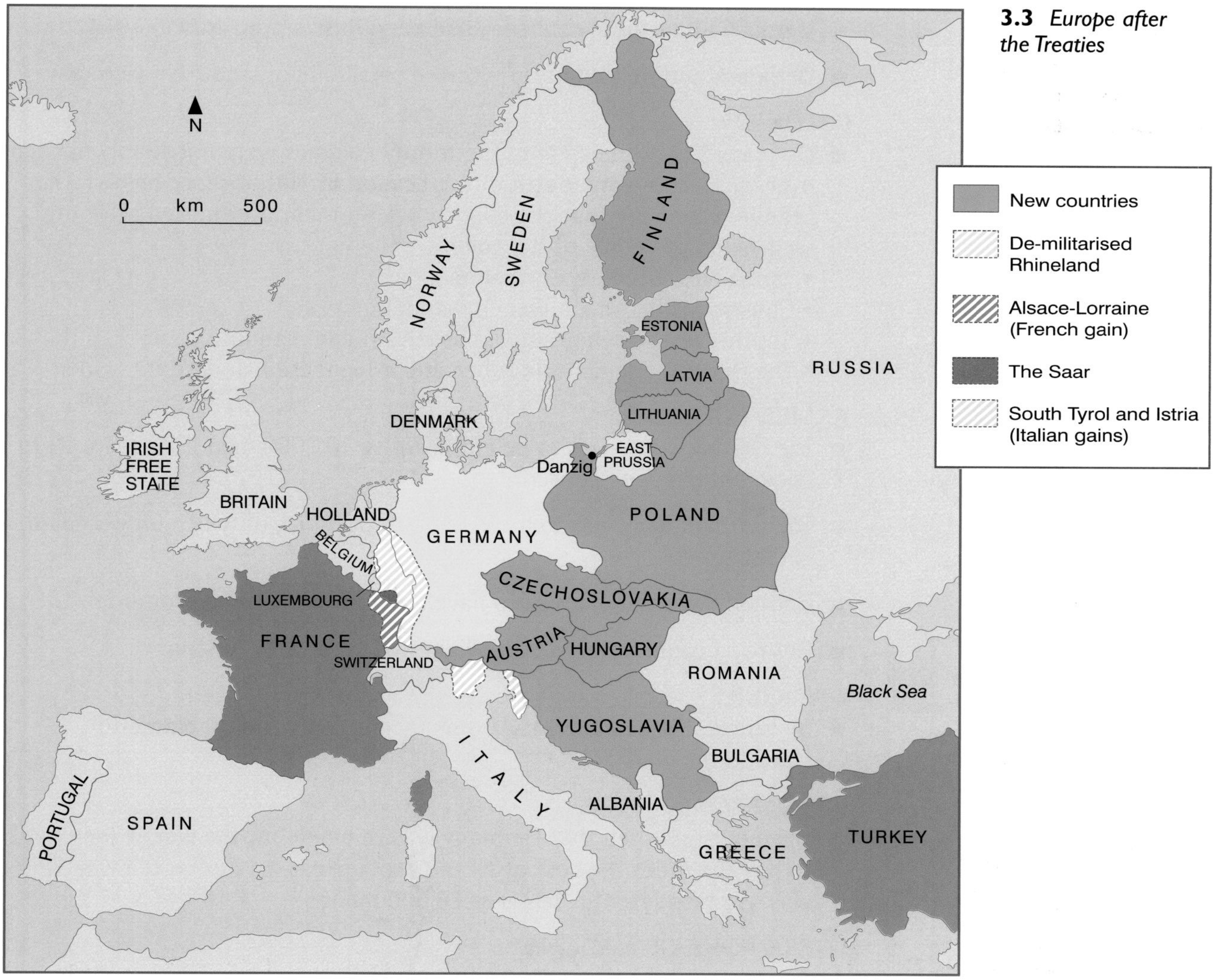


**3.3** *Europe after the Treaties*

TERRITORY (see 3.3)

- Alsace–Lorraine was returned to France.
- The left bank of the River Rhine was to be occupied by the Allies. A strip 50 kilometres wide on the right bank was to be **de-militarised** (no German bases or soldiers would be allowed in it).

- **The Saar**, with its important coalfield, was to be handed over to France for 15 years. After that time, its people would be asked to vote, in a **plebiscite**, whether they wanted to stay French or return to Germany.
- **Poland** became an independent country. Most of Poland was Russian in 1914 but the new country also took land from Germany, including the coalfield of Upper Silesia, and a 'corridor' of land to the sea. This split off the German province of **East Prussia** from the rest of Germany (as the map shows). The former German port of **Danzig** was made a free city in order to give Poland access to the sea.
- **Finland**, **Estonia**, **Latvia** and **Lithuania** became independent countries. Virtually all of these countries had been Russian territory in 1914.
- **Denmark** and **Belgium** also received small bits of land from Germany.

### COLONIES

- Germany lost all its empire. The former colonies were not simply handed over but became **mandates** of the **League of Nations** (see below). The League made sure that the country taking them over looked after the well-being of people of the colony.
  - Tanganyika became a British mandate.
  - Cameroons became a French mandate.
  - South-West Africa became a South African mandate.
  - The German Pacific islands became a Japanese mandate.

### ARMED FORCES

- The German army was to be cut down to 100,000 men. They were all to be volunteers – no conscription.
- The German navy was to be reduced to 36 ships, of which only 6 could be battleships.
- Germany was not allowed to have any tanks, submarines or aircraft.
- Germany could not make an alliance or unite with Austria.

### WAR-GUILT

- By article 231 of the Treaty, Germany had to accept all **blame** for starting the war.

### REPARATIONS

- Having established that Germany was to blame for the war, it then had to pay the Allies the cost of all the damage caused during the war. This was assessed later (in 1921) as £6,600 million.

### THE LEAGUE OF NATIONS

- An international peace-keeping organisation, the League of Nations, was set up as part of the Treaty.
- Once the Treaty of Versailles had been signed, Clemenceau, Lloyd George and Woodrow Wilson went home. The 4 remaining treaties dealt with Germany's 4 allies and were worked out by diplomats on the same basis as the Treaty of Versailles.

**QUESTION SPOTTER**

Typical exam questions on this topic:

- How did Woodrow Wilson's ideas of 'self-determination' affect the map of Europe?
- In what ways was Germany punished by the Treaty of Versailles?
- Which of the terms of the Treaty of Versailles were a result of Woodrow Wilson's ideas? Which terms were not?

## What were the terms of these other treaties?

AUSTRIA: TREATY OF ST GERMAIN, 1919

- Two new countries were set up out of the old Austria–Hungary: **Czechoslovakia** and **Yugoslavia**.
- Austria handed over land to Italy.
- Austria had to reduce its army and was forbidden to ally with Germany.

Austria became a small, second-rate power. It had severe problems re-adjusting to the new boundaries as much of its former industrial areas were now in different countries.

HUNGARY: TREATY OF TRIANON, 1920

- Hungary also lost territory to Czechoslovakia and Yugoslavia.
- Hungary lost territory to Romania.
- Hungary also had to disarm and lost land and people, as well as industrial raw materials.

BULGARIA: TREATY OF NEUILLY, 1919

- Bulgaria lost land to Greece, Romania and Yugoslavia. As a result, it had no access to the Mediterranean Sea.
- Bulgaria also had to disarm.

TURKEY: TREATY OF SÈVRES, 1920

- Turkey lost what was left of its empire.

1 Britain took over Palestine, Iraq and Jordan as mandates.

2 France took over Syria and Lebanon as mandates.

3 Greece took Smyrna (Izmir).

### A* EXTRA

These treaties marked an important moment in European and world history. They reorganised the boundaries of Europe. They altered the lives of millions of people all over the world. They provided a baseline for the rest of the 20th century. There had been nothing like it since the Congress of Vienna in 1815. The end of the Second World War in 1945 did not bring anything like so many changes, but rather re-established most of the boundaries laid out in 1919–20.

## CHECK YOURSELF QUESTIONS

**Q1** What were:
**a** the de-militarised Rhineland
**b** mandates
**c** war-guilt
**d** reparations
**e** the League of Nations?

**Q2** **a** What new countries were set up by the Treaties?

**b** Do these countries still exist?

*Answers are on page 186.*

# Reactions to the treaties

## How have historians commented?

- Germany had opened negotiations with the Allies on the basis of Wilson's 14 Points. The eventual terms of the Treaty were far removed from the 14 Points.
- The German people under the Kaiser were subjected to **propaganda** about the war more than the British people. They had been told that they were fighting a defensive war against attacking nations. They did not know that, in autumn 1918, the German Army was in retreat and almost defeated. The tough terms came as a surprise and were hard to swallow.
- **Reparations** payments punished the people of Germany and their new Weimar government, not the Kaiser and the old rulers.

However:

- Germany did not, in fact, lose that much by the Treaty of Versailles. It was still the largest country in western Europe. Its economy was still powerful. As you will see in unit 4, Germany experienced an economic revival in the 1920s despite all that the Treaty had done.
- The complaints about not being fair, and not in line with the 14 Points, are a bit weak. Germany had ignored Wilson's 14 Points when he first produced them. Only when defeat was staring them in the face did they appeal to the USA for peace.
- Their own treatment of Russia at the **Treaty of Brest–Litovsk** in March 1918 (see unit 5) was extremely harsh. Their plans for the Allies, if Germany had won the war, were very tough.

## How did the German people react?

When the terms of the Treaty of Versailles were revealed in May 1919, the German people were angry because:

- the terms had not been negotiated. They were simply told to sign or the war would re-start.
- they thought the terms were harsh.

  1. They had to lose 13% of their land, 12% of their population, 16% of their coalfields, 48% of their iron industry and 10% of their manufacturing industry.
  2. They had to lose all their colonies.
  3. They had to lose most of their proud army and navy.
  4. They had to accept total blame for the war.
  5. They would be crippled by reparations for years to come.

- they thought the terms were unfair.
  1 Although the 14 Points said that every nation should disarm, the Allies were not doing so.
  2 Self-determination did not seem to apply to Germans. The new countries set up by the treaties left 3.5 million Germans in Czechoslovakia and 1 million in Poland.
  3 Germany was treated as some kind of outcast by not being allowed to join the League of Nations.

**3.4** *'Bayern', a ship in the German High Seas Fleet, scuttled at Scapa Flow*

- In protest, the German High Seas Fleet, captive in Scapa Flow in the Shetlands, **scuttled** (sank) their ships rather than let them fall into British hands (see 3.4).
- The Kaiser, whose government had taken Germany into the war, had fled. Germany was now run by democratically-elected politicians. **Ebert**, the new Prime Minister, thought about fighting on, but was told by his generals that Germany would only be crushed, with more loss of life. He decided that the German people were suffering enough and agreed to sign the treaty.

## What happened next?

- The reparations payments were fixed in 1921 at **£6,600 million**, to be paid in instalments.
- The German economy was in a poor state after the war. In 1922, the German government said they could not pay that year's instalment, pointing out that people were starving in Germany (see 3.5).
- France and Belgium did not believe them. In 1923 – as agreed in the terms of the Treaty of Versailles – they sent troops into **the Ruhr** (Germany's main industrial area). They took over every mine, factory, railway and shop in the Ruhr.

**3.5** *Street soup kitchen for poor people in Germany at the end of the First World War*

- The German response was '**passive resistance**': everyone refused to work or cooperate in any way with the occupying forces. The French were furious. They deported 150,000 people for disobeying orders and 132 Germans were killed.
- German resistance to the occupation cost the country dearly. Its **currency** collapsed completely and **hyper-inflation** resulted: by November, a dollar was worth 4 billion marks (see unit 4, p36). This was no use to France either and talks began which led eventually to the Dawes Plan (see unit 4, p37).

### QUESTION SPOTTER

Typical exam questions on this topic:

- What did many Germans object to in the terms of the Treaty of Versailles?
- Was the hostility of many Germans to the Treaty of Versailles justified?

## How did others react?

### THE ALLIES

- **The British** soon began to have second thoughts about the peace terms. In his book *The Economic Consequences of the Peace*, J. M. Keynes showed that the treaties were bad for everyone.

- When Woodrow Wilson returned to the USA, he found that the mood had changed there, too. **The US** public and politicians wanted nothing to do with Europe. They refused to agree the treaties and did not join the League of Nations.

- **France** had wanted a tougher treaty for Germany. The French still feared Germany and needed reparations payments to pay off their huge debts. But the alliance of 1917, already crumbling in 1919, was over. The USA had pulled out. Britain was lukewarm. After the failure of the Ruhr invasion, France looked for allies elsewhere.

### OTHER REACTIONS

- **Hungary** had lost two-thirds of its pre-war territory by the Treaty of Trianon. Anger fuelled a Communist uprising and then a right-wing dictatorship.

- The other country to protest loudly at the terms of the Treaty (of Sèvres) was **Turkey**. A nationalist army under Mustafa Kemal drove the Greeks out of Smyrna. A new treaty – the Treaty of Lausanne – was signed in 1923 to recognise this.

- **Italy** had expected to do better from the treaties and felt aggrieved.

- **The Chinese** were furious that German ports in China were not handed back in 1919, but became Japanese mandates. There were huge protests: one of the key stages in the growth of Chinese nationalism.

### A* EXTRA

The peacemakers have been criticised for setting up small, weak nations in eastern Europe and for the failure to achieve real self-determination (e.g. 30% of the people in Poland in 1919 were non-Poles). It is also true that most of these new nations fell easy prey to Hitler in 1939–41 and to the USSR in 1945. But their nationhood was an important factor in throwing off Communism in 1989. Only two have completely disappeared: Czechoslovakia peacefully and Yugoslavia in a terrible civil war. It remains to be seen how successful the new small nations of eastern Europe will be in the immediate future.

## ? CHECK YOURSELF QUESTIONS

**Q1** **a** Why did the Germans call the Treaty a 'diktat' – a dictated peace?

**b** If they were so angry about it, why did Germany sign the Treaty of Versailles?

**Q2** Why did France occupy the Ruhr in 1923?

*Answers are on page 186.*

REVISION SESSION 1

# Germany after the War, 1918–1923

## How did Germany become a democratic country?

By late 1918, Germany was in a terrible state.

- The country's pride and joy, the German army, was on the verge of defeat.
- The German people were nearly starving, living on handouts of potatoes, turnips and sawdusty bread.
- The Kaiser and his advisers had lost the support of many of the German people.
- Germany was in financial ruin as a result of the cost of the war.

In late October 1918 – in a last, desperate throw – the Navy commanders ordered their ships to attack the British Navy. The sailors in the port of Kiel **mutinied**. This was followed by risings of workers and soldiers all over the country. The **Kaiser** fled to Holland. He left Germany as a **republic** in the hands of the men he most hated, the democratically-elected politicians.

### THE POLITICAL PARTIES

The leader of the biggest party, the **Social Democrats**, was Ebert. He made an **armistice** (ceasefire) on 11 November 1918 and called an election for January 1919.

**4.1** *Striking workers and soldiers on the streets of Berlin, 1918*

The **Spartacists**, a smaller group of socialists, were admirers of the revolution which had taken place in Russia a year earlier. They wanted a similar revolution in Germany, based on the **soviets** of mutinying soldiers and striking workers which had sprung up across Germany. Led by **Rosa Luxemburg** and **Karl Liebknecht**, they could see that elections would put power back into the hands of more moderate, middle-class politicians. Armed Spartacists took to the streets of Berlin.

Ebert and the Social Democrats also turned to violence. They formed groups of armed anti-socialist ex-soldiers, called the **Freikorps**, to crush the Spartacists. Luxemburg and Liebknecht were murdered and hundreds of Spartacists killed.

- The Spartacists called themselves **Communists** and began to take part in democratic politics. They were always the enemies of the Social Democrats.
- Many Germans remained deeply afraid of the Communists.

### THE WEIMAR REPUBLIC

As the capital of Germany, Berlin, was still in chaos, the new democratic government met in the town of Weimar. It was called the **Weimar Republic**. The new constitution said:

- Everyone over 20, men and women, had the vote.
- Freedom of speech, of travel, of religious belief were all guaranteed.
- The elected Parliament was called the **Reichstag**. There was also an elected upper chamber, called the Reichsrat. The **Chancellor** (or Prime Minister) had to have the support of a majority of members of the Reichstag.
- The **President** was to be the elected head of the country. It was expected that the President would be merely a figurehead, although with the power to rule without the Reichstag's support in emergencies.
- Elections were held by **proportional representation**, so a party with 25% of the votes cast all over Germany would get 25% of the members of the Reichstag. (Proportional representation means that each party gets members according to its proportion of the vote.)

This system leads to the growth of small parties. No party, throughout the life of the Weimar Republic, ever got more than 50% of the votes cast, so all governments had to be **coalitions**. (A coalition is where 2 or more parties agree to work together and form a government.) It was rare for these coalitions to last very long, so governments were always changing.

**A* EXTRA**

The main parties in the Weimar Republic in the 1920s:
1. The Nazis (see p40).
2. German Nationalist Party: right-wing party of the landowners and industrialists who had supported the Kaiser.
3. German People's Party: not quite as right wing as the Nationalists; a party of business.
4. Centre Party: a party of Roman Catholics.
5. Democratic Party: a middle-of-the-road party with support from the German Jewish community.
6. Social Democratic Party
7. Communist Party.

Parties (1), (2) and (7) were all totally opposed to the Weimar system of government.

## What problems were there in the early years of the Weimar Republic?

### THE TREATY OF VERSAILLES

In 1919, the Weimar government was faced with the choice of signing the Treaty of Versailles or resuming the war. The latter would have brought the destruction of Germany, so they signed.

The anger of many Germans was transferred to the Weimar politicians. They were called 'November Criminals', by Hitler and by others, for making the armistice of November 1918. They were accused of 'stabbing the army in the back' (when, in fact, the army was quite incapable of fighting on).

> **QUESTION SPOTTER**
>
> Typical exam questions on this topic:
> - Describe the problems facing Germany at the end of the First World War.
> - What difficulties did the Weimar Republic have in trying to establish democratic government?
> - What is hyper-inflation? What problems did the hyper-inflation of 1923 cause for the people of Germany?

### RIGHT-WING VIOLENCE

Many Germans remained loyal to the old system of rule by the Kaiser. They hated democracy and the Weimar politicians. The years 1918–23 were full of violence:

- The Kapp **putsch**, 1920, was an attempt by the Freikorps to seize power in Berlin. They were defeated when the workers held a general strike.
- There were nearly 400 political murders between 1919 and 1923, including 2 government ministers.
- Hitler's beer-hall putsch, 1923 (see p41).

### THE FRENCH OCCUPATION OF THE RUHR (see p32)

- The French occupation of the Ruhr was met by **passive resistance**:
  - postal, telegraph and telephone services stopped
  - trains and boats didn't run
  - factory production came to a halt.
- This was effective in resisting the French, but the workers and those expelled from the Ruhr had to be fed. However, Germany was not making anything to sell. So the government printed more money. Soon this got out of control.

> 1 mark = 100 pfennigs

- Prices in a restaurant changed while you were eating a meal. Wages were paid in basketfuls of paper notes. A loaf of bread which cost 29 pfennigs in 1913, cost 1,200 marks in summer 1923 and 428,000,000,000 marks by November 1923. People with debts were able to pay them off easily, but those with savings found they had become worthless. People on fixed incomes were in real distress.
- The result of this **hyper-inflation** was that middle-class Germans who had lost their savings never forgave the Weimar government.

## CHECK YOURSELF QUESTIONS

**Q1** Why did the following hate the Social Democrats and the Weimar Republic?

**a** the Communists

**b** many patriotic Germans

**Q2** **a** What is a coalition?

**b** Why were coalitions in the Weimar Republic difficult to operate?

**Q3** Why did the massive inflation of 1923 cause chaos and distress?

*Answers are on page 187.*

## REVISION SESSION 2 The Weimar Republic, 1923–1930

### What did Stresemann achieve for Germany?

The problems of Germany in 1923 were:

- **economic** – the massive inflation
- **diplomatic** – Germany's bad relations with its ex-enemies.

From 1923 to 1929, German politics was dominated by **Gustav Stresemann**. He was Chancellor briefly in 1923 and then Foreign Minister until his death in 1929. He dealt effectively with both these problems.

#### ECONOMIC RECOVERY

- Stresemann called off passive resistance to the French invasion of the Ruhr.
- He introduced a new currency, the *rentenmark*, cancelling the old, inflated mark.
- Inflation stopped; industry began to pick up, unemployment began to fall.
- He negotiated the **Dawes Plan**, 1924, named after the US banker, Charles Dawes.

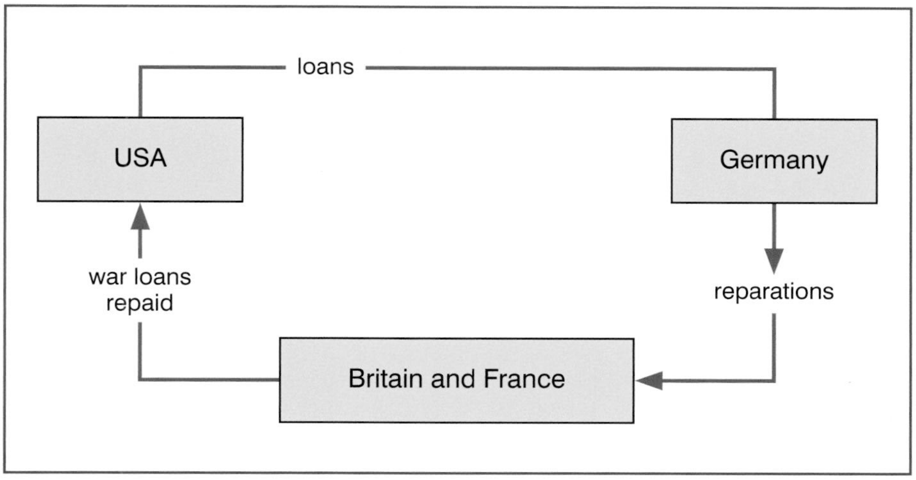


**4.2** *The Dawes Plan*

- The Dawes Plan agreed that Germany should pay a lower amount of **reparations**. It also arranged loans to German industry from US bankers. With Germany beginning to recover, some reparations could be paid to the Allies, who could then pay off some of their wartime debts to the USA.
- The **Young Plan**, 1929, negotiated a further reduction of the amount of reparations to one-third of the 1921 figure.

#### DIPLOMATIC RECOVERY

- The French could see that the invasion of the Ruhr had not got them what they wanted. In 1923, they withdrew. They also agreed to the Dawes Plan: better to receive some reparations than none at all.

- **Locarno Pact**, 1925: Stresemann increased the new mood of cooperation by agreeing to respect the boundaries with France and Belgium agreed at Versailles. He agreed not to re-militarise the Rhineland, from which Allied troops were gradually withdrawn. In turn, France agreed not to invade Germany.
- In this new atmosphere of trust – sometimes called the 'Locarno Honeymoon' – Germany was admitted to the **League of Nations**, 1926.

**Results:**

- The diplomatic recovery helped Germany's economic recovery: now that it was behaving normally, investors poured money into Germany, which prospered.
- Stresemann showed that Germany could be trusted to behave like any other democratic nation.
- Parties which fed on desperate conditions in Germany declined: votes for the Nazis fell. In 1928, they were reduced to just 13 members of the Reichstag.

## Were these 'golden years'?

### ECONOMIC PROSPERITY

Germany prospered in these years.

- 25,000 million marks of foreign loans were invested.
- New industries sprang up.
- Cars, telephones, radios, airships, ocean liners were built.

After the USA, Germany was the most up-to-date country in the world in the 1920s.

### THE ARTS

- Censorship had been tough under the Kaiser. Under the Weimar Republic, there was freedom and the arts flourished. New techniques were developed in:
  - film-making by Fritz Lang
  - drama by Bertold Brecht
  - song by Kurt Weill
  - architecture by Walter Gropius and the Bauhaus school.

### ENTERTAINMENT

- **Berlin** became a 'good time' city, with hundreds of night clubs and jazz bands. For some at least, sexual freedom replaced the repression of the Kaiser's Germany. Many Germans, and stuffy **puritans** like Hitler, hated this aspect of Weimar. They thought it was decadent.

## What happened in the Great Depression?

Stresemann died in 1929. In October of that year, the bubble of German prosperity burst.

- The Wall Street Crash (see unit 7) brought disaster for US financiers. They called in their loans.
- German companies closed down.
- **Unemployment** rose fast. By 1932, 1 worker in 3 was out of work, including clerks and teachers, as well as manual workers. With their dependants, this meant that 23 million people had no wages to live on.
- The government paid **unemployment benefit** for 26 weeks. After that, there was a handout, not really enough to survive on. Many could not afford to pay their rents and became homeless. Even those in work suffered pay reductions and shortened hours. Germany was deep in crisis again.

## What did Stresemann achieve?

By negotiation, he had:

- lowered the amount of reparations
- reached agreement over Germany's western boundaries – with the implication that the eastern boundaries, therefore, were not so fixed
- achieved the removal of foreign troops from German soil.

### A* EXTRA

Stresemann had achieved, peacefully, a good deal of what right-wing Germans wanted. Recent research has shown his aims were the same as theirs: to improve on the terms made at Versailles, but by negotiation rather then defiance.

Nevertheless, they hated him. For Hitler, and others, nothing less than total defiance of the Versailles Treaty would do.

### QUESTION SPOTTER

Typical exam questions on this topic:

- What did Stresemann do to improve the situation of Germany (a) economically and (b) diplomatically?
- Why did the Wall Street Crash affect Germany so deeply?

## CHECK YOURSELF QUESTIONS

**Q1** What was the 'Locarno Honeymoon'?

**Q2** Why did the Depression hit Germany so hard?

**Q3** Was the Weimar Republic doomed to failure?

*Answers are on page 188.*

REVISION SESSION 3

# Hitler and the Nazis, 1918–1930

## Who was Hitler?

### ADOLF HITLER (THE EARLY YEARS)

| | |
|---|---|
| *Born:* | 1889 |
| *Family:* | He did not get on with his elderly father, an Austrian customs official on the German border, but loved his mother. |
| *Education:* | He failed to get into art school in Vienna in 1907. |
| *Jobs:* | Barely scraped a living as an artist. |
| *First World War:* | When war broke out in 1914 he joined the German Army (16th Bavarian Infantry Regiment) and served on the Western Front. Loved army life. As a messenger, he twice won the Iron Cross for bravery. In hospital recovering from a gas attack, when the war ended. Like many Germans, he could not believe that Germany had lost. |
| *After the War:* | In 1919, still in the army, he was sent to investigate the German Workers Party (one of the many tiny political parties which sprang up after the war). Although Hitler did not ask to join, he was sent a membership card. He decided he could mould this little party into his own organisation. |

### A* EXTRA

The founder of the German Workers Party was a railwayman, Anton Drexler. It was intended to appeal to working-class patriotism. Its nationalist, socialist and anti-Semitic policies contained nothing new, but the combination of all three in one party was new.

**4.3** A swastika

## Who were the Nazis?

In 1920 the German Workers Party changed its name to the National Socialist German Workers Party (*National Sozialistische Deutsche Arbeiter Partei*, NSDAP, or **Nazis**). The Nazis' 25-point programme contained elements of:

- **Nationalism**: union with Austria, abolition of the Treaty of Versailles, seizure of land from Poland and Russia.
- **Socialism**: old age pensions, profit-sharing in industry, abolition of big business, protection for small shopkeepers.
- **Anti-Semitism**: Jews to lose their right to German citizenship.

In 1921, Hitler became leader of the Nazi Party. It adopted the **swastika** symbol he had designed. The party became quite successful in Bavaria, in southern Germany, with 50,000 members by 1923.

### REASONS FOR EARLY SUCCESS

- Hitler was a powerful speaker. In packed meetings in Munich, he was able to play on the anger felt by many Germans over their defeat in the First World War and the hardship they were suffering. Many leading Nazis were moved to join at this time: Roehm, Goering, Hess, Himmler, Streicher, Rosenberg.
- Hitler formed the ***Sturm Abteilung*** **(SA)** (stormtroopers, or brownshirts, from their uniforms). Many were unemployed ex-soldiers (see 4.4). They kept order at Hitler's meetings and broke up other parties' meetings.

**4.4** *SA – Sturm Abteilung (stormtroopers)*

Their violence demonstrated their rejection of democratic and peaceful methods and, supposedly, their determination to take action to solve Germany's problems.

## What happened at the beer-hall putsch?

By 1923, Hitler's 35,000 brownshirts were pressing him to seize power. When Stresemann ended passive resistance to the French invasion of the Ruhr, all nationalist Germans were furious. What happened next is shown in diagram 4.5.

**4.5** *The beer-hall putsch, and what followed*

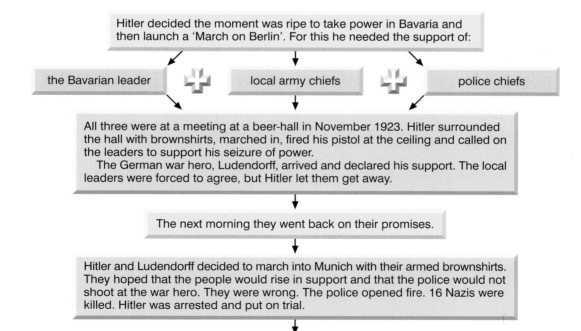

Hitler decided the moment was ripe to take power in Bavaria and then launch a 'March on Berlin'. For this he needed the support of:

↓

the Bavarian leader + local army chiefs + police chiefs

↓

All three were at a meeting at a beer-hall in November 1923. Hitler surrounded the hall with brownshirts, marched in, fired his pistol at the ceiling and called on the leaders to support his seizure of power.

The German war hero, Ludendorff, arrived and declared his support. The local leaders were forced to agree, but Hitler let them get away.

↓

The next morning they went back on their promises.

↓

Hitler and Ludendorff decided to march into Munich with their armed brownshirts. They hoped that the people would rise in support and that the police would not shoot at the war hero. They were wrong. The police opened fire. 16 Nazis were killed. Hitler was arrested and put on trial.

↓

Hitler was allowed to give a long speech in his own defence, which was fully reported in the papers, giving him national publicity. It is a sign of conditions in Weimar Germany that he was sentenced to 3 years in prison, of which he served only 9 months (April–December 1924), in comfort in Landsberg Prison.

→

In prison, Hitler wrote his book, *Mein Kampf* ('My Struggle'): a long-winded account of his life and beliefs.

## What were Hitler's beliefs?

- The German people belonged to a superior race, the **Aryans**. They were the master-race, the *herrenvolk*, while other races – like Slavs, Jews and black people – were inferior.
- **Germany** must be great again. The Treaty of Versailles should be overthrown. Germany should seize more land in the east, by war if necessary.
- **Communism** was evil because it was international.
- **Democracy** was feeble. Germany needed a **dictator** to lead it to the great future Hitler had promised.

### WHAT HAPPENED TO THE NAZIS IN THE 'GOLDEN YEARS' 1924–1930?

On his release, Hitler fought off a challenge to his leadership from Gregor Strasser, who emphasised the more socialist aspects of Nazism. Hitler then began re-organising the party:

- Having failed to seize power by violent means, the Nazis would win it democratically, through the Reichstag.
- Local Nazi Party branches were started.
- A youth organisation, the **Hitler Youth**, was set up.
- The black-uniformed ***Shutz Staffel* (SS)** was set up in 1925, personally loyal to Hitler.
- Goebbels was put in charge of **propaganda**.

However, this change of policy did not bring Hitler immediate success. Nazi Party support fell in the 'golden years'. In 1928, they gained just 2% of the votes. Hitler seemed to be offering desperate remedies to problems which the German people did not have any more.

**QUESTION SPOTTER**

Typical exam questions on this topic:

- What contribution did Adolf Hitler make to the early success of the Nazis?
- What is National Socialism? How far did Hitler's personal beliefs fit in with Nazi ideas?
- In what ways, and with what success, did Hitler change Nazi Party policy after the failure of the beer-hall putsch?

## CHECK YOURSELF QUESTIONS

**Q1** How did the Nazis get their name?

**Q2** 'Instead of working to achieve power by armed conspiracy, we shall have to hold our noses and enter the Reichstag. Sooner or later we shall have a majority and after that we shall have Germany.' (Hitler, in Landsberg Prison, 1924)

**a** What changes in policy for the Nazis does Hitler describe in this source?

**b** Why do you think he was making this change?

**c** What does the source tell you about Hitler's attitude to democracy?

*Answers are on page 188.*

# REVISION SESSION 4 How Hitler won power in 1933

The single most important factor in Hitler's rise to power is the **Depression** (see p39). By 1932, there were 6 million Germans out of work.

## Reaction of the Weimar governments

- The Weimar government, like most governments in the world, seemed unable to deal with the Depression. However, in Germany democracy itself began to crumble.
- It was difficult to take decisive action with coalitions of several parties. When bankers and financiers wanted to cut the **dole**, the Social Democrats, the largest party, left the coalition.
- Under the Weimar constitution, the President had the power to **rule by decree** (without the agreement of the Reichstag) in an emergency. From 1930 President Hindenburg, with the advice of his friends in the army, began to use these powers on a regular basis.

### REACTION OF THE GERMAN PEOPLE

- For many Germans the Depression was the last straw. They blamed Weimar for the defeat and humiliation at the end of the war in 1918–19, for the inflation of 1923, and now this.
- In the 1930 elections, the Nazis increased their support to 107 seats and Communist support went up from 54 to 77 seats. People were turning to 2 parties, both utterly committed to overthrowing the Weimar Republic.
- The 1932 Presidential elections gave Hitler a tremendous opportunity for publicity. He won 13 million votes to Hindenburg's 19 million.
- In the 1932 Reichstag elections, the Nazis won 230 seats and were the biggest party.

## Why did the Nazis win support at elections?

### VIOLENCE

- The SA (brownshirts) grew in size, from 30,000 in 1929 to over 440,000 in 1932. Many were full-time members, living in SA hostels and paid out of Nazi funds. They continued to use violence, breaking up opponents' meetings and beating people up. This had three results:

  1. It increased the impression of lawlessness and the Weimar government's inability to keep law and order.
  2. It increased the impression that the Nazis were ready to take tough action.
  3. Many middle-class and rich business people were scared stiff at the increase in support for the Communists. They liked the Nazis' hostility to Communists and gave them lots of money for their campaigns.

### LAW AND ORDER

- Nazi uniforms and processions gave an impression of order and purpose. They reminded older Germans of the great days of the Kaiser.

### NAZI POLICIES

Nazi policies began to appeal to people who had lost faith in Weimar:

- They gave people someone to blame: Jews and Weimar politicians.
- They offered strong leadership and strong government instead of the deals and incompetence of Weimar.
- They promised to make Germany great again by rejecting the Versailles peace terms.
- They offered an end to unemployment by putting men into the army.

### PROPAGANDA AND HITLER'S ORATORY

- Nazi **propaganda**, especially at election times, was far ahead of their opponents. Goebbels organised torchlight processions, huge rallies, radio broadcasts, films, records, concerts, sports days, theatre groups. Hitler used **aeroplanes** to travel about. It was all exciting, impressive, modern, purposeful.
- Many Germans were won over to the Nazis by hearing Hitler speak. They began to think only he could save Germany.

**QUESTION SPOTTER**

Typical exam questions on this topic:

- Describe how this Nazi poster (4.6) was designed to appeal to the German people.
- Use this poster to describe how the Nazis won over many Germans to vote for them in 1932 and 1933.

**4.6** Nazi election poster, 1928. It says 'Work, Freedom and Bread. Vote for the National Socialists!'

## What happened in 1932–33?

### JULY 1932 ELECTIONS

Although the Nazis were the biggest party after the July 1932 elections, Hindenburg refused to make Hitler Chancellor. Instead he chose his friend **von Papen** and ruled on his own, by decree, when von Papen could not get support in the Reichstag.

### NOVEMBER 1932 ELECTIONS

In these elections the Nazis lost some support, but remained the biggest party. Still Hindenburg refused to appoint Hitler. Then, in January 1933, von Papen came up with the idea of making Hitler Chancellor, but in a **coalition** with only 3 Nazi ministers and 9 from other parties. Von Papen thought he could control Hitler, while Hitler supplied him with the votes in the Reichstag.

### MARCH 1933 ELECTIONS

New elections were called for March 1933 – the third in 9 months. Goering was now in charge of much of the police and enrolled SA members as special constables. There was massive Nazi violence: at least 50 anti-Nazis were killed and many injured.

A week before the election, the Reichstag building was set on fire and a Communist was found inside. (It may be that the Nazis set it on fire in order to blame the Communists.) 4,000 Communists were arrested. Hindenburg was persuaded to suspend **basic rights** and in the last week before the election only Nazi candidates were heard or seen.

In this undemocratic situation, the Nazis won 17.3 million votes and with 288 seats were the biggest party, but still 22 million Germans voted for other parties. However, by outlawing the Communists, Hitler got a majority in the Reichstag.

### QUESTION SPOTTER

Typical exam questions on this topic:

- Why was the Weimar government unable to deal with the effects of the Depression in Germany?
- Why did many Germans turn to the Nazis in the period 1930–1933?
- Describe how Hitler came to power in 1933.

### A* EXTRA

**Was the Weimar Republic doomed from the start?**

1. The Weimar Republic came into existence out of defeat and hardship, and carried the blame for them to the end.
2. Germany had little experience of democracy and how to make it work. Many Germans never supported it. Although the Kaiser fled in 1918, leading figures from his government and army remained in power under Weimar. Even President Hindenburg, who should have upheld democracy, was quite ready to rule undemocratically. Democracy really ended in Germany in 1930.
3. The constitution led to coalition governments. These demanded a high level of agreement and willingness to work together. This was never achieved.

However:

4. Weimar worked quite well under Stresemann and the country prospered.
5. No one could have foreseen the Wall Street Crash and Depression.
6. No one could have foreseen Hitler. He was determined to overthrow Weimar and very successful at turning events to his advantage.

## CHECK YOURSELF QUESTIONS

**Q1** Why did the Depression help the Nazis?

This looks a big question at first sight: there is the Depression itself, the Nazis, and the country as a whole. Use this plan to sort out your answer:

*'The worldwide Depression hit Germany hard. Its effects were...'*

*'The Nazi Party had little support when the Depression started. But...'*

*'People rejected Weimar because...'*

*'People turned to the Nazis because...'*

**Q2** How did the Nazis appeal to:

**a** the unemployed

**b** ex-soldiers

**c** business people?

*Answers are on page 189.*

# Hitler's dictatorship

Hitler had plans to change Germany completely and build a new **Reich** (Empire). This Third Reich (the others were the Kaiser's rule and the Weimar Republic) would last for a thousand years. These plans were sometimes called the 'Nazi revolution'.

## What were Hitler's plans for Germany?

- To take over complete control of the country (see below).
- To build a community in which everyone had a place, which Hitler had decided for them. If people agreed, they would benefit (see p50).
- To make Germany strong, economically and militarily (see p54).
- To make Germany racially pure (see p58).

These four aims overlap. In this revision session, we shall see how Hitler took over complete control of Germany.

After the March 1933 elections, Hitler rapidly went about making himself **totalitarian dictator** of Germany. (Totalitarian means the total control of the lives of everyone in the state; dictatorship is rule by one person.)

### REMOVAL OF OPPOSITION

- **Enabling Act, March 1933**: gave Hitler the right to pass laws without consulting the Reichstag. It was passed with the agreement of some other parties while SA and SS members surrounded the building. President Hindenburg was thus sidelined and democracy ended.
- Local government was brought under Nazi control. In April 1933, each of the 18 provinces of Germany was given a Nazi Governor appointed by Hitler, with the power to make state laws. In January 1934, state parliaments were abolished.
- Trade unions were abolished in May 1933.
- Other parties' leaders were attacked, their offices raided. In July 1933, all parties apart from the Nazi Party were banned.
- Opponents fled abroad or were arrested. They were beaten up or put in **concentration camps** (the first of which, at Dachau, was opened in 1933). Concentration camps were run by the SS. Inmates did hard labour, with poor food and harsh discipline.

### RIVALS TO HITLER

- By early 1934, the only rival to Hitler's personal power over the German people was the **SA**:

  1 There were now 3 million of them.

  2 They thought Hitler owed them a debt for having helped him to power. They wanted jobs and rewards.

  3 They were more left-wing than Hitler and wanted to carry out some of the Socialist points of the Nazis' 25-point programme (see p40).

4 Their leader, **Ernst Roehm**, had a plan to merge the SA and the army. As head of both, he would be more powerful than Hitler.

- Hitler had to act. The army was horrified at the idea of being swallowed up in the SA. One weekend in June 1934 Hitler ordered his SS to execute 400 SA leaders, including Roehm. This was called the '**Night of the Long Knives**'.
- A few weeks later, Hindenburg died. Hitler combined the jobs of President and Chancellor, calling himself simply ***Der Führer*** (the Leader). The Army now swore its loyalty oath to Hitler. In return for their support, Hitler had removed the SA. He now promised to increase the size of the army to half a million men, contrary to the Treaty of Versailles.

> **A* EXTRA**
>
> Hitler's other rival for power in Germany was the army. He settled this in 1938, when he sacked his War Minister, the Chief of Staff and 60 other generals for opposing his war plans.

## THE CHURCHES

The other big organisations in Germany to which lots of people belonged were the Churches. Hitler and many leading Nazis were hostile to Christianity, but about two-thirds of Germans were **Protestants** and one-third were **Roman Catholics**. At first, Hitler did not feel strong enough to attack the Churches. Many church members, particularly Protestants, supported the Nazis.

- Hitler made a '**concordat**' (agreement) with the Pope in 1933 not to interfere in the life of the Roman Catholic Church. However, his drive to establish total control led to shutting down monasteries and Catholic Youth groups. The Pope protested but it did no good. Several Catholic bishops were imprisoned.
- Hitler attempted to set up a 'Reich Church' of Nazi supporters, 'with the swastika on our chests and the cross in our hearts'. Many Protestants could not agree to this and left the Reich Church. Many were arrested and put in concentration camps, including their leader, Martin Niemoeller.
- Some smaller religious groups had firmly-held beliefs which were completely contrary to Nazism. Jehovah's Witnesses, for example, did not believe in serving in the army. Thousands of them were arrested and died in concentration camps.

## POLICE CONTROL

- Germany became a country where it was unsafe to do, or say, anything against the government.
- After 1936, the **Gestapo** (secret police) were under the control of **Himmler**, who also ran the SS. They could arrest and imprison anyone without trial.
- A network of informers ensured that no one dared to step out of line. People were encouraged to inform the police about neighbours or even their own family.
- They were helped by the members of the Nazi Party (grown to 5 million by 1938).

QUESTION SPOTTER

Typical exam questions on this topic:

- Describe how Hitler became dictator of Germany, 1933–1934.
- Describe how Hitler dealt with his opponents after he came to power in 1933.

- Every block, every village street, had its 'block leader' – 400,000 of them – to report on suspicious behaviour. 'Suspicious behaviour' could mean not giving the 'Heil Hitler' salute, or not letting their children join the Hitler Youth.
- There was an atmosphere of fear. Local police were run by Nazis. Judges swore an oath of loyalty to the Nazis.

### THOUGHT CONTROL

- Once Hitler was dictator of Germany, Goebbels turned his skill at **propaganda** to controlling the German people. Books, plays, films, newspapers, art and music – so free under the Weimar Republic – were now strictly controlled. In 1933, Nazi students held huge bonfires of books by authors of which the Nazis disapproved (see 4.7). No rival newspapers, magazines, radio stations were allowed. No material criticising Hitler or the Nazis was allowed to be published.

**4.7** *'Un-German' books being thrown on to a pyre, May 1933*

- Cheap radios were made and radio ownership went up four times in the 1930s. On their radios German people only heard what Goebbels wanted them to hear: how Hitler and the Nazis were making Germany great again. The message was even broadcast from loudspeakers in the streets.
- Hitler was almost worshipped. His picture was everywhere: in schools, offices, law-courts. He was portrayed as Germany's saviour from all its enemies.
- Huge rallies were held at the specially-built stadium at Nuremberg (see 4.8). Thousands of uniformed Nazis lined up, focused on the rostrum from which Hitler spoke. Whether seen in person, or on film, these rallies:

  1 showed the power of the Nazis

  2 gave a sense of discipline and order

  3 made people feel that everyone thought the same.

**4.8** *Nazi rally at Nuremberg*

## A* EXTRA

Do you think that Hitler's Germany was efficiently run? Many historians have pointed out that it was in fact quite chaotic. All power, in theory, lay with Hitler, but he only worked in the afternoons and did not try to know everything that was going on. His close colleagues could take their own decisions, and spent most of their time building up their own positions. Himmler, for example, built up the SS to be the biggest organisation in Germany. By 1945, he controlled the Gestapo, the 'Death's Head Units', which ran the concentration camps, the Waffen SS, fighting units which rivalled the army during the war years and some 150 factories using slave labour.

## QUESTION SPOTTER

Typical exam questions on this topic:

- Why were rallies such as the one shown in 4.8 important for building support for the Nazis?
- Analyse the ways in which this rally is designed to create loyal Nazis.

## CHECK YOURSELF QUESTIONS

**Q1** What were:
**a** the Enabling Act
**b** the Night of the Long Knives
**c** the Reich Church?

**Q2** 'Hitler became dictator of Germany quite legally.'
**a** When did Hitler become dictator?
**b** Is the statement above true?

**Q3** Using the photographs 4.7 and 4.8, explain how the use of 'thought control' and propaganda worked together to crush opposition in Germany.

*Answers are on page 189.*

REVISION SESSION 6

# Women and children

## What were Nazi plans for women?

- Hitler and the Nazis had clear ideas about what they wanted from women in the Third Reich. They used 'the stick' (passing laws) and 'the carrot' (encouragement and propaganda) to achieve what they wanted. In both cases, they were not completely successful.

**A* EXTRA**

The position of women in Nazi Germany contrasted with the relative freedom women had had in the Weimar Republic and were having in Britain and the USA at this time.

- The Nazis were, in many ways, old-fashioned in their views. The Nazi Party was a man's party, with no women in any senior positions. They did not like the idea of women's **equality** in jobs. Instead, they believed that women should stay at home, support their husbands and have lots of children:
  - for racial reasons, to build up the numbers of German people by increasing the birth-rate;
  - for economic reasons, to free jobs for unemployed men.
- The Nazis started by passing laws:
  - Women were removed from state employment. This meant they could not be employed as civil servants, lawyers, judges or doctors. Many women teachers and all Germany's 3,000 women doctors were sacked. Women could not serve on juries.
- Women were also encouraged to follow Nazi policy:
  - **Jobs: sex discrimination** was encouraged.
  - **Marriage and child-breeding:** couples received a loan of 1,000 marks on getting married. The more children you had, the less of this loan you had to pay back. They also gave medals for child-bearing: bronze for 4 children, silver for 6 and gold for 8. In 1938, childlessness was made grounds for divorce.
  - 'Racial purity' was ensured by **sterilising** women with hereditary diseases, or mental illness, even colour blindness (because soldiers need to be able to recognise colour). Unmarried women could also volunteer to have a child by an 'Aryan' SS member.
  - **Fashion:** Nazi propaganda discouraged wearing make-up, dyeing or perming your hair, wearing high heels, smoking in public. Posters encouraged peasant styles of fashion, flat shoes, hair in plaits or buns.
  - The propaganda image of women was thus one of the devoted wife, mother and home-builder. The traditional German '3Ks': *Kinder, Kirche, Küche* (children, church, cooking) summed up the Nazi ideal.

### PROBLEMS

- There were problems with the Nazi ideal. By 1937, Germany was short of workers. When the war got under way and men were called up into the armed forces, the shortage was even greater. So women were encouraged to take jobs. However, even at the height of the war, German women were never mobilised as much as women in Britain. German industry relied on slave labour from all over Europe.

**4.9** *Nazi poster of an 'ideal' family*

**QUESTION SPOTTER**

Typical exam questions on this topic:

- In what ways does poster 4.9 support Nazi ideas about women, children and the family?
- Why did the Nazis oppose equality for women?

## What were Nazi plans for children?

Young people were particularly important to the Nazis. They knew that they could never win over all Germans, but a new generation was growing up who would not know anything but the Third Reich. The lives of young people, especially boys, were controlled both in and out of school.

### IN SCHOOL

- Schools were taken out of the hands of local government and put under central government control. All teachers had to swear an oath of loyalty to Hitler and join the Nazi Teachers League. Jewish teachers were sacked.
- The curriculum was changed. The key subjects were History, Biology and PE.

  1 In History, all pre-Nazi textbooks were banned. Pupils were to be taught only about the greatness of the German race. The Nazi version of events was taught, including the so-called 'stab in the back' of 1918 and Hitler's great mission to restore Germany.

**A* EXTRA**

At school, Nazi ideology got into every part of the curriculum, even maths, as this problem shows:

'It costs 4 marks a day to keep a mentally ill person in care. There are 300,000 mentally ill people in Germany. How much, in total, do these people cost the country each year? How many marriage loans at 1,000 marks each could be granted from this money?

2 In Biology, they were taught a false 'race science', concerned with the superiority of the Aryans and the inferiority of races such as Jews, Slavs and black people.

3 The amount of PE in the timetable was tripled and boxing was made compulsory for boys. Hitler wanted fit people more than clever people, the boys to become soldiers and the girls to breed lots of Aryan babies.

### OUT OF SCHOOL

- Young people were expected to join one of the Nazi youth movements. From the age of 6 they could join the 'Pimpfen'. Then, from 10 to 14, they joined the Young Girls or the Young German Folk. Girls then joined the **League of German Girls** and boys joined the **Hitler Youth**.
- The Hitler Youth went camping, learnt Nazi songs and played games. They were taught how to overcome fear by doing things like jumping over fires.

**4.10** *Hitler Youth members jumping a bonfire at camp*

- They also had lots of Nazi political talks and films. Girls were given lectures on health, racial purity and child-rearing. Boys learnt to clean and fire rifles, read maps, go on long marches and throw hand grenades. In both cases, it was clear how the Nazis saw their future.
- There were 2.3 million youngsters in the Nazi Youth movements in 1933, about 30% of all young people in Germany. Only about half as many girls had joined their organisations as boys.
- Hitler appointed **Baldur von Schirach** to build up the numbers. From 1936, it became almost impossible not to join. Many young people were fanatical supporters of the Nazis. By 1939, there were 8 million members, about 82% of German young people.

**QUESTION SPOTTER**

Typical exam questions on this topic:
- Why did the Nazis try to win over children?
- What methods did the Nazis use to indoctrinate children?
- Were the Nazis successful in winning over children and young people to their ideas?

PROBLEMS

- By the late 1930s, when membership was virtually compulsory, nearly 1 in 5 young Germans had avoided joining. Those who were members were often fed up with the long, boring talks and readings from *Mein Kampf*, which they had heard many times before, about the Nazis and how Hitler was saving Germany. Many young people wanted to be left alone to lead their own lives. It was now more exciting to join rebel groups like the Swing or the Edelweiss Pirates (see p56).

## Check Yourself Questions

**Q1** How were German women under the Nazis encouraged to get married and have lots of children?

**Q2** Hitler, speaking about young people: 'Weakness has to be knocked out of them. The world will shrink in alarm from the youngsters who grow up in my schools: a masterful, dauntless, cruel, younger generation. Then I shall have in front of me the pure and noble natural material. With that I can create the new order. They shall learn to overcome the fear of death by the severest of tests.'

(adapted from *Hitler Speaks* by Hermann Rauschnigg, published in 1939)

Use this source and the information in this book to describe Hitler's educational aims.

*Answers are on page 190.*

REVISION SESSION 7

# The Nazi economy/resistance to Hitler

## What were Hitler's aims for the German economy?

Hitler had 3 aims for the German economy under 'the Nazi revolution':

- To **reduce unemployment** – one of his main election promises.
- To **re-arm Germany** – he always said he would do this, despite the restrictions in the Treaty of Versailles.
- To **make Germany more self-sufficient** – he knew that Germany was dependent on imported goods like rubber, textiles and petrol and so could be strangled in a wartime blockade (as the Allies had done in the First World War).

> **A* EXTRA**
>
> 1. Hitler did not know much about economics. He appointed Schacht as Minister of the Economy. Schacht did very well, fulfilling all 3 of Hitler's economic aims. However, he fell out with Hitler in 1938 because Hitler wanted to re-arm Germany faster than Schacht said the country could afford. He was sacked and sent to a concentration camp.
>
> 2. Goering took over the economy. He was also head of the *Luftwaffe* (the air force), but not an economist. Goering introduced a Four-Year Plan in 1937 to build up the economy so that Germany would be ready for war in 4 years.

## How was unemployment reduced?

- Before the Nazis came to power, a **National Labour Service** had been set up. This used government money to pay unemployed men to do public works, like planting forests, building houses and schools. Hitler expanded these schemes. He was especially keen on building 'autobahnen' (motorways). 80,000 men worked on these. These had great propaganda, as well as military, value – transporting motorised armies rapidly around the country.
- From 1935 all 18–25 year olds had to spend 6 months in the National Labour Service. They were paid only pocket money, wore uniforms and did drill, like soldiers. The scheme took millions off the unemployment figures.

### RE-ARMAMENT

- As soon as he came to power, Hitler ordered the building of aircraft, tanks, battleships and submarines, at first secretly and then, from 1935, openly. This military build-up provided work in factories, ironworks, coalmines and other industries. Hitler also increased the size of the army, from 100,000 in 1933 to 1,400,000 by 1939.
- The re-armament campaign also helped to reduce unemployment. It was down to 1 million by 1936 and by 1938 Germany needed more workers. However, quite a number of people had disappeared from the list of unemployed but were not actually in paid work: Jews, many women, soldiers, many 18–25 year olds.

### SELF-SUFFICIENCY

- Tough controls were put on imports. Industry was told to try to find substitutes for imported rubber, petrol, cotton and coffee.
- Agriculture was stepped up to try to feed all Germans without food imports. There were often shortages of some foods as a result, even before the war. It soon became clear that this was impossible unless Germany seized more land from other countries.

### WORKERS' LIVES

- Nazi policies for workers, like those for women and children (see p51), were that they should do as they were told, shut up, not complain, and the Nazis would make them happy.
- All workers had to join the **Labour Front**. There were no trade unions, so no way of negotiating better wages or conditions. Businesses and employers liked this, of course. Wages were low and hours long, but at least workers now had secure jobs. The standard of living of German workers remained quite low.
- The Nazis organised **'Strength through Joy'**. This campaign gave workers cheap holidays, foreign cruises, theatre trips, concerts, sporting facilities.
- The Nazis also promised workers a cheap 'workers' car', the **Volkswagen**. This was designed, and many workers began to pay for theirs, but none were delivered.

**4.11** *Men in the Labour Front*

## Did people like what Hitler was doing?

### PUBLIC OPINION

In a country with no free elections and no free media it is difficult to tell what public opinion is. Until the middle of the war – when rationing, bombing and high casualties brought increasing disillusionment – many Germans were quite happy with Hitler.

- He had carried out many of his promises.
- Most people had jobs.
- Germany was strong and successful.

Unless you were Jewish, or a Socialist or Communist, or a strong believer in personal freedom (and most Germans were none of these), you had little to complain about.

- People grumbled about the endless propaganda and the interference in their private lives.
- They attended the parades and meetings if their job depended on it.
- Anti-Nazi jokes were as far as most people dared to go.

### RESISTANCE

Caught between the fear of the Gestapo and the pressure of propaganda, resistance to Hitler was very difficult.

- The Communists and Social Democrats set up underground organisations. They published secret newsletters and sent information to friends abroad. Some workers **sabotaged** factories or railway lines. But they would not work together.

**QUESTION SPOTTER**

Typical exam questions on this topic:

- In what ways did Hitler try to put the German economy on a war footing?
- Did the Nazis improve the lives of ordinary Germans?

- Several priests and bishops spoke out against the Nazis. They managed to have the **euthanasia** campaign (see p58) stopped. Some hid Jews or helped them get out of the country. Some were imprisoned or executed. Martin Niemoeller, for example, was held in a concentration camp (1938–45). Some resisted more actively: Dietrich Bonhoeffer was executed in 1945.
- Later, in the war years, some in the army could see that Hitler was leading their country to destruction.
- In 1944, an attempt was made to assassinate Hitler: the Bomb Plot. It failed and 5,000 people were executed in retaliation.
- Some young people rejected the boring, restricted life in Nazi Germany.
  1. **Swing groups** were mainly middle class and admired British clothes and American jazz.
  2. Working-class young people joined a variety of groups all of which the Nazis called **Edelweiss Pirates**. They hung around together, drew anti-Nazi graffiti on walls and mocked the Hitler Youth.
  3. The **White Rose group** were students at Munich University, led by Hans and Sophie Scholl and Christoph Probst. They published anti-Nazi leaflets and posters. They were arrested and executed in 1944.
- Upper-class Germans despised Hitler at first, but agreed with his nationalist policies. Later they became disgusted with the Nazis' corruption and greed. Although this class was not firmly committed to democracy under Weimar, many came to see that strong democracy was a better system than dictatorship.

**QUESTION SPOTTER**

Typical exam questions on this topic:
- Who resisted Hitler and the Nazis in the years 1933–39?
- What difficulties did those who opposed Hitler and the Nazis face?
- How did the Nazis deal with those who opposed them?

## How did German people cope in the war years?

Germany was prepared for a short war, not a long one. Goebbels' wish for total war was only implemented from 1943 (see 4.12).

**4.12** *How German people fared during the war*

**German family**

**Rationing** introduced from start of war in 1939. Gradually got more severe until most Germans were living on a monotonous diet of potatoes, vegetables and cheap bread. Clothes were rationed too. The German people had been promised that they would get food from lands they conquered, but most of the loot from these territories went to Nazi Party members and to the **black market**.

German people faced the choice of fighting on or being overrun by their enemies, so they could only fall in with this.
- All non-essential shops and industries were closed.
- All sporting events stopped.
- Slave labourers were brought in from all over Europe to work in the factories.

Germany was bombed by the Allies with increasing intensity after 1942. Huge raids towards the end of the war devastated large parts of German cities. 150,000 people were killed in one night's raid on Dresden in 1945 – more than in Hiroshima. Millions of people were made homeless.

The hardship got worse as the war went on. There were almost no doctors, as Jewish doctors and women doctors had been sacked and most of the rest had been sent into the army.

So many men were called up that there were not enough left to work the land. In the towns and cities there was often no water, no power, no light, no food.

- From 1944 refugees began to pour into Germany from the East, fleeing from the Soviet Army. By 1945 there were 16 million refugees, of whom 2 million died.
- When Hitler committed suicide on 30 April 1945 Germany and its people were in a state of total devastation.

## ? Check Yourself Questions

**Q1** List the ways in which Hitler solved the unemployment problem.

**Q2** Look at the photograph of men in the Labour Front (4.11, p55). Use this source to describe the Labour Front.

**Q3** What were the motives of the various groups opposing Hitler?

*Answers are on page 191.*

# Hitler and racism

We have seen that Hitler was, in many ways, a clever politician, realistic and clear-thinking. When it came to **racism**, however, he was obsessive, with an unthinking hatred. Racism, particularly **anti-Semitism**, was something that Hitler had picked up early in his life, and carried with him to the end. Anti-Semitism had been present in Europe for centuries, but Hitler had the power and technology to take it to extremes.

## What were the results of Nazi racial beliefs?

- The Nazis believed in the superiority of the **'Aryan' race**. They encouraged women to breed more 'Aryan' babies (see p50). They also prevented certain people from having children: handicapped people, prostitutes and habitual thieves were sterilised.
- **Euthanasia** was secretly introduced for the mentally ill: 72,000 patients in mental hospitals were gassed between 1939 and 1941, until a campaign led by the church resulted in its being called off.

## What about Hitler and the Jews?

- About 1% of the population of Germany were **Jews**. Their ancestors had lived there for centuries and they were full German citizens.
- Hitler's attack on them began in his first few weeks in power. It was, like many of Hitler's measures, haphazard and unsystematic, but it became increasingly violent. As in other campaigns, he combined propaganda and law-making.

### PROPAGANDA

- In schools, **'race-science'** was put on the curriculum. Pupils were encouraged to identify and despise Jews.
- A campaign of hate was waged in Goebbels' propaganda newspapers, posters and films, with crude and vicious stereotyping of Jews.

### LAWS

- April 1933: a **boycott** of Jewish-owned shops. Shop windows were scrawled with Jewish symbols, SA and SS stood outside and intimidated anyone trying to go in.
- April 1933: Jews banned from all state jobs, as civil servants, broadcasters, teachers, journalists, lawyers.
- **Nuremberg Laws, 1935**: Jews could not be German citizens. Jews could not marry or have sexual relations with a German citizen.
- Over the next few years many other laws were passed. Some took away basic civil rights – like the right to vote, attend a state school, go to university, own a shop or business, or travel. Others affected small but important aspects of everyday life – like not being allowed to own a radio or a pet, not being allowed to go to the theatre, the cinema or a sporting event.

- In 1939, all Jews had to add the name 'Sara' (for women), or 'Israel' (for men), to their own names. From 1941, every Jew had to wear the Star of David badge.

### KRISTALLNACHT, 1938 ('THE NIGHT OF BROKEN GLASS')

- Angry at the treatment of Jews in Germany, a young Jewish student assassinated a German diplomat in Paris. This was made the excuse for a vicious attack by SS and other Nazis on Jews, their homes, businesses and synagogues all over the country. The police did nothing. 91 Jews were killed, 20,000 put in concentration camps. Jews in Germany were forced to pay the government a fine of one billion marks.

### THE 'FINAL SOLUTION'

- Hitler and the Nazis had various plans for German Jews. One idea was to transport them all to the African island of Madagascar. The war, and the huge conquests of land Germany had made by 1941, changed the situation. To the half million German Jews under Nazi rule were now added 4 million more in Poland and Russia. There were also the Slav populations of these areas, whom Hitler also considered to be 'inferior'.
- At first, the Nazis treated these people with casual violence. Jews were forced to live together, separately from the rest of the population in **ghettoes**. These were desperately overcrowded (e.g. the Warsaw ghetto held 400,000 people in an area where 100,000 people used to live).
- Then, in July 1941, came the proposal for the **'Final Solution'**. This was probably proposed by Goering and agreed by Hitler. Himmler was responsible for carrying it out: killing all 11 million Jews in Europe. It is a sign of the racist views at the heart of the Nazi Party that such an evil plan was talked of as a 'solution' to a 'problem'.
- It is not easy to kill millions of people one by one. At first they were shot by special units of the SS called *Einsatzgrüppen* (see 4.13).
- Then the Nazis turned to 20th-century technology to find a way of killing as many people as possible at once. **Gas chambers** were built at Auschwitz in 1941, which could kill 2,000 people at a time. Five other **death camps** were built, all in Poland. Auschwitz was the largest because of its position on the railway network.
- Jews were collected from all over Europe, put on trains (where many died), and taken to these camps. This went on until the end of the war, taking up fuel and trains which might have been put into the war effort. By then, 6 million Jews and 5 million others – including Slavs, gypsies and homosexuals – had been killed.

#### A* EXTRA

It was difficult, almost impossible, for Jews to resist what was happening, but some did. In April 1943, there was a rising in the Warsaw ghetto which held out for 42 days. There were rebellions and escapes at several concentration camps, including Treblinka.

#### A* EXTRA

On arrival at the death camps, families were separated. Most women, children, the elderly and the ill – about 80% of arrivals – were sent at once to the gas chambers. It took up to 20 minutes for them to die. The doors were then opened and special prisoners took out the bodies and burnt them. Those who were selected as fit to work toiled at the SS-run factories attached to the camps. With poor food and harsh treatment, they lasted about 2 months on average. At some camps gruesome 'medical' experiments were carried out on inmates.

## QUESTION SPOTTER

Typical exam questions on this topic:

- Describe how Hitler and the Nazis gradually deprived Jews in Germany of their rights as citizens.
- How did Hitler and the Nazis try to win over the German people to their anti-Semitic ideas?
- How did the Second World War change Nazi policy towards the Jews?
- What was the 'Final Solution'? How did the Nazis put it into effect, 1941–1945?

**4.13** *Jews being shot and put in a mass grave.*

## CHECK YOURSELF QUESTIONS

**Q1** What were:

**a** Kristallnacht?

**b** Nazi euthanasia policies?

**c** The Final Solution?

*Answers are on page 191.*

REVISION SESSION 1

# Russia before the Revolution

## Why was Russia in 1900 so difficult to rule?

- Russia was a vast country, 6,500 kilometres wide – 100 times bigger than Britain. On the long Trans-Siberian Railway, completed in 1904 (see 5.1), it took a week to make the whole journey from Moscow to the far East.
- Travel was difficult. Roads were full of mud in summer, blocked by snow in winter. Great rivers ran north-south and were used a lot. Railways were beginning to help the situation, although total railway mileage in Russia was only the same as in Britain.
- Only 40% of the people were Russian-speaking. The country was an empire of at least 16 different nationalities, many of whom resented being forced to adopt the Russian language and customs.
- Apart from these national divisions, Russia was deeply divided socially as well, with a huge gulf between the rich and the poor.

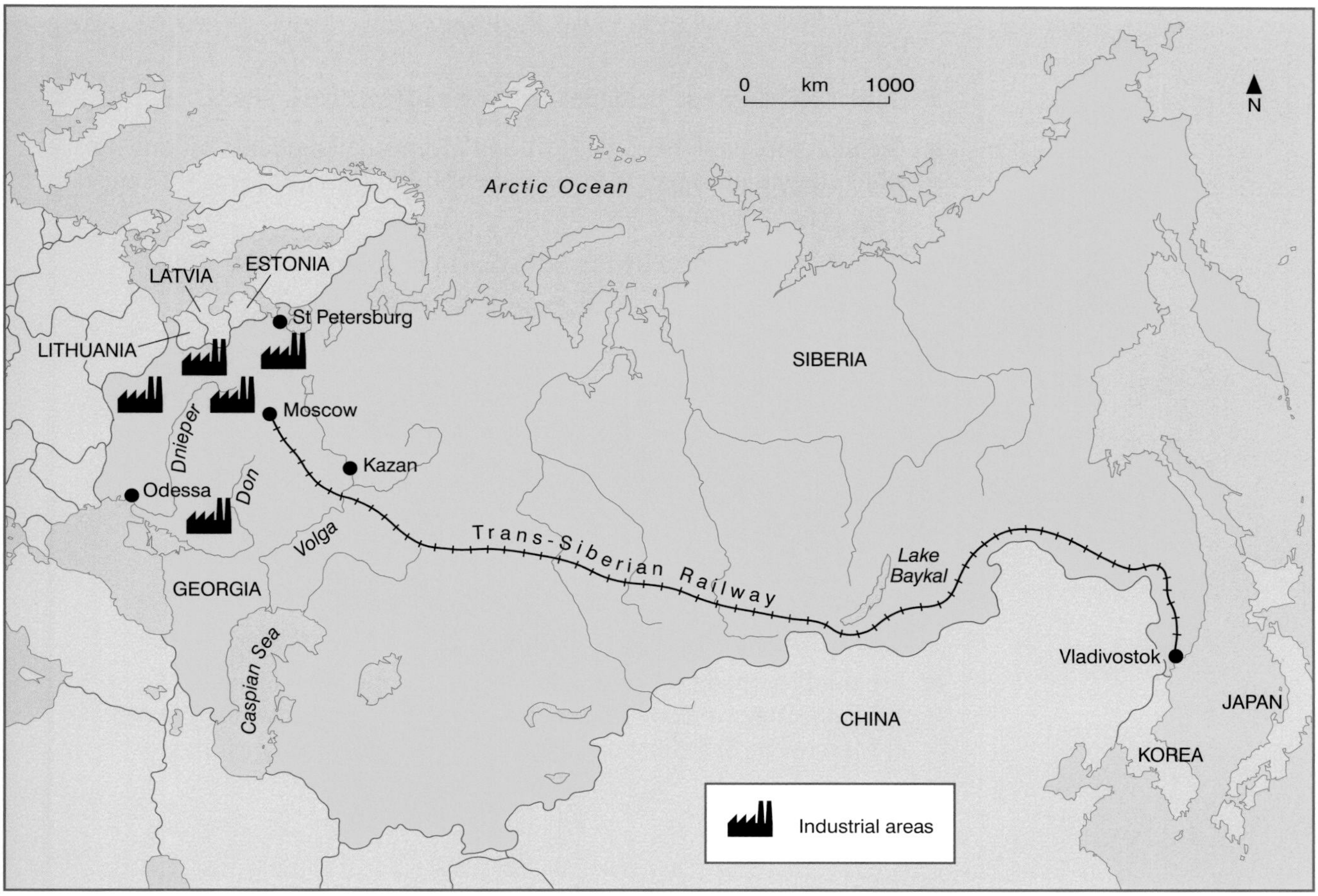


**5.1** *Map of Russia in 1900*

**5.2** *Peasants in a Russian village in about 1900*

## PEASANTS

- **Peasants** made up 80% of the people, living in villages, isolated by bad transport.
- Until 1861 they had belonged to their masters, like animals.
- The peasants were freed in 1861 and given small amounts of land, for which they had to pay the government back. The result was that they were very poor, with heavy debts.
- This was made worse by the 50% rise in population, 1860-1900.
- Peasants divided and sub-divided their land between their family, so their plots were very small.
- Most peasants could not read or write and still used old-fashioned farming methods, working their plots by hand.
- They were envious of the huge estates owned by the nobility (see below), but deeply suspicious of change.
- Disease was common and in years of bad harvest many died of starvation.

## NOBILITY

- The **nobility** made up only 1% of the population but owned 25% of the land. They were well-educated and rich, usually owning houses in Moscow or St Petersburg as well as on their country estates.

**5.3** *Guests at a countess' palace in St Petersburg*

## INDUSTRIALISTS

- Russia had industrialised later than most European countries and was not so developed. However, by 1900 there were huge textile factories, ironworks and other industries (see 5.1). Many were partly owned by foreigners or the government, but **industrialisation** did bring a new and growing class of bankers and factory-owners. They were often resentful of the power and influence of the old nobles.

## INDUSTRIAL WORKERS

- Conditions for the workers in these new factories were as bad as, if not worse than, those in Britain in the early Industrial Revolution: low pay, long hours (15–16 hours a day), terrible living conditions. Many of the workers were peasants who only came to the cities to work for a few months. Housing was overcrowded and unhealthy.

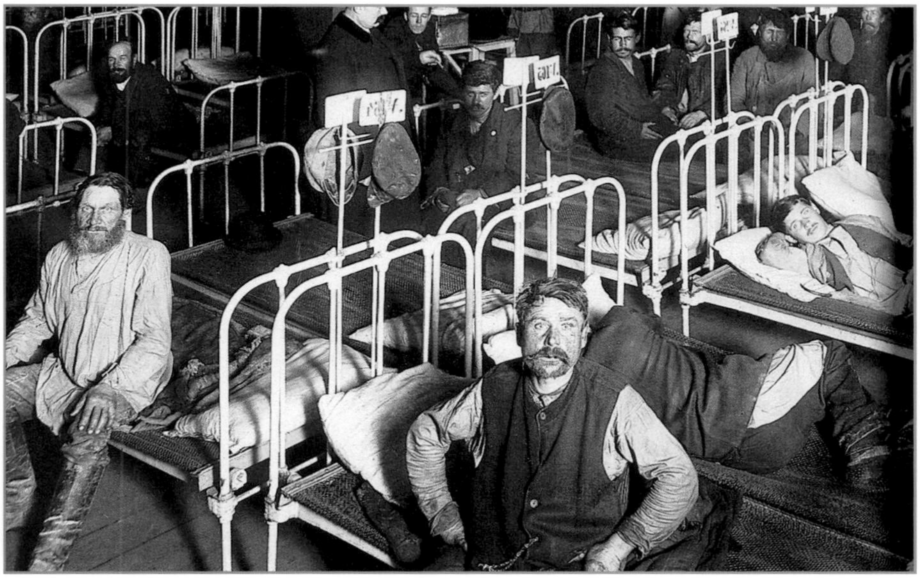

**5.4** *Industrial workers' living conditions in Moscow*

## A* EXTRA

Tsar Nicholas was strongly supported in his views by his wife Alexandra. She discouraged him from giving way to anyone. She later came under the influence of Rasputin (see p69), which further discredited the Tsarist government. Her influence over her weak husband helped to bring about his downfall.

## Who ruled Russia?

- The ruler of Russia was called the **Tsar**. He had complete power over the country. The Tsar appointed ministers to advise him but he did not have to take their advice. He took all decisions himself. There were no elections, no democracy at all. This system is called an **autocracy** (rule by one person).
- The Church supported this autocracy by teaching the Russian people that God had chosen the Tsar to be their 'little Father on earth' to look after them.
- Nicholas II had become Tsar in 1896. In an autocracy the personality of the autocrat is important.

**5.5** *Tsar Nicholas II and his family*

| Nicholas' good points: | Nicholas' bad points: |
|---|---|
| ▸ He was a kind and devoted family man.<br>▸ He believed he had been appointed by God to rule Russia well.<br>▸ He genuinely wanted the best for his people. | ▸ He had no idea how his people really lived and made no effort to find out.<br>▸ He could not rule alone, but employed large numbers of officials, many of whom were corrupt.<br>▸ He was weak: he usually agreed with the last person he had been talking to.<br>▸ He was cruel and obstinate. He clung to every bit of his power, hated opposition and used force to crush it.<br>▸ There was no free speech; there was censorship of newspapers and publishing; trade unions were banned; the secret police, the Okhrana, could arrest and imprison people without trial. |

## QUESTION SPOTTER

Typical exam questions on this topic:

- What problems did the Tsar face in 1900 in trying to rule Russia?
- How was Russia ruled in 1900?
- What were the main features of the rule of Tsar Nicholas II?

## Who were the opposition?

The key factors in Russia likely to cause change were the hardship of the peasants and the workers and a harsh, undemocratic government. All opposition groups were small, with little support among the masses of Russian people.

- **Cadets** (from the first letters of the Russian words Constitutional Democrats) were admirers of the democracies of Britain, France and the USA. They wanted Russia to have the same constitution. They were supported mainly by the small Russian middle class.
- **Social Revolutionaries** wanted to seize the land of the rich and share it out among the peasants. They had some peasant support. Their tactics, in the absence of any democratic elections, were to try to cause a revolution by assassinating government ministers.

- The Russian **Social Democrats** were a **Marxist** party split in 1903 over tactics:

  1 The **Mensheviks** wanted to set up a mass party, including industrial workers and trade unions.

  2 The **Bolsheviks** wanted to build a party of dedicated professional revolutionaries. Their leader was **Lenin**. Because of the Tsar's police, most of the Social Democrats lived in exile abroad. Lenin published his newspaper, *Iskra* (Spark) from London.

## Karl Marx (1818–1883)

A German writer who analysed society and political systems in Europe at the time. He explained that:

1. The economic system called capitalism is unfair because the **capitalist** (investor) makes huge profits out of the labour of the **proletariat** (workers) who actually do the work.
2. All history shows struggles between different classes, e.g. the struggle between middle classes and landowners which, he said, had led to parliamentary democracy in Britain and elsewhere in the 19th century.
3. The next stage in the class struggle would be a violent revolution in which the proletariat would throw out the capitalists and take over the country themselves.

## Check Yourself Questions

**Q1** What problems were faced by

**a** the peasants

**b** industrial workers

in Russia in about 1900?

**Q2** What were the main features of Tsarist autocracy under Nicholas II? How did he deal with opposition?

**Q3** Look again at photographs 5.2 to 5.5. Describe the differences you can see between the classes.

*Answers are on page 192.*

REVISION SESSION 2

# Russia 1905–1914

## Why was there a revolution in 1905?

### KEY FACTORS

The key factors for change outlined in the previous revision session came together in the early years of the 20th century to cause a revolution in 1905:

- Bad harvests brought hunger in the countryside.
- Depression in industry brought unemployment and wage cuts in the cities.
- The Tsar's government was seen to be incompetent and cruel.

### THE RUSSO–JAPANESE WAR, 1904–5

- The Tsar declared war on Japan in 1904, partly to distract the Russian people from their problems. He expected to do well. Instead, Russia suffered a series of humiliating defeats, culminating in the naval battle of Tsushima in May 1905, in which the Russian fleet was defeated in less than an hour.

### THE 1905 REVOLUTION

- Apart from what the war revealed about the Tsar's government, it brought further shortages and hardships for the people. Nicholas had decided that it would be better to allow some trade unions to be formed, under people he approved of (such as priests), as a way of avoiding more extreme protests.
- In January 1905 one of these leaders, **Father Gapon**, led a huge procession in St Petersburg to deliver a petition to the Tsar, asking for his help. They were met by troops who charged into the crowd and then fired at them . Many, perhaps thousands, were killed. It was called '**Bloody Sunday**'.

**5.6** *Troops fire on workers, St Petersburg, 22 January 1905*

- This was followed by a year of protests by all kinds of different groups, with different grievances.
  1 There were demonstrations all over the country calling for democracy in Russia.
  2 Peasants seized land for themselves and burnt their landlords' houses.
  3 Non-Russians protested against Russian rule.
  4 In June, sailors on the battleship 'Potemkin' mutinied.
  5 In September, there was a **general strike** (a strike of all workers).
  6 In October, a **soviet** (council) of workers was set up in St Petersburg.
- There was no attempt by the different groups to work together, but Nicholas was put under pressure. He issued the **October Manifesto**. This promised:
  1 a **Duma** (Parliament)
  2 free speech and freedom of the press
  3 freedom to set up and join political parties.
- This achieved just what Nicholas hoped: his opponents split. Some, like the Cadets, called off their protests because this was just what they wanted; others did not trust Nicholas.
- Meanwhile the Tsar had made peace with Japan, brought his best troops home and paid them well. With his opponents divided, Nicholas used them to crush the revolution. Its leaders were put in prison or fled abroad and the revolution fizzled out.
- Nicholas then passed the **Fundamental Law**. According to this law, the Duma would have little power, with its elections fixed to give more influence to the Tsar's supporters: there was to be 1 member per 2,000 nobles; there was only 1 member per 90,000 workers.
- Then, when the Duma met and began criticising him, Nicholas dismissed it. He did the same with the second Duma. Elections to the third Duma were even more weighted in the Tsar's favour and it sat, doing little, until 1912.
- The Tsar's opponents reached these conclusions about the situation:
  1 The Tsar was not to be trusted.
  2 There would be no revolution in Russia as long as the soldiers were loyal to the Tsar.

## 1905–1914: A new future for Russia?

Nicholas then appointed an able minister: **Stolypin**. His policies had two angles:

1 Repression of all opposition

2 Land reform.

### A* EXTRA

Some think that Stolypin's ideas might have led Russia to a different future and so avoided revolution. They point out that Russia was now more prosperous, and did have the beginnings of democracy, the Duma.

Others think that these reforms do not amount to much. Nicholas never really backed Stolypin and did not continue with his reforms after he was assassinated. The Duma was almost powerless, Nicholas would always resist change and Tsarism was doomed whatever happened.

## QUESTION SPOTTER

Typical exam questions on this topic:

- What were the short-term and long-term causes of the 1905 Revolution?
- How successful was Tsar Nicholas in dealing with the 1905 Revolution?
- What were the lessons of the 1905 Revolution for the opponents of Tsarism?

### TOUGH REPRESSION OF ALL OPPOSITION

- Contrary to the October Manifesto, **censorship** was re-introduced. The Okhrana increased its power. 20,000 opponents were exiled to Siberia. Over 1,000 were hanged.

### LAND REFORM

- Better-off, more enterprising peasants (called **kulaks**) were allowed to buy up land from other peasants. Special banks were set up to help them. By this **privatisation** of land, Stolypin hoped to create a middle class of well-off farmers, supporters of Tsarism. He called it 'A wager on the strong and sober'.

**Results:**

- About 15% of peasants took up the offer and agricultural production went up rapidly.
- Industrial production doubled, 1900–14. Russia became the fourth largest producer in the world of coal, pig iron and steel, and second largest producer of oil.
- Many peasants became poorer. Having sold their land, they were reduced to landless labourers.
- Industrial workers were still doing long hours, for low pay, in bad conditions.
- Stolypin was assassinated in 1911. Nicholas did not appoint anyone as able as Stolypin to follow him.

## CHECK YOURSELF QUESTIONS

**Q1** Make a list of the long-term and short-term causes of the 1905 Revolution.

**Q2** Why did the Tsar survive the 1905 Revolution?

**Q3** Strikes in Russia, 1905–14:

| | |
|---|---|
| 1905 | 13,995 |
| 1906 | 6,114 |
| 1907 | 3,573 |
| 1908 | 892 |
| 1909 | 340 |
| 1910 | 222 |
| 1911 | 466 |
| 1912 | 2,032 |
| 1913 | 2,404 |
| 1914 | 3,534 |

Suggest reasons for the differences in the figures shown here.

*Answers are on page 193.*

# The revolution of 1917

## How did the First World War help to cause the March 1917 Revolution?

When war broke out in August 1914, there was a wave of patriotic and pro-Tsarist emotion in Russia. Two and a half years later, Nicholas was forced off the throne. How did this happen?

### Short-term causes of the Revolution

- Before the end of 1914 the Russians had experienced two massive defeats, at Tannenberg and the Masurian Lakes. One million men were dead, wounded or taken prisoner.

  The war showed up huge faults in the Tsarist system. Soldiers were short of guns and boots. Many died from lack of medical supplies. Military leaders panicked and retreated. In September 1915, Nicholas decided to take over command of the army in person. Army morale improved, but it meant that he became associated personally with these faults.
- Soldiers began to mutiny. Some formed soviets (councils). Some simply deserted and went home.
- Nicholas and Alexandra's only son, Alexis (5.7), had **haemophilia** (hereditary blood condition in which the blood does not clot properly and the subject can bleed to death). Alexandra found that **Rasputin**, a strange peasant, had the power to stop Alexis' bleeding. She began to believe that Rasputin had been sent by God to help them. With Nicholas away at the war, Russia was run by Alexandra, who was under Rasputin's daily influence. In this situation even the upper classes lost support for **Tsarism**. Rasputin was murdered by a noble in 1916, but the damage had been done.
- **Shortages:** with 13 million men called up by 1916, the peasants were short of people to work the land. Less food was grown. Even worse, food was not getting through to the cities because the railways were in chaos. Food prices shot up in early 1917. There were also shortages of fuel.

**Note:** At this time Russia still used the old calendar, which was 13 days behind the rest of Europe. Thus the 'March revolution' took place at the end of February by the Russian calendar, and the 'November revolution' was called the October Revolution by Russians.

## A* EXTRA

The behaviour of the troops on the streets of Petrograd in March was a crucial difference from 1905. They were actually raw recruits – peasants in uniforms – and so likely to sympathise with the demonstrators. The Tsar dared not call up more disciplined, experienced troops for fear of weakening the battle front.

## THE MARCH 1917 REVOLUTION

- There were increasing strikes and protest demonstrations at the beginning of 1917.

1. On 7 March, there was a strike at the huge Putilov steelworks. Women, protesting about bread shortages, joined it.
2. On 12 March, some soldiers refused to fire at the demonstrators and shot their own officers instead.
3. At this point, the ruling classes decided that something had to be done in order to prevent a total revolution in which they would be swept away. They therefore told Nicholas he had to **abdicate** (give up being Tsar).
4. On 15 March, Nicholas agreed.

**5.7** *Tsarina Alexandra (left), Tsar Nicholas and their son, Alexis, aged 8 (carried by a soldier) on tour in 1913.*

## How did the Bolsheviks take over Russia?

- The Tsar's abdication left 2 different authorities in Russia:

  1 The Duma became the **Provisional Government**; it was called 'provisional' (= for the time being) because they wanted to hold full democratic elections to a proper parliament.

  2 But the **Petrograd Soviet** also had a lot of influence, as the council of workers and soldiers representatives. (The name St Petersburg sounded too German so it had been changed to Petrograd at the beginning of the war.) The Soviet agreed that, for the time being, the Provisional Government should be the government of Russia.

- A key minister in the Provisional Government was Kerensky, who was also on the Soviet and so acted as a bridge between them.

### THE FAILURE OF THE PROVISIONAL GOVERNMENT

- The March Revolution was an **abdication** by the Tsar. The real revolution now followed:
  - peasants seized land
  - workers took over control of factories
  - soldiers mutinied and deserted.
- For a little while – April and May 1917 – the **Provisional Government** had a chance of seizing the initiative. The Bolsheviks were weak – Lenin was actually in Switzerland. They could have led the revolution to become the new popular, democratic government of Russia. They failed to do so.
- The Provisional Government wanted to do everything properly and legally. They therefore decided:
  - Russia should have free speech, and free elections.
  - To stand by Russia's alliances with France and Britain and so continue with the war.
  - To leave all the other problems until the elections had been held.
- These things were not what the people wanted to hear.

**A* EXTRA**

Many Bolshevik leaders disagreed with Lenin in April and October 1917. They expected the next stage of Russia's history, ruled by democratic parliament, to last a long time. They thought Lenin was rushing things, and this would lead them only to disaster. Lenin had to use all the force of his personality to persuade them to act.

### LENIN

- At this point Lenin, the leader of the Bolsheviks, returned to Russia. The Germans had allowed him to travel by train through their country in the hope that he would stir up trouble in Russia and take it out of the war. They were not disappointed.
- As soon as he arrived in Russia in April 1917, Lenin called on the Bolsheviks to seize power. His slogans were: 'All Power to the Soviets!' and 'Peace, Land and Bread!'

**5.8** *Lenin*

- Lenin's ideas were written up as the **April Theses**. Most Bolshevik leaders disagreed with him, but it was soon clear that his ideas were popular:

  1 the soldiers wanted peace,

  2 the peasants wanted land,

  3 the workers in the cities wanted bread, and they were all getting increasingly impatient.

## THE JULY DAYS

- In July, **Kerensky** ordered a new advance against Austria but it brought another defeat.
- Soldiers began to desert the army in thousands. They were mostly peasants, who had heard that the peasants at home were seizing land from landlords and they wanted to be there.
- There were anti-war demonstrations in Petrograd. The Bolsheviks tried to use them to seize power, but did not have enough support. Kerensky used soldiers to crush them and nearly arrested Lenin, who had to flee abroad again.

## KORNILOV

- In September, **General Kornilov** began to send his army towards Petrograd to remove the Provisional Government and restore the Tsar.
- In panic, Kerensky gave weapons to anyone who would use them to defend him. Many Bolsheviks formed **Red Guard** units (see 5.9).
- In fact, Kornilov's advance was stopped by Bolshevik railway workers who sabotaged his trains.

### QUESTION SPOTTER

Typical exam questions on this topic:

- How important was the First World War in bringing about the March 1917 Revolution?
- How did the First World War affect: (a) peasants, (b) industrial workers, (c) soldiers?
- Why did the Provisional Government fail?

**5.9** *Armed Red Guard units*

## THE BOLSHEVIKS SEIZE POWER, NOVEMBER 1917

- By October, Russia was in chaos. The Provisional Government had failed to end the war. It had tried to stop peasants seizing land and had failed to deal with food shortages.
- The Bolsheviks, on the other hand, had increased their support among soldiers, sailors and workers.

  1 They alone seemed to be willing to give people the changes they were looking for.

  2 They were armed.

  3 They had a leader, **Lenin**, who knew exactly what he wanted and an organiser, **Trotsky**, who could carry it out.

- On the night of **6 November 1917**, Red Guard units took control of key points in Petrograd: post office, stations, bridges over the rivers. They then took over the Winter Palace where the Provisional Government was, and arrested them. Kerensky fled abroad.

### A* EXTRA

The 'November Revolution' was not a revolution of the people on the streets like the March revolution. It was really a Bolshevik seizure of power, or 'coup'.

**5.10** *Trotsky*

## CHECK YOURSELF QUESTIONS

**Q1** Look at the four factors listed as the short-term causes of the March Revolution (p69). Write a sentence on each one, showing how it was linked to the war.

**Q2** Why did the Provisional Government only last 8 months?

*Answers are on page 193.*

REVISION SESSION 4

# The Communists and the Civil War, 1917–1921

Although they had seized power in Petrograd, the Bolsheviks were far from being in control of the whole of Russia. There were only 250,000 of them and they had little support in the countryside. They only took over Moscow after several days' fighting.

## How did the Bolsheviks take over Russia?

### THE BOLSHEVIK GOVERNMENT

- They set up a government, called the **Council of People's Commissars** ('Sovnarkom' for short). Lenin was chairman, Trotsky was Commissar for War, Stalin was Commissar for Nationalities and there was one woman, Alexandra Kollontai. Several far-reaching decrees were passed quickly:
  - All class distinctions were abolished. Instead of 'Your Grace', Your Excellency' etc., everyone now called each other *Tovarich* (comrade).
  - All distinctions of rank in the armed forces were abolished.
  - All land belonging to the Tsar, the Church and the nobility was taken over by the peasants.
  - Workers should not work more than 8 hours a day and 48 hours a week.
  - All factories were taken over by the workers. All banks and foreign trade were taken over by the government acting in the name of the workers.
  - Equal rights for women.
- All these decrees were simply telegraphed out to other parts of Russia in the hope that they would be obeyed.

### THE CHEKA

- Lenin also set up his own secret police – the **Cheka**.
- All non-Bolshevik newspapers were closed down.
- After three attempts to kill Lenin, the Cheka were given the power to arrest and execute opponents without trial. The **'Red Terror'** began.

### THE CONSTITUENT ASSEMBLY, 1918

- Lenin had to hold free elections to a **Constituent Assembly**, which met in January 1918. The Bolsheviks only won 175 seats out of 707. The Social Revolutionaries (see p64) won 370.
- Lenin surrounded the building with Red Guards and closed the Assembly after 1 day. So ended Russia's first freely-elected government – the last for another 74 years.

### THE TREATY OF BREST-LITOVSK, 1918

- Lenin had to get Russia out of the war by making peace with Germany. He hoped that the revolution in Russia would spark off Communist revolutions elsewhere, but they did not happen. He was forced to sign harsh terms.

> **A* EXTRA**
>
> Lenin devised an idea called 'The Dictatorship of the Proletariat' to defend his own dictatorial rule. He claimed that, in the crisis Russia was going through, the Communists had to act dictatorially on behalf of the workers (proletariat) to ensure that the Bolshevik revolution was not crushed. This explained the Cheka and the rest of the 'Red Terror'. In time, he said, government would not be necessary. It would 'wither away'.

- As map 5.11 shows, Germany seized lots of territory from Russia – some, but not all, of which was returned at the Treaty of Versailles. Russia lost 25% of its people, 27% of its best farmland, 26% of its railway system and 70% of its iron and coal industries.

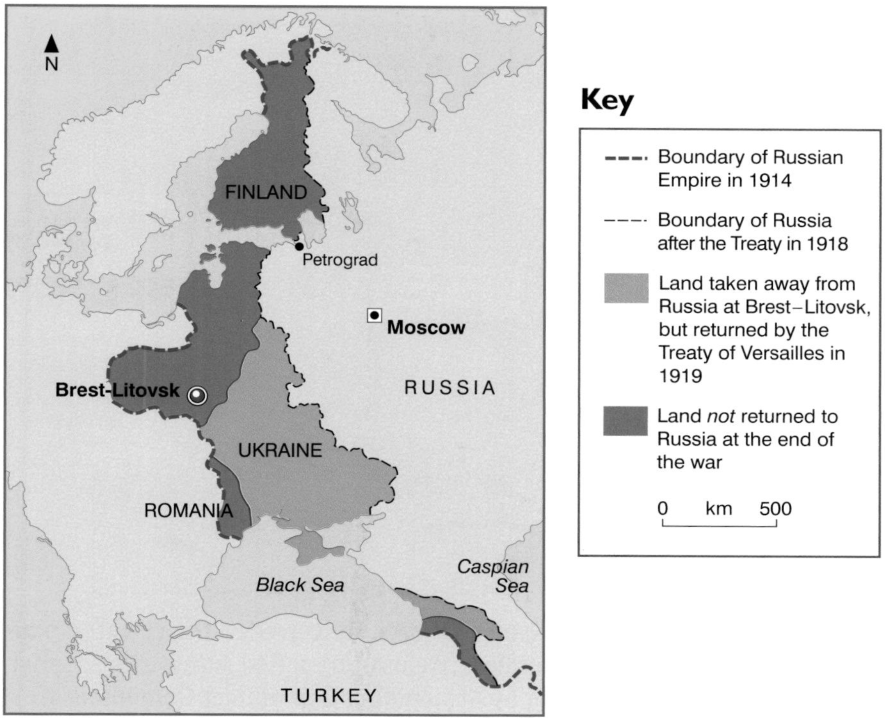


**5.11** *Russian losses at the Treaties of Brest-Litovsk and Versailles*

## Why was there a civil war 1918–1921?

- By 1918, there was civil war in Russia. On one side were the **Communists** (Reds), as the Bolsheviks were now called. On the other were all kinds of groups, called **Whites**, wanting to overthrow them. At one point there were 30 governments in different parts of Russia. The Whites were helped by other countries – Britain, France, USA – angry at Russia pulling out of the war and determined to stop the spread of Communism. Japan and Poland invaded to see what they could get. There was also a legion of Czech prisoners-of-war who seized control of part of the Trans-Siberian Railway (see 5.12).
- It took over three years' fighting for the Communists to remove all their enemies from the country.

### REASONS FOR THE COMMUNISTS' VICTORY IN THE CIVIL WAR

- The Reds were united in wanting to hold on to power in order to build a Communist state. The Whites were not united. There were all kinds of groups: Tsarists, Cadets, Social Revolutionaries – who did not work together.
- The Reds held the central heartlands of Russia. This meant they could use the core of the railway system to supply their armies. The Whites were huge distances apart (see 5.12), and had problems supplying their armies.

**A* EXTRA**

1. Foreign help to the Whites was rather half-hearted. Allied soldiers were not keen to fight on behalf of Tsarism to crush a workers' government.

2. The situation in Russia was very confused in the Civil War. Some forces, often called 'Greens', supported neither the Reds nor the Whites but fought to be free of outside control. These were Anarchists and Nationalists.

**5.12** *Russia in the Civil War, 1918–21*

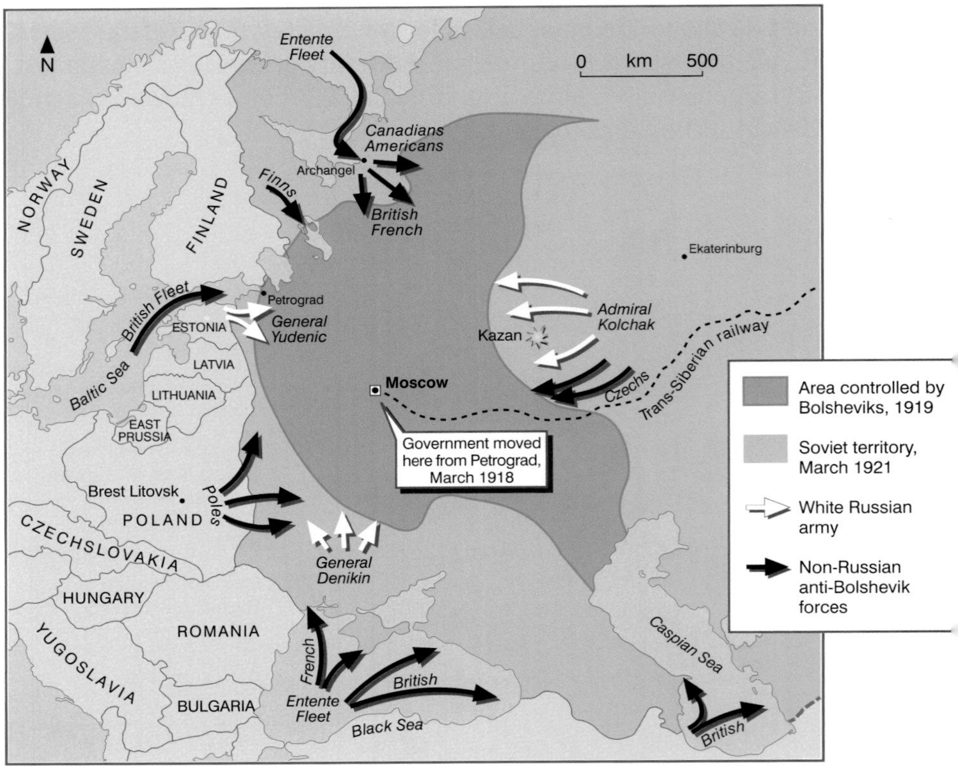


## QUESTION SPOTTER

Typical exam questions on this topic:

- What changes did the Bolsheviks make in Russia in the first few months after they seized power in November 1917?
- Why did the Whites fail to overthrow the Bolshevik Government?
- What were the results of the Civil War of 1918–1921 for the people of Russia?

- The Reds had one dynamic leader, Trotsky. He travelled the country in an armed train, urging on his soldiers. He built up a Red Army, using Tsarist officers but controlling them by attaching a Communist Commissar to each one and sometimes by holding their families hostage.
- The three main White leaders – General Denikin, General Yudenich and Admiral Kolchak – did not cooperate.
- The Reds got more support from patriotic Russians as the Whites were helped by foreigners.
- The Communists had given the peasants the land they wanted. The peasants were not sure about the Communists, but they knew that if the Whites won the landlords would demand their land back.
- The Reds used **War Communism** (see p77) to get the supplies they needed. This included 'Red Terror' measures. In 1918, the Tsar and all his family were murdered at Ekaterinburg. The Whites used 'White Terror' which was just as bad.

## CHECK YOURSELF QUESTIONS

**Q1** Why did Lenin do the following things in 1917–18:

**a** Give up so much land to Germany at the Treaty of Brest-Litovsk?

**b** Put factories under the workers' control?

**c** Take over all banks and foreign trade?

**d** Set up the Cheka?

**Q2** What part did Trotsky play in the Civil War?

**Q3** Who supported the Reds in the Civil War?

*Answers are on page 194.*

# REVISION SESSION 5 Lenin's rule, 1917–1924

## WAR COMMUNISM

**'War Communism'** is the name given to the particularly harsh Communist measures Lenin introduced in the Civil War, while the Communists were fighting for their survival.

- All factories were taken over by the government. They were told what to make, at what price. Everyone had to work: men and women, aged 16–60. There was strict discipline and strikes were illegal.
- Peasants were not allowed to trade the grain and other food they grew. The government simply took what they wanted. Detachments of soldiers, armed with machine-guns, went out into the country to seize grain.
- Food was rationed and only workers could have a ration card. Hoarding food was a crime for which you could be shot by the Cheka.

**Results:**

- The peasants refused to cooperate, and grew less grain.
- Coming on top of the First World War and civil war, this led to a famine in 1921 in which perhaps 7 million people died.
- In 1921, there was a mutiny of the sailors at the Kronstadt naval base near Petrograd. Sailors had previously been Bolsheviks and now demanded 'soviets without Communists', free speech and free elections. Trotsky's soldiers crushed the mutiny, but it was a blow to Lenin and the Communist leadership.

## NEW ECONOMIC POLICY (NEP)

Lenin introduced **NEP** in 1921. It was a dramatic change as it allowed several aspects of capitalism to return. Lenin said it was only temporary, to revive the country until it was 'ready' for Communism.

- Small factories were given back to private ownership.
- Peasants were allowed to sell their grain and other food on the open market.
- Heavy industry like iron, steel and coal, as well as railways, banking and foreign trade, were kept in the hands of the government. However, 'experts' were called in to manage them, and paid high salaries.

**Results:**

- Some Communists were angry. They said it was a retreat for the Communist revolution.
- The Russian economy revived, rapidly and steadily. Food was on sale in the streets. Restaurants opened. Consumer goods reappeared in the shops.
- Some people got rich: **'Nepmen'** were rich business people; **kulaks** were better-off peasants.

**A* EXTRA**

Note how governments had to pay attention to the demands of the peasants. Kerensky's failure to let them have the land they demanded led to his downfall. Lenin gained support by supporting their demands. He then had to deliver his promise, even though Communists did not accept private ownership of land. After War Communism Lenin had to give in and introduce NEP in order to halt the famine. As they made up 75% of the population, the peasants' demands could not be ignored or over-ruled.

UNION OF SOVIET SOCIALIST REPUBLICS (USSR)

- In 1923, a new constitution was introduced. In theory, it set up separate republics for each national group; in practice, the whole country was run by the Soviet Communist Party.

## Did Lenin change the lives of the Soviet people?

As we saw on page 74, the Communists were not widely supported in 1917.

In the next few years they made a big effort to win people over.

- **Propaganda in art:**
  1 New ideas in art – particularly poetry, music and painting (especially posters) – were encouraged.
  2 New techniques in film-making were developed by Eisenstein.
  3 Propaganda trains went out across the USSR with theatre groups and films.
- The Communists tried to bring about **equality for women** but met lots of resistance, especially in the countryside.

**5.13** *Peasants watching the first electric lights in their village*

- The **Church** was attacked. Many Russians chose not to have a church wedding. Divorce was made easier.
- **Education:** a mass literacy campaign began; peasants' children could go to university free.
- A large-scale **electrification programme** began, to bring electric power to every village in Russia. Lenin said 'Soviet Power plus electrification equals Communism'.
- Most people remained unsure of Communism, but many were won over and became devoted party activists.

DEATH OF LENIN

- Lenin had been shot in 1918. The doctors were not able to remove two bullets from his head. In 1922, he suffered a severe stroke and was unable to work. He died in 1924, aged only 54. He was made a hero: his body was laid out in state and then embalmed.

## CHECK YOURSELF QUESTIONS

Q1 Why was the Kronstadt Mutiny so serious for Lenin?

Q2 What was new about NEP?

Q3 Look again at 5.13. What did Lenin mean by 'Soviet Power plus electrification equals Communism'?

*Answers are on page 193.*

# REVISION SESSION 1 — How Stalin became leader

Lenin died in 1924. He had no automatic successor: several of the leading Communists were able and popular. The least likely to succeed was **Joseph Stalin**, the General Secretary of the Communist Party. Yet by 1929 he had become undisputed ruler of Russia, a position he held until his death in 1953.

To outwit Trotsky and the others, Stalin used:

- trickery
- rivalry between other Communist leaders
- his support in the Party
- policy differences.

**6.1** *Lenin with Stalin. Lenin and Stalin were not actually close friends and this picture may be a fake.*

**Josef Stalin (1879–1953)**

*Real name:* Josef Djugashvili

*Born:* Georgia, of middle-class parents

*Background:* Began to train as a priest but soon became a Bolshevik revolutionary. Tsarist secret police arrested him several times. He changed his name to Stalin ('man of steel') in prison.

*Political involvement:* Took part in 1917 Revolution and was made Commissar of Nationalities.

*Main role:* Took on boring but important job of General Secretary of Communist Party (1922). Used his position to build up support in the Communist Party: after a few years his supporters held key positions at all levels.

*Character:* Not a great thinker, but very hard-working. The one thing at which he showed tremendous skill was in out-manoeuvring his rivals, particularly Leon Trotsky.

**Leon Trotsky (1879–1940)**

*Real name:* Lev Bronstein

*Born:* son of Jewish farmers

*Background:* Leader of Petrograd Soviet in 1905 Revolution, but was a Menshevik and only joined the Bolsheviks in 1917. Most well-known Bolshevik after Lenin.

*Political involvement:* Played important part in 1917 Revolution and a crucial role in creating the Red Army in Civil War (see Unit 5).

*Main role:* Commissar for War (1922).

*Character:* Powerful speaker, thinker and organiser. However, he was arrogant and made no effort to build up support. Other Bolsheviks mistrusted him: they were suspicious that he was such a recent Bolshevik and feared he would use the army to become a dictator. He was ill for much of the time following Lenin's death

FIRST STAGE, 1924–25

- Stalin told Trotsky that Lenin's funeral was a day earlier than the real date. Trotsky did not turn up; Stalin did, and made a great show of being Lenin's keenest follower. He made sure pictures like 6.1 were published.

| | |
|---|---|
| **Stalin** put forward 'Socialism in One Country': developing Communism in the USSR first. | **Trotsky** put forward a policy of 'World Revolution'. He said Communism in the USSR would only survive if other countries became Communist too. This meant promoting revolutions elsewhere. |

- Stalin managed to out-vote Trotsky with the support of:
  - other Communists, anxious to see Trotsky pulled down
  - his supporters in the Party
  - ordinary Communist Party members, who feared that 'World Revolution' would involve them in more wars. They were fed up with war and keen only to get on with building Communism in the Soviet Union.
- In 1925, Trotsky was removed from his post as Commissar for War.

SECOND STAGE, 1925–27

- The USSR still faced the problem of how to develop industry and modernise peasant farming. The Communist Party was split over how to do this:
  - Right-wing Communists wanted to keep on with NEP, slowly building up industry with peasant cooperation.
  - Left-wing Communists wanted a crash programme of rapid industrialisation, forcing the peasants to join collective farms (see p86).
- For a while Stalin held the balance, then threw his weight in favour of the right-wingers. In 1927, Trotsky was expelled from the Communist Party, along with other leading left-wingers, and their supporters.

**A* EXTRA**

1. The leaders of the left-wing Communists were Zinoviev and Kamenev, both ex-Bolsheviks who had worked with Lenin for years. The leading right-winger was Bukharin, also a former Bolshevik and a popular leader and thinker.

2. Lenin, in his 'Testament', said Stalin was 'too rude', 'not cautious enough' and should be removed. Lenin also criticised Trotsky and other leading Communists. The 'Testament' was not made public, much to Stalin's relief.

THIRD STAGE, 1928–29

- Stalin then turned on the right wing and began forcing **collectivisation** through. (Farms and factories were to be brought under state ownership and control.) All right-wingers were removed from important positions. By 1929, all his opponents – to right and left – and their leaders, were out of power. Only Stalin's supporters remained.

- Stalin was not a man to forgive and forget. Trotsky was sent to Siberia in 1928, expelled from the USSR in 1929 and murdered by one of Stalin's agents, in Mexico, in 1940. You can read what happened to his other former rivals on page 88.

## Check Yourself Questions

**Q1** Make a list of points for and against Trotsky in the clash for the leadership of the USSR after Lenin's death.

**Q2** Give an example of each of the 4 tactics used by Stalin to outwit his rivals between 1924 and 1929.

**Q3** What have you learnt about Stalin's personality so far?

*Answers are on page 195.*

REVISION SESSION 2

# Stalin and industry

When Stalin won the struggle to be leader in 1928, the USSR was not a heavily industrialised country. By 1941, it had the industry to support a massive and victorious war against Hitler's Germany. After that, the USSR challenged the might of the USA in the Cold War.

## Why did Stalin decide to industrialise so fast?

INDUSTRY IN THE USSR IN 1928

- Some industry had been built up under the Tsars, but it was restricted to only a few areas (see 5.1, p61).
- This early growth had been severely disrupted by the First World War, the Revolution (see p70) and the Civil War (see p74).
- Industry was not a big part of the USSR's economy. Only about 20% of people worked in industry.

> **A* EXTRA**
>
> The Tsars had tried to encourage the growth of Russian industry. Ever since they came to power, the Communists had been discussing how to industrialise. After all, they were the party of industrial workers. More industry would, they thought, mean more industrial workers, so more support among the people.

In 1928, Stalin decided to industrialise the USSR as rapidly as possible. His reasons were:

- fear of other countries invading Russia. In fact, although many governments were hostile to Communism, no one had any plans to invade the USSR at the time. However, Stalin was naturally suspicious and found threats everywhere. It is true that other countries were hostile to the Communists and some had supported the Whites against the Communists in the Civil War.

> It is worth learning the italicised sentences from this famous speech of Stalin's from 1931, which explains his attitude:
>
> 'The history of old Russia consisted in being beaten again and again because she was backward. If you are backward you may be beaten and enslaved. If you are powerful, people must beware of you. *We are 50 or 100 years behind the advanced countries. We must make up this gap in 10 years. Either we do it or they crush us.*'

- Stalin was fed up with the peasants charging high prices for food under NEP. Like several leading Communists, he suspected the peasants were cutting the supply of food to the cities in order to keep prices up. He was determined to smash their resistance. Rapid **industrialisation** would need rapid changes in agriculture and these would break their power.

## How did he industrialise?

Stalin set up a **planned economy** with targets for each industry.

- The state planners, **Gosplan**, set each industry a national target (see 6.2).

| | 1928 output | 1932 target | 1932 actual production | 1937 actual production |
|---|---|---|---|---|
| Coal | 36 | 76 | 65 | 130 |
| Iron | 3 | 10 | 6 | 15 |
| Oil | 2 | 22 | 22 | 29 |

**6.2** *The Five-Year Plans (output in millions of tonnes)*

This was divided into further targets, so that:

- each region set a target for each factory
- each factory set a target for each shift
- each shift set a target for each worker
- each worker had to produce the target.

Each industry had a Five-Year Plan to increase production:

- **First Five-Year Plan (1928–32)**: concentrated on heavy industry: coal, iron, oil, electricity.
- **Second Five-Year Plan (1933–37)**: concentrated on heavy industry, but also on transport (new roads, railways, canals and the Moscow underground were built) and on mining, particularly in new areas.
- **Third Five-Year Plan** (started in 1938 but was abandoned in the war): concentrated on re-arming for the war.

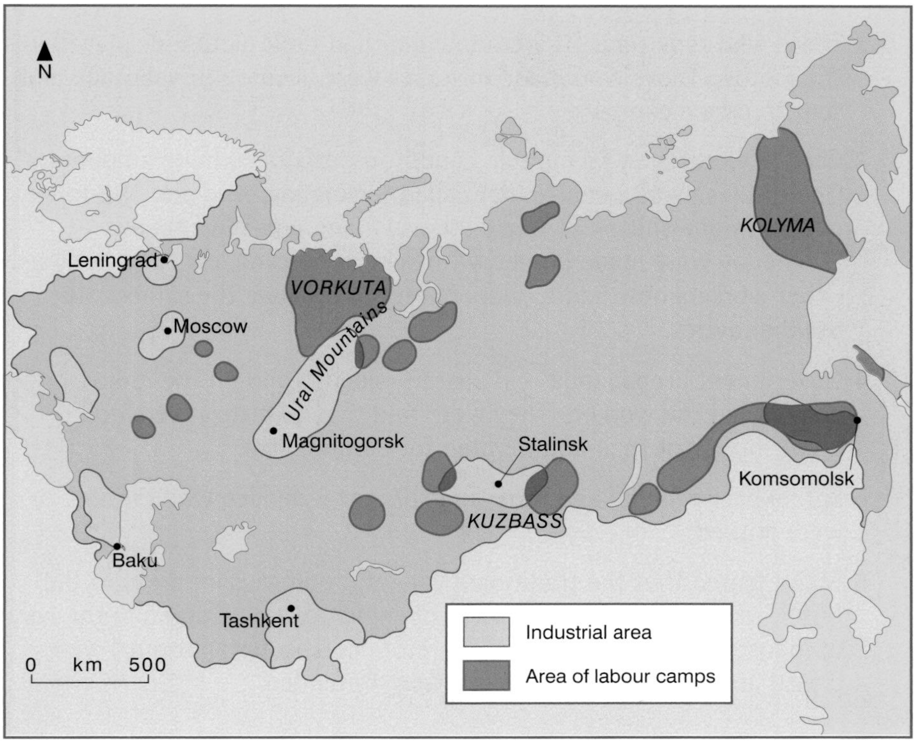


**6.3** *The USSR under the Five-Year Plans*

> **A* EXTRA**
>
> The system of central planning was very rigid. Local factories had no room to use their initiative: all they had to do was fulfil their targets. It might have been a good way to 'kick-start' industrial growth, but it made Soviet industry inefficient and slow to react to change. It was always unable to produce consumer goods in quantity and quality and was a major reason for the collapse of Communism in the late 1980s.

> **QUESTION SPOTTER**
>
> Typical exam questions on this topic:
> - Why did Stalin want to industrialise the USSR?
> - How did Stalin set about getting more work out of the Soviet people?

## How were the targets to be achieved?

The increases in production in the targets were so great that it was not going to be enough just to work a little bit harder.

The whole Soviet Union was transformed:

- New areas of industry were opened up (see 6.3). There were new towns, with new factories and houses for those who worked in them.
- Millions of new workers were needed.

  1 Some were **foreigners** – skilled workers paid high wages to show the Russians what to do.

  2 **Women** were recruited in large numbers; factories had nurseries so that women could soon return to work after their children were born. 80% of new workers in the second Five-Year Plan were women. 40% of industrial workers in 1937 were women, compared with 28% in 1927.

  3 **Peasants** were encouraged to leave the land to work in industry.

  4 On many schemes Stalin used **forced labour** by convicts in the prison camps.

- These millions of workers had to be made to work hard to achieve their targets.

  1 Hours were long.

  2 Those who took time off were fined, or had their picture displayed in the factory. Those who made mistakes were accused of sabotage and sent to prison camps.

  3 Certain workers, in favourable conditions, produced huge amounts. One of these was a coal-miner called Stakhanov, who dug 102 tonnes of coal in one shift – 14 times the usual amount. Workers like Stakhanov were made heroes, with special housing, cars and honours. Other workers now had to work harder to produce the same as the **Stakhanovites**.

  4 Government propaganda – in posters, slogans and on the radio – bombarded the workers. They were told that that they were doing great things for their country and for Communism.

  5 Safety was minimal and thousands of inexperienced workers died or were injured.

  6 Stalin feared that the traditional way of life in Muslim areas of the USSR, where new industries were opening up, would stand in the way of industrialisation. Islam was therefore persecuted: mosques were closed and pilgrimages to Mecca were forbidden.

RESULTS

- The USSR became an industrial giant. The table 6.2 (p83) shows that the 1932 targets were rarely achieved, but that production by 1937 was way ahead of what it had been 10 years earlier.
- Workers' standard of living fell.
  1. The concentration on heavy industry meant a shortage of **consumer goods** (the things people need, like shoes, clothes, household appliances).
  2. '**Real wages**' (what you can actually buy for your money) fell.
  3. Conditions in the new towns were appalling.
  4. People lived in over-crowded flats, with expensive food and few amenities.
- On the other hand, there was no unemployment, there was free health care and free education.

**A* EXTRA**

**Compare the growth in Soviet industry in the 1930s with depression and unemployment throughout the capitalist world at this time.**

## CHECK YOURSELF QUESTIONS

**Q1** **a** What were the Five-Year Plans?

**b** How did they work?

**Q2** How did Stalin make his workers work harder?

**Q3** What were the effects of industrialisation on the people of the USSR?

There is quite a lot you could write about here, but it needs to be planned if it is not to look haphazard. Various ways of splitting it up could be used: you could divide your answer into good and bad effects; or you could look at working and living conditions separately, as in this plan:

'At work, the Soviet people had to...'

'People's home life was changed because...'

'There were some improvements to their out-of-work lives because...'

*Answers are on page 196.*

REVISION SESSION 3

# Stalin and agriculture

## QUESTION SPOTTER

Typical exam questions on this topic:

- In what ways was the collectivisation of agriculture intended to help the industrialisation of the USSR?
- Why was there so much opposition to the collectivisation programme from the peasants?
- Was the collectivisation of farms a failure?

## Why collectivise?

- Stalin could not turn the USSR into a modern industrialised state without changing agriculture. He needed:
  - more food to feed the people in the new cities he was building.
  - more workers for the new factories he was setting up.
  - more food to sell abroad (this would give him the money to buy foreign industrial machines).
  - more control over the countryside.

## What was agriculture like in the USSR in 1928?

- Farming methods were old-fashioned, with few machines and lots of small farms. Many peasants had little or no land and so were very poor. Some peasants owned more land. These were called **kulaks** and were doing quite well under NEP. However, they grew what they liked and were only interested in making a profit for themselves.

### COLLECTIVE FARMS

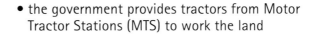

- A collective farm was called a **kolkhoz**. It should be more efficient because:
  - all land is farmed together in much larger units
  - the government provides tractors from Motor Tractor Stations (MTS) to work the land
  - all tools and animals are pooled
  - peasants work the land together.
- The government would tell the collective what to grow and then buy a fixed amount. The peasants would be paid a share of the profits. In addition, they were allowed to keep small plots of land of their own to grow their own food.

**6.4** *A government propaganda poster which says 'Come and join our kolkhoz, comrade!'*

### OPPOSITION

- At first, Stalin tried to persuade the peasants to join collectives voluntarily. Few did so. Then collectivisation was imposed by force. The peasants opposed collectivisation because it was the end of their whole way of life:
  1. They lost control over how they farmed: what they grew, when they planted, when they harvested, etc.
  2. They knew that the government would take their share of the crop in bad years and in good (Stalin called this 'The First Commandment'). This could leave them without food.

3 They objected to control from the Communist Party. The chairman of every collective was a Communist; every MTS had a secret policeman on the staff.

- The peasants hated the idea of collectivisation. Many refused to hand over their farms and animals. In an attempt to win over poorer peasants, Stalin attacked the kulaks. Anyone who resisted collectivisation was labelled a 'kulak' and driven from their homes. They were put in labour camps or forced to settle on poor land. Most of the 4 million kulaks died. The rest of the peasants worked the land reluctantly.

### RESULTS

- Farming routines were disrupted. Animals were slaughtered. Government experts made bad decisions. There was a serious decline in agricultural output.

| | 1928 | 1933 |
|---|---|---|
| Grain harvest | 73.3 million tonnes | 68.4 million tonnes |
| State grain demands | 10.8 million tonnes | 22.6 million tonnes |
| Numbers of cattle | 70.5 million | 38.4 million |
| Numbers of pigs | 26.0 million | 12.1 million |

**6.5** *Agricultural output at the start of first Five-Year Plan (1928) and the second Five-Year Plan (1933)*

- The government always took its share, as the figures in 6.5 show, and this share increased. Armed convoys took food from starving villages. In 1932–33, at least 5 million died.
- Stalin had what he wanted: agriculture was under his control.

## A* EXTRA

These points set Communist agricultural policy in a wider setting, looking back and forward over Soviet history.

1. The Communists had never been popular in the countryside. The Revolution of 1917 had been city-based. The Communists also resented the fact that, under NEP, cities were often short of food as the kulaks restricted the supply in order to keep prices up. Changing agriculture would give Stalin more control over the peasants.

2. The long-term results of collectivisation for the USSR were bad:
a) Peasants remained resentful; in the Second World War, in 1941, the German invading army was welcomed in the Soviet countryside.
b) Agriculture under Communism remained inefficient in spite of efforts by other Communist leaders after Stalin to improve things. Although the USSR is a vast and fertile country there were always food shortages in the cities. (This failure was a major cause of the collapse of Communism in the late 1980s.)

## CHECK YOURSELF QUESTIONS

**Q1** Fill in the blanks at (a), (b), (c) and (d) on this chart.

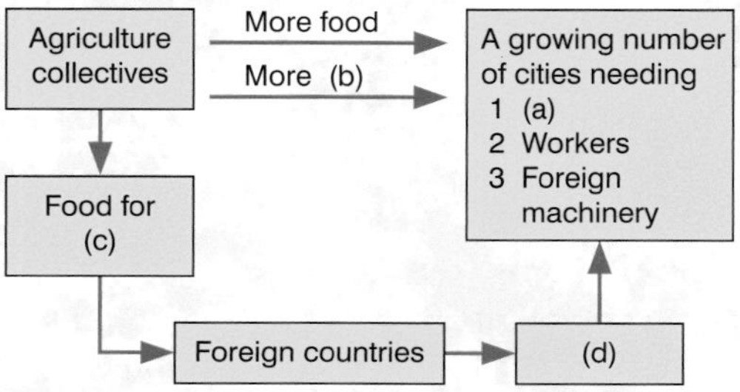


**Q2** Give as many reasons as you can why the peasants opposed collectivisation.

**Q3** What does the story of collectivisation of Soviet agriculture tell you about Stalin's methods?

*Answers are on page 197.*

# Stalin's dictatorship

In the years after 1929, Stalin built up a **totalitarian dictatorship** in the USSR. (For comparisons with Hitler's totalitarian dictatorship, see p46).

### 1. SECRET POLICE

- The Cheka, which Lenin had set up, changed its name over the years: to OGPU, NKVD and then, after the war, KGB. Their job was to seek out and arrest anyone who was in any way critical of Stalin.

### 2. PURGES

- Since 1918, the Communist Party had been the only party allowed, so Stalin's only critics were inside the Party.
- **Kirov**, the popular party boss of Leningrad (as Petrograd was re-named in 1924), was murdered in 1934. Historians have accused Stalin of his murder, but he may not have been to blame. Nonetheless, Stalin took the opportunity to arrest many of his old rivals and their followers.
- '**Show-trials**' were held, in which lifelong Bolsheviks were accused of amazing things – spying for the West, or taking part in Trotskyite plots. They all 'confessed' and were executed. By 1938, all of the Bolshevik leaders of 1917 had died or been executed, except Stalin. 98 of the 139 members of the Central Committee of the Communist Party of 1934 were shot. Half a million Party members were arrested.
- The other possible power-base for opposition was the Red Army, created by Trotsky in the Civil War. Stalin purged the army in 1937–38. One-fifth of all officers, including 90% of all generals, were executed.

> **A* EXTRA**
>
> The purges were a way of explaining things that went wrong in the Five-Year Plans. If there was a fault, or a train went off the lines by accident or bad work, for example, it was called sabotage and people were arrested, tried and executed. This happened in the Shakhty trial as early as 1928.

### 3. TERROR

- Ordinary Soviet citizens suffered too. NKVD men would call early in the morning and take victims away. They interrogated people for days on end, without sleep, after which they would confess to anything.
- To be a kulak, or the son of a kulak, or to have supported one of Stalin's rivals in the leadership contest in the 1920s, was enough.
- Trying to spread religious ideas or being a member of a church group could get you arrested.
- Teachers, doctors, scientists and poets all feared the knock on the door.
- The secret police encouraged informers to make accusations, and arrested people as a result. Sometimes members of a family informed on each other.
- No one really knows exactly how many people were arrested, or what happened to them all. Some historians suggest 10 million, others 20 million. Perhaps 1 million were shot.

### 4. LABOUR CAMPS

- The rest were sent to **labour camps** (see 6.3, p83). Here they toiled, unpaid, poorly fed, often in appalling conditions, building dams, canals, roads and other important projects. The Moscow Underground was built in this way. Millions died in the camps.

## 5. PROPAGANDA AND CENSORSHIP

- The press, radio, cinema and publishing were all heavily controlled.
- The churches were not allowed to publish books.
- No critical word was ever heard. Only successes and achievements were described.
- Most Soviet citizens were not allowed to travel abroad to see what other countries were like for themselves.

## 6. 'PERSONALITY CULT'

- Stalin was the focus of the propaganda campaign. His picture was everywhere: in stations, offices, classrooms, factories (see 6.6). Huge statues of Stalin were set up.
- Several towns were named after him. Slogans gave him credit for everything: 'The country is being led from victory to victory by the steersman of the Party, the great Stalin.'

## 7. THE ARTS

- In the first few years of Communism, the arts had flourished under new freedom. Now **censorship** was imposed and every novel, painting, musical composition, film or play had to serve the state.

**6.6** *Painting of Stalin talking with peasants and workers at a new dam.*

## 8. YOUNG PEOPLE

- Special efforts were made to **indoctrinate** young people. In school, the curriculum was changed to explain the Communist Revolution and the heroic roles of Lenin and Stalin. Stalin himself wrote the history book all pupils used.
- Pictures of other Bolsheviks in old library books had paper glued over them. Instead of religious education, pupils had anti-religion lessons.
- There were youth movements for young people: Octobrists from 8–10, Pioneers from 10–16 and Komsomol from 16–23.

### QUESTION SPOTTER

Typical exam questions on this topic:

- What is meant by the 'personality cult' of Stalin? Give examples of what it meant for the Soviet people.
- What methods did Stalin use to make himself dictator of the USSR?
- What problems, and what improvements, did the Soviet people meet in the years up to 1941?

## How did lives in the USSR change under Stalin?

### WOMEN AND THE FAMILY

- In the early years of Communism, divorce and abortion had been made much easier. Now restrictions were restored and the family was promoted, with the woman as wife and mother.
- At the same time, the industrialisation programme needed lots of women workers. The USSR took the lead in providing crèches, nurseries and child-minding facilities at every workplace.
- Women continued to enjoy more equality in theory than in the West, but few reached top positions.

### HEALTH SERVICES AND EDUCATION

- Health services were provided, free. By 1939, the USSR had more doctors per head than Britain.
- Education also improved, although it was full of Communist propaganda (see above). A big effort was made to bring literacy to the mass of Soviet people.

### LIVING STANDARDS AND LEISURE

- Living standards rose, although they remained considerably below Britain and the USA.
- Food shortages, lack of consumer goods and lack of housing in cities (94% of Russians lived in one room per family) were a continual hardship.
- Party members and senior officials had extra privileges in food, shopping and housing.
- Leisure facilities improved: every factory and new town had sports grounds, swimming pools, theatres, cinemas and social clubs.

### A* EXTRA

In the war, 1941–45, Stalin relaxed some of the censorship. He allowed the churches to open again as they encouraged Russian patriotism. After the war, the terror and censorship returned. Returning prisoners of war were especially at risk as they had seen that the West was not as awful as Stalin's propaganda said. Stalin was planning new purges when he died in 1953.

## CHECK YOURSELF QUESTIONS

**Q1** Look at points 1–8. Which are examples of terror and which are examples of indoctrination?

**Q2** Look at 6.6. What message is it trying to give about Stalin?

*Answers are on page 197.*

REVISION SESSION 1

# Isolationism

The First World War ended with over a million US soldiers fighting on the Western Front. The US President, **Woodrow Wilson**, was adoringly welcomed when he arrived in Europe to take part in the peace negotiations. He was the first US President to visit Europe during his term of office. His '14 Points' for a better, peaceful world after the war, played a big part in drawing up the Treaty of Versailles. (For more on these issues, see unit 3.) Yet when Wilson returned to the USA, he found that the mood of the country had changed. Many American people seemed to want to return to **isolationism**. This meant that they did not want the USA to join any foreign alliances or take much part in world affairs.

## Reasons for isolationism

### TRADITION

- Isolation was the traditional US policy towards the rest of the world. Woodrow Wilson had in fact been re-elected President in 1916 on a promise to keep the USA out of the First World War. In a world before air travel, the USA was cut off from the rest of the world far more than it is today. Apart from other countries in the Americas, everywhere else was at least 6 days' journey away by sea.

### DISLIKE OF THE 'OLD WORLD'

- The USA is a country of **immigrants**. In 1919, the majority of US citizens had been born in Europe and their experiences and memories of Europe were not happy ones. For them, Europe spelt poverty, lack of freedom, exploitation, and oppressive governments. Not surprisingly, they wanted to forget Europe and get on with building new lives for themselves.

### DANGEROUS IDEAS

- The Europe of 1919 was full of revolutionary ideas – Socialism, Communism and Anarchism. There had been the Communist Revolution in Russia in 1917 (see unit 5) and attempted Communist revolutions in Germany, Hungary and elsewhere. Many people in the USA hated and feared these ideas. Any further contact with Europe was therefore to be avoided.

### US SOLDIERS IN THE FIRST WORLD WAR

- Many Americans regretted that 100,000 US soldiers had died in the First World War, and wanted to pull out of any more entanglements that might lead to further wars.

## What did isolationism mean in practice?

### REJECTION OF THE PEACE TREATIES

- Under the US **Constitution**, peace treaties have to be agreed by the **Senate** – one of the elected houses of the US Congress (Parliament). The Senate was isolationist and would not agree to the Treaty of Versailles because it involved joining the League of Nations. The Treaty, into which Wilson had put so much, was rejected. The USA never joined the League of Nations.

**A* EXTRA**

1. Wilson was very keen on his League of Nations. On his return from Europe, he made an exhausting speaking tour of the USA by train, trying to whip up support. He suffered a stroke and the important negotiations with the Senate were conducted from his sickbed. He could have got the Senate to agree to sign the treaty if he had compromised, but he refused to budge at all and lost the vote.

2. Quite often a different party from the one the President belongs to controls the Congress, including the Senate. Wilson was a Democrat, but the 1918 elections gave the Republicans a majority in the Senate. The Republicans were more isolationist than Wilson.

7.1 *Immigrants from Italy arrive in the USA*

## RESTRICTIONS ON IMMIGRATION

- 13 million immigrants had come into the USA, 1900–19. Many of these were 'new' immigrants from southern and eastern Europe: Italy, Greece, Poland and Russia (see 7.1). They were often Catholics and some were socialists.
- Immigrants who had arrived in the 18th and 19th centuries were mainly from countries in northern and western Europe, like Britain, Germany, Scandinavia and the Netherlands. They were nicknamed **'WASPs'** (White Anglo-Saxon Protestants). WASPs were worried about these new immigrants and restrictions were placed on immigration in 1921:

  1 The total number of immigrants let in was limited.

  2 In 1917, a literacy test was imposed on all immigrants.

  3 A 'quota' system was introduced: numbers were only let in according to the proportion of people from that country already in the USA (e.g. a large quota from Britain, which was hardly ever filled, while the countries of 'new' immigrants only had small quotas).

- The 'open door' which the USA had always offered to anyone who wanted to come had closed.

## TARIFFS

- The **Fordney–McCumber tariff** put high duties on 28 products coming into the USA from other countries. This made them expensive for US customers.

### QUESTION SPOTTER

Typical exam questions on this topic:

- Why did the USA adopt isolationist policies after the First World War?
- Why did Woodrow Wilson oppose the US policy of isolationism?
- How did the US policy of isolationism affect: the League of Nations? immigration? international trade?

## CHECK YOURSELF QUESTIONS

**Q1** What are:
**a** isolationism
**b** WASPs
**c** tariffs?

**Q2** Why didn't the USA join the League of Nations?

*Answers are on page 198.*

# REVISION SESSION 2 The US economy in the 1920s

The US economy was booming in the 1920s.

**Table 7.2 Sales of goods in the USA**

| | 1919 | 1929 |
|---|---|---|
| Cars | 9 million | 26 million |
| Telephones | 10 million | 20 million |
| Radios | 60,000 | 10 million |

The figures give you two main features of this boom:

- There was a huge increase in production in the 1920s. It has been called a second Industrial Revolution.
- It was a boom in **consumer goods** (i.e. goods which people bought and used themselves). This compares with the first Industrial Revolution, which took place in the USA in the last part of the 19th century and was a boom in heavy industry: coal, iron, steel etc.

## Why did the US economy boom in the 1920s?

### RAW MATERIALS

- The USA is rich in the raw materials industry needs, like coal, iron and oil.

### THE RESULTS OF THE FIRST WORLD WAR

- The USA had stayed out of the First World War for 3 years, until 1917. This meant:
  - US industry did well selling weapons, ammunition and food to the warring countries of Europe.
  - While the European countries were busy fighting, the USA took over many of their colonial markets.
  - The German chemical industry, which led the world before 1914, was held back by the war. The US chemical industry developed in its place, making fertilisers, dyes, plastics and explosives.
  - US investors and bankers did well out of the war, so they had money to invest in new industries in the USA.

### TARIFFS

- Tariffs on imports protected US industry from foreign competition (see p92).

### LAISSEZ-FAIRE

- President Woodrow Wilson had put restrictions on US industry to protect the public. His successors as president in the 1920s (Harding 1920-23, Coolidge 1923-28, Hoover 1928-33) believed in leaving industry and business alone and kept taxes low. This policy is called ***laissez-faire***.

**A* EXTRA**

People believed that the USA was 'the land of opportunity'. Being optimistic about the future actually helped business grow: if things were going to get better then it was worth expanding your factory, or buying something more on hire purchase. And for the years 1920 to 1929, things *did* get better.

> **A* EXTRA**
>
> The system of production which Henry Ford and other industrialists used, in which making something was broken down into lots of small tasks, was called **Taylorism**.

### NEW TECHNOLOGY

- Many of the successful industries of the 1920s were based on **new technology**: telephones, radio, artificial fibres, fridges and other electric goods. There was a huge electrification programme so that most US citizens, at least in the cities, could use electric home appliances.

### THE FILM INDUSTRY BOOMED

- California, with its months of sunshine, was ideal for filming. A suburb of Los Angeles called **Hollywood** grew up as the home of the industry. By 1930, 80 million cinema tickets were being sold a week in the USA, and Hollywood films were entertaining the world.

### PRICES PEOPLE COULD AFFORD

- Not many of the goods sold in the 1920s were new, but the effect of new technology was to make them cheap. Cars, radios, vacuum cleaners and so on had existed before 1920, but were expensive luxuries. Now lots of people could afford them (see 7.3).

The Ford Model T was produced from 1908 to 1927: 15 million were made.

In 1908, a basic Model T cost $850; in 1917, $360; in 1925, $250.

**7.3** ***Henry Ford****'s assembly-line. The bodywork is just about to be slid on to the chassis.*

### ADVERTISING AND SALES

- Selling millions of goods to a mass market needed new techniques of **advertising**. Posters and magazines told the US public about the new goods on offer in glowing terms. Radio commercials brought the desire for new goods into every home.

- Teams of **commercial travellers** took samples to persuade local stores to order them. Shopping habits changed as **chain stores**, like Woolworths, expanded: there were 29,000 chain stores in 1918, 160,000 by 1929. Many more people began to buy on **hire purchase**: 60% of cars were bought this way.

## Did everyone share in this prosperity?

- Foreign visitors were flabbergasted by what they saw of the USA in the 1920s, with its bustling cities, full of cars. But that was not the whole picture.

### FARMERS

US agriculture was not prospering in the 1920s.

- Farmers had increased production during the First World War to sell food to Europe, but by the 1920s Europe was growing its own food again.
- High US tariffs protected US industry, but meant that foreigners did not have any dollars to buy US farm produce. Many countries put up their own tariffs in retaliation.
- US farmers suffered competition from Canadian farmers.
- US farmers were really the victims of their own success: they had cultivated new land, taken on new machines, so that they were **over-producing** food: they grew more farm produce than they could sell. The result was lower and lower prices for their produce: wheat which sold for $1.83 a bushel in 1920, only fetched 38 cents a bushel in 1929.

> The average annual income per head in the USA in 1929 was $681; the average farmer's income was $273. Nor were these just a small group: half of all US citizens lived in rural areas. Those people in rural areas who were not farmers worked in businesses dependent on agriculture, and shared the hard times. Not for them the new fridge and vacuum cleaner: even if they could afford it, very few rural areas had electricity. Rural Americans felt isolated; 6 million left the land for the cities in the 1920s. Many of these were black farm labourers and small farmers from the southern USA.

### THE POOR

- Historians estimate that 42% of US citizens were living below the poverty line. That is, they did not have enough money to feed, clothe and house themselves.
- New technology in industry often replaced jobs with machines. There were around 2 million **unemployed** throughout the 1920s.
- Workers in old industries – coal, textiles – were facing stiff competition for their goods. Wages were low. At a time when $48 a week was considered a minimum, male coalminers were earning $18 and women $9 a week.

**QUESTION SPOTTER**

Typical exam questions on this topic:
- Which industries prospered in the USA in the 1920s?
- Why was the US economy so successful in the 1920s?
- How important was advertising to the boom in the US economy in the 1920s?

**A* EXTRA**

Low food prices were bad for farmers, but good for business, because it meant that workers did not have to be paid high wages.

## QUESTION SPOTTER

Typical exam questions on this topic:

- Why did US agriculture not share in the boom in the USA in the 1920s?
- Why were so many people in the USA living in poverty in the 1920s?

- Those in unskilled or casual jobs did not share in the boom, their wages were low and jobs uncertain. Only 3% of semi-skilled workers owned a car. Many of these poor workers were 'new' immigrants: Italians, Poles, Mexicans and black Americans recently arrived in the cities of the north from the southern states.

## CHECK YOURSELF QUESTIONS

**Q1** Look at 7.3 again.

**a** Use this picture to explain what an assembly line is.

**b** How did assembly-line methods change industry?

**Q2** How widespread was prosperity in the USA in the 1920s?

**Q3** Which groups did *not* take part in the boom?

*Answers are on page 198.*

REVISION SESSION 3

# The Roaring Twenties

## What was life like in the USA in the 1920s?

### THE CITIES

- It was in the huge, bustling cities of the USA that the Twenties seemed to roar the most. Just before 1920, the number of US citizens living in towns and cities exceeded the number living in rural areas for the first time in the history of the USA.
- Cities were:
  - bigger – as people moved out to new suburbs and travelled in to work in their cars or by train
  - higher – as **skyscrapers** were built.
- In the streets of the cities there were:
  - lots of cars and lorries
  - shops, especially large chain stores and department stores – where all the new consumer goods were on display
  - cinemas – where Hollywood films were shown
  - bars – where you could get a drink (illegally)
  - clubs – where people danced new and lively dances, like the Charleston, to Jazz music, often played by black musicians (the other name for this period is 'The Jazz Age').
- Rural Americans looked at this situation with dismay. They disapproved of what they saw as a new immorality: more freedom for women (see below), easy sexual relations in films, divorce, buying things on hire purchase rather than paying for them outright.

**7.4** *Skyscrapers in New York in the 1920s*

### WOMEN

- Before 1920 women in the USA, as in Britain, were not equal with men and were subject to many restrictions. Girls were expected to get married and stay at home looking after their children. For working-class women this was not possible as their families needed money, but most jobs were closed to them and any others were low paid. They did not have the vote in most states. In New York, it was illegal for women to smoke in public. Fashion reflected their restricted lives, with long dresses, tight waists and elaborate hairstyles.
- Then along came the First World War. Women took on new jobs, while the men were away. In 1920, all women were given the vote. By 1929, 10 million more women were working than in 1920 – a 25% increase. Divorce was made easier and the number of divorces doubled.

> **QUESTION SPOTTER**
>
> Typical exam question on this topic:
> - How widespread were changes in women's lives in the USA in the 1920s?

- **'Flappers'** was the name given to young, liberated women of the 1920s. They wore short hair, short skirts, smoked in public, drove cars, danced wildly, had their own sex lives.
- As with other aspects of the 1920s, the evidence can be misleading. Women did not enter a new age of equality. In spite of having the vote, hardly any women made careers in politics. They may have had jobs, but they were paid less than men for the same work and were unable to get promotion. The 'flappers' were well-off city girls. Most girls, especially in rural America, still had less personal freedom than boys, got married and stayed at home.

### PROHIBITION

- One cause which rural and small-town women took up passionately was the banning of alcoholic drink. **Prohibition** was introduced because organisations like the Anti-Saloon League (a saloon is an American word for a bar) and the Women's Christian Temperance Union believed that alcohol damaged family life. They said that:

  1. Men spent money on alcohol which should have gone to buy the family food and clothes.
  2. Alcohol ruined their health.
  3. It caused them to lose their jobs.

Many religious organisations and politicians supported Prohibition.

- In 1919, the **18th Amendment** to the US Constitution made the sale, manufacture or transport of alcohol illegal. At the same time, the **Volstead Act** made the buying of alcohol illegal.
- The Prohibitionists may have been right about the dangers of alcohol, but millions of US citizens were used to having a drink. They were not going to change their habits because of a change in the law. So ways were found of getting round it, especially in the cities:

  1. Speakeasies: illegal bars.
  2. Moonshine: illegally-made alcohol.
  3. Bootlegging: smuggling alcohol into the USA.

- A new police force had to be set up to enforce the law. In 1929, they poured over 50 million litres of illegal alcohol down the drains – though this was only a tiny fraction of the amount made.
- The problem with Prohibition was that it made ordinary citizens into criminals. Police officers were reluctant to enforce the law and took bribes to 'turn a blind eye'. Gangsters took the place of ordinary drink manufacturers. They controlled speakeasies and illegal alcohol supplies. The Chicago boss, **Al Capone**, made $100,000 a year from illegal businesses and openly murdered 400 of his rivals. He claimed: 'All I do is supply a public demand' and, in the circumstances of Prohibition, he was right. (In 1933, the government judged Prohibition to have failed and the 21st Amendment abolished it.)

> **QUESTION SPOTTER**
>
> Typical exam questions on this topic:
> - Why was Prohibition introduced?
> - What were the results of the introduction of Prohibition in the USA in 1919?

## INTOLERANCE

- Some powerful Americans were scared of left-wing, or **'red'**, ideas. Known Socialists or Anarchists were harassed by police. Some immigrants with these beliefs were deported back to Europe. Trade unions were attacked and some industrialists, like Henry Ford, refused to allow their employees to join a trade union. Trade union membership fell from 5 million to 3 million over the 1920s.
- The **Ku Klux Klan** increased in membership in the 1920s.
  1 The roots of the Klan were among poor whites in the South, but it also had members in northern cities.
  2 They wore white sheets with pointed hoods, and marched with burning crosses.
  3 They attacked mainly black Americans, but also Roman Catholics, Jews and foreigners.
  4 Victims were bullied, beaten up, even lynched (see 7.6).
  5 The Klan had 5 million members by 1925.

### A* EXTRA

Among the scandalous examples of intolerance in the 1920s were:
a) The trial of two Italians, Sacco and Vanzetti. They were accused of robbery and murder, but the evidence against them was slim. However, the judge was biased against them because they were **Anarchists**. They were executed in 1927.
b) In some states it was made illegal to teach **Darwin's theory of evolution** because it conflicted with a literal interpretation of the Bible.

## BLACK AMERICANS

- There were 12 million black Americans in the USA in 1920, the descendants of African slaves. Three-quarters of them lived in the South, where they suffered not only at the hands of the Ku Klux Klan, but also from poverty and **discrimination**. They had been freed from slavery in 1865, but southern whites still kept black farmers in debt.
- **'Jim Crow' laws** ensured that black Americans did not have the right to vote. They had separate and poorer schools and were barred from using the same restaurants, transport, cinemas, toilets, beaches, parks, even the same drinking fountains as whites.

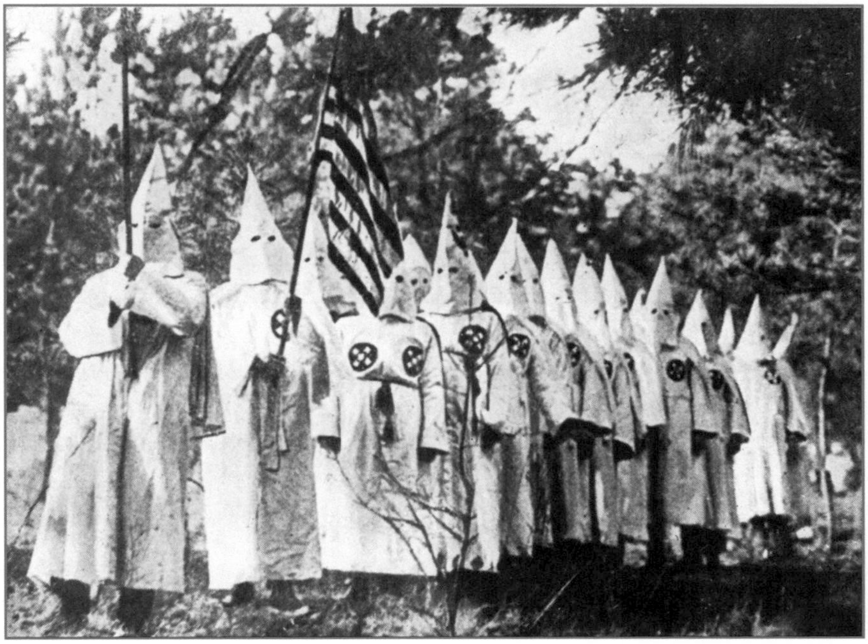

**7.5** *Ku Klux Klan*

'Jim Crow' was a music-hall character invented by Thomas D. Rice in the 1820s. Dressed in rags and with his face blacked up, 'Jim Crow' came to represent a white view of happy-go-lucky blacks; his name was later applied to the laws regulating the lives of black Americans in the South.

## QUESTION SPOTTER

Typical exam question on this topic:

- How much improvement was there to the lives of black Americans in the 1920s?

■ Over the 1920s, 1.5 million black Americans left the South for the cities of the North. In many ways their lives improved:

1 They had a chance of getting a job.

2 Some blacks did well and formed a new black middle class.

3 They could get educated at black universities and colleges.

4 There were black newspapers, magazines, literature.

5 Popular black heroes appeared – sportsmen and jazz musicians. Jazz, created by black musicians, swept the USA first and then became the popular music of the western world.

6 There was less obvious discrimination – no segregated buses or restaurants, for example.

**7.6** *Lynching in Indiana, 1930*

■ In other ways black Americans still faced difficulties. There was discrimination in:

1 jobs – blacks were the last to be taken on, the first to be fired.

2 housing – blacks were forced into **ghettoes**, like Harlem, New York and South Side, Chicago. Even recent immigrants, discriminated against by most whites, were hostile to blacks.

## CHECK YOURSELF QUESTIONS

**Q1** What were:
**a** skyscrapers
**b** flappers
**c** speakeasies
**d** jazz?

**Q2** Prohibition was called 'A great social experiment'. What does this mean and why did Prohibition fail?

Think about the word 'experiment'. What do you think it means? Think about the reasons *why it failed* – this is not a description of what happened. Make a list. Which do you think is the most important reason? Now use this writing plan:

Start paragraph 1 by writing: 'Prohibition was an experiment because...'

Start the next paragraph by writing: 'The main reason it failed was...'

Put any other reasons you can think of into a paragraph starting: 'Other reasons for the failure of Prohibition are...'

**Q3** What problems are there in deciding whether the 1920s brought improvements to the lives of
**a** American women
**b** black Americans?

*Answers are on page 199.*

# The Wall Street Crash and the Great Depression

## THE OVER-PRODUCTION CRISIS

- As the 1920s ended, the US economy faced a crisis, although few people recognised it at first. It was a crisis of **over-production** (i.e. US industry was producing more than it could sell). The boom had been based on selling consumer goods; this meant finding more and more people to buy fridges, telephones, vacuum cleaners etc. By the late 1920s, the market was running out of customers.
  - Probably more than half of all Americans were too poor. Farmers, unemployed and low wage-earners had no money to spare for consumer goods after they had fed, clothed and housed themselves.
  - Even the well-off could not go on buying and buying. There are limits to how many fridges you need.
  - US industry could not sell abroad because other countries had put up tariffs on US imports in response to the Fordney-McCumber tariff (see p92).
- The most spectacular sign that all was not well was the **Wall Street Crash**.

> **A* EXTRA**
>
> Clearly one of the reasons for the over-production crisis was the distribution of wealth in the USA. This can be put statistically: the richest 5% of the population earned 32% of earnings, while the poorest 42% earned only 10% of earnings.

## THE BOOM IN SHARES

- Suppose you want to start a company. Diagram 7.7 shows what you need to do.

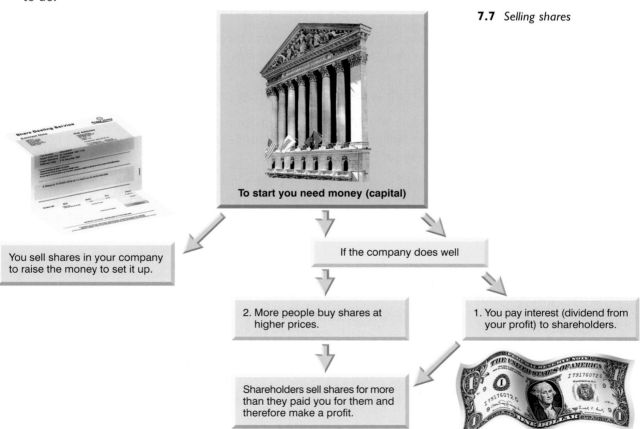

**7.7** *Selling shares*

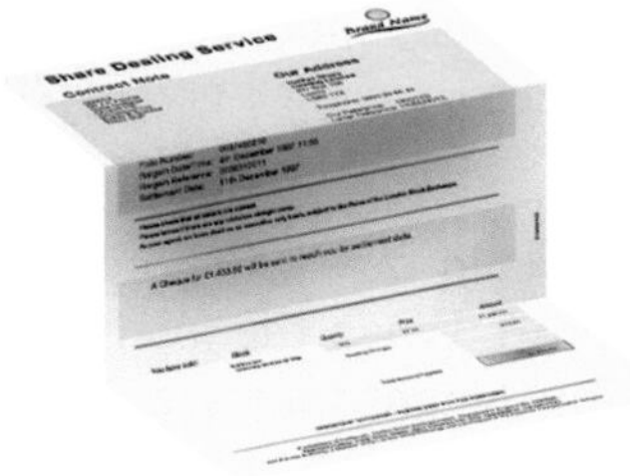

To start you need money (capital)

You sell shares in your company to raise the money to set it up.

If the company does well

1. You pay interest (dividend from your profit) to shareholders.

2. More people buy shares at higher prices.

Shareholders sell shares for more than they paid you for them and therefore make a profit.

- In the USA, shares are bought and sold in **Wall Street**, in New York. In the 1920s, dividends went up and share prices went up, year after year. It seemed an easy way to make money: you bought some shares, perhaps on borrowed money, and sold them again 6 months later at a profit. Lots of people were eager to join in: in 1920, 4 million Americans owned shares; by 1929, it was 20 million.
- Then, in autumn 1929, some people began to get rid of their shares. Suddenly, there was a panic: everyone rushed to sell and prices fell fast.

  1 On 24 October 1929, 13 million shares were sold.

  2 Prices plummeted. A share in one cigar company, for example, fell from $113 to $4 in a day.
- This was the Wall Street Crash.

## What caused the Wall Street Crash?

- Shares are only worth a lot of money if people believe things are going to go on getting better. As soon as there is any doubt, everyone loses confidence, no one will buy and prices drop. Some investors could see that the over-production crisis was looming and began to sell, sparking off the crash.
- Some people had bought shares 'on the margin' (i.e. they had only paid 10% of the price), expecting to pay off the rest when they sold them at a profit. When prices began to fall, these **speculators** were in trouble and rushed to sell in order to cut their losses.
- Some banks had lent money to speculators to buy shares. They needed to cover their loans and rushed to sell.

### A* EXTRA

The Crash, when it came, was also made worse by the fact that some companies did not really make anything at all: they just made money by buying and selling shares. When confidence in these companies collapsed, it brought down proper companies too.

## What were the results of the Wall Street Crash?

- People who had invested heavily in shares were ruined. Speculators who had bought shares on the margin – at higher prices than they could sell them for – were bankrupted.
- **Banks** began to fail. There were lots of small banks in the USA. Some had lent out more money than they had on deposit. When the loans could not be paid back, the bank went broke. This meant that people who had put money in the bank, believing it to be safe, lost it all. Between 1929 and 1933, 5,000 banks went broke.
- There was a tremendous loss of confidence and fall in demand, which helped to cause the **Great Depression**.

THE GREAT DEPRESSION

By 1933, the worst year of the Depression:

- industrial production had fallen by 40%
- wages had fallen by 60%
- share prices had fallen by 80%
- 14 million Americans were unemployed.

- Diagram 7.8 shows how the US economy became locked into a downward spiral. The main cause was over-production, but the Wall Street Crash made it all worse.

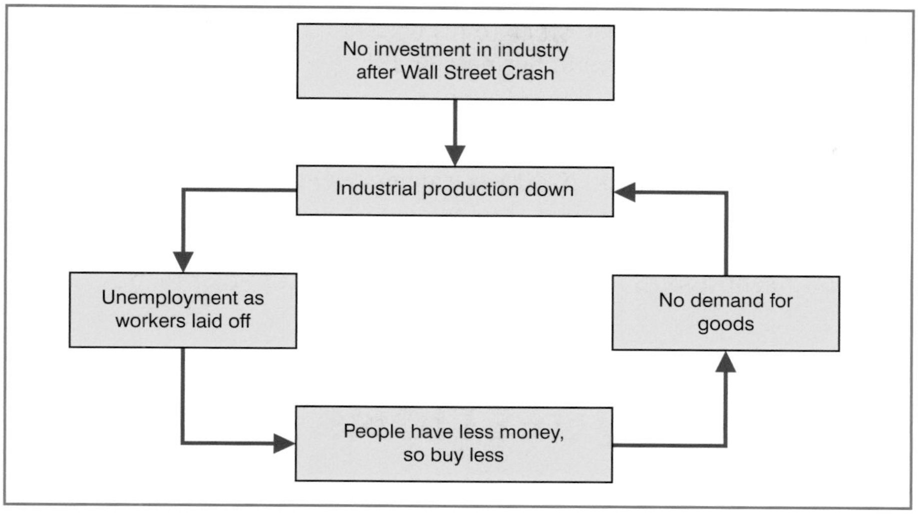


**7.8** *Causes of the Great Depression*

## How did the Great Depression affect the American people?

### FARMERS

- Farmers were already in an over-production crisis in the early 1920s. In the Depression, things got worse. It was not worth some farmers taking crops to market, because the price they would get was less than the freight charges. Many could not meet their mortgage repayments and had to sell the farm they had worked on all their lives. In some cases, farmers ganged up and forced banks at gunpoint not to put the farm up for sale.
- In parts of the Mid-West soil erosion led to a **'dust bowl'**, in which the over-cropped soil on the farms blew away. Some farmers, forced off their land, loaded up their family and belongings and headed for California, hoping to find work fruit picking. These 'Okies' (from Oklahoma) or 'Arkies' (from Arkansas) found lots of others had the same idea.

### IN THE CITIES

- Americans believed in **'rugged individualism'** (i.e. each person should look after his/her own future). There was no system of unemployment benefit ('dole'). Americans had grown up believing that in their 'land of opportunity' anyone could succeed. Now that things had gone wrong, they thought it was their fault and felt ashamed.
- The busy streets were now quieter, with people who had lost their jobs begging or selling small items. Many had to resort to picking over the city rubbish dumps in search of food or something to sell. Those who could not pay their rent were forced out to sleep in the parks, on benches or in cardboard shacks. They queued for charity soup kitchens or bread handouts. Some left home and travelled around, looking for work. These **'hoboes'** often rode illegally in railway goods wagons.

**QUESTION SPOTTER**

Typical exam questions on this topic:
- How did the crisis of over-production in the USA help to cause the Wall Street Crash?
- Why did the Wall Street Crash affect the lives of so many Americans?
- How did the Great Depression affect
  (i) farmers
  (ii) industrial workers?

THE GOVERNMENT

- **President Hoover** had been elected just before the boom ended. He believed it would go on forever and claimed that the USA was going to be the first country in the world to put an end to poverty. When the Depression came, he stuck to his belief that it was not the job of government to interfere in business and things would get better in time. He also insisted it was the job of charities to help those in poverty.
- Hoover was deeply unpopular. People in cardboard shacks called them **'Hoovervilles'**. In 1932, 20,000 ex-soldiers went to Washington to ask for their 'bonus' (war pension) to be paid early, as they were in financial trouble. Some of this **'Bonus Army'** camped outside the White House. Hoover sent troops, with guns and tear-gas, to get rid of them.

## CHECK YOURSELF QUESTIONS

**Q1** Describe in one sentence each:

**a** The Wall Street Crash

**b** The Great Depression

**Q2** Look at the main central spiral in 7.8 and explain it in your own words.

**Q2** Explain President Hoover's attitude to the Depression crisis.

*Answers are on page 199.*

# Roosevelt and the New Deal

- Hoover's opponent in the 1932 Presidential election was Franklin D. Roosevelt.

## FRANKLIN DELANO ROOSEVELT (1882–1945)

| | |
|---|---|
| *Nickname:* | 'FDR' |
| *Born:* | Came from a rich family and led an easy life as a young man. |
| *Background:* | In 1921, he caught polio. For 3 years he struggled to regain the use of his limbs, to sit and then to stand. |
| *Character:* | His own suffering seemed to give him more understanding of other people's. |
| *Main roles:* | Elected Governor of New York in 1929 and made the state government do what it could to relieve the hardship of Depression. |

- **'FDR'** ran an inspiring campaign. He did not have any detailed plans, but he seemed ready to try something new to improve the situation. He was prepared to spend government money to start the economy going again – something Hoover regarded with horror. Above all, 'FDR' seemed optimistic. His most striking promise was 'I pledge you, I pledge myself, to a new deal for the American people'. He won the election easily and immediately began his **New Deal**. His aims were:
  - relief for those in hardship
  - recovery of the economy so that people could get jobs
  - protection of people's homes and savings
  - improvement of the USA.

As you look at the New Deal measures described below, try to see which of these 4 aims he was trying to meet with each one.

## What happened in the first 100 days?

- FDR began a whirlwind of activity. New government agencies were set up, often known by their initial letters.

### EMERGENCY BANKING ACT

- On the second day of his presidency, he ordered all the banks to be closed. Government officials looked at their records and those that were financially sound were allowed to re-open. Public confidence in the banks was restored.

### FERA (FEDERAL EMERGENCY RELIEF AGENCY)

- $500 million was made available to help those in dire need. It was spent on soup kitchens, blankets, free nursery schools for children of the unemployed, etc.

### CCC (CIVILIAN CONSERVATION CORPS)

- Young people were given a job for 6 months at a time so that they could get used to the idea of work.
- They did environmental work: planting trees in National Parks, digging drainage ditches, flood prevention schemes.
- The government paid them a wage of $30 a month, of which they had to send $25 home to their families.
- 2 million people (of whom only 8,000 were women) worked on CCC schemes.

### AAA (AGRICULTURAL ADJUSTMENT ADMINISTRATION)

- Prices of farm produce were raised by setting fixed quotas for most products, so that they did not grow too much.
- The cotton crop was ploughed into the ground, and pigs slaughtered in order to keep up the price.
- Farmers were paid not to cultivate some land. Farm incomes rose by 50% by 1936.

### NIRA (NATIONAL INDUSTRIAL RECOVERY ACT)

- This had two parts:
  1. PWA (Public Works Administration) – which spent $3.3 billion on building schools, roads, bridges, airports, etc. and giving jobs to millions of people.
  2. The government worked with employers in setting decent wages and working conditions. Goods made under this agreement displayed a 'Blue Eagle' badge.

### TVA (TENNESSEE VALLEY AUTHORITY)

- The land of the Tennessee River valley was badly eroded. There were frequent floods. Farmers were poor, hardly any had electricity. Seven states were involved, so no one was able to deal with it.
- The TVA was set up to cover the whole area. Dams were built on the rivers.

**7.9** *Dam in the Tennessee Valley*

#### PROBLEMS

- FDR believed in spending government money – even more than he could raise through taxes – to get the economy going again. Diagram 7.10 shows the idea.

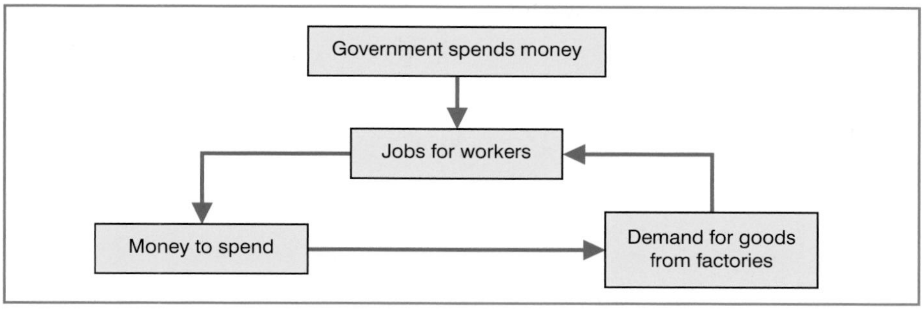


**7.10** *New Deal spending*

- The British economist **J.M. Keynes** approved of this way of 'spending your way out of trouble'. Many conservative Americans and business people did not. They argued that FDR should not spend what he did not have.
- Under the US Constitution drawn up in 1787, the **Supreme Court** can review laws passed by the government. It takes time, but in 1935 the Supreme Court declared the NIRA illegal and did the same to the AAA in 1936.
- Despite these problems, FDR won the 1936 election easily. 'Everyone is against the New Deal except the voters,' he joked. With this support, FDR thought of adding enough new judges who agreed with him to the Supreme Court in order to out-vote the others, but his supporters warned him that he should not meddle with the constitution. In fact, NIRA and AAA had done most of what they were set up to do and new laws were passed in a Second New Deal. Gradually, the Supreme Court changed its views anyway.

## What did the Second New Deal do?

- **Wagner Act, 1935** – gave US workers the right to join a trade union.
- **Social Security Act, 1935** – began a basic system of welfare (old age pensions, unemployment benefit and sick pay). It did not cover health care, and was set at a lower level than welfare in Europe, but it was better than nothing.
- **WPA** (Works Progress Administration) involved more public spending to provide jobs. 8.5 million people worked on WPA schemes, for parks, hospitals and schools. Writers, artists and photographers were also employed.

#### CRITICISMS OF THE NEW DEAL

- It was inconsistent (e.g. measures intended to help farmers actually made life harder for the poor by making food more expensive).

## QUESTION SPOTTER

Typical exam questions on this topic:

- What were the aims of the New Deal?
- How did the New Deal try to restore confidence in the US economy?
- How did the New Deal try to deal with unemployment?
- How successful was the New Deal?

- Right-wing Americans complained that the New Deal was spending money FDR did not have and just turning millions of Americans into government employees. In 1937, FDR decided to try to meet these criticisms by cutting government spending. Unemployment immediately rose again.
- Left-wingers criticised the New Deal for not doing enough to change the USA.

  1 The New Deal did little for the very poor.

  2 Black Americans continued to be disadvantaged and made no progress towards civil rights in these years. FDR was dependent on support from white southern Democrats, who would have blocked any attempt to help black people. New Deal laws allowed blacks to be paid lower than whites. The AAA quota system led to millions of poor black farmers being pushed off their land.

  3 Women made little progress towards equality. For example, they were still paid less than men for the same work. FDR did appoint one woman to a senior position in his government – Frances Perkins, Secretary of Labor.

  4 Revolutionary ideas like the TVA were not copied elsewhere.

- Recovery was only partial: spending in 1937 was only 75% of what it was in 1929. Unemployment was still 9.5 million when the Second World War broke out in 1939. Contracts for war industries began to bring down the figures.

In spite of these criticisms, the New Deal did:

- restore the confidence of the American people in their country and in their capacity to deal with their problems
- retain democracy and most of the basics of US economy and way of life intact.

Roosevelt was immensely popular. He was able to communicate with ordinary Americans, especially through his 'fireside chats' – radio broadcasts. He is the only US President to have been elected four times: 1932, 1936, 1940 and 1944.

## CHECK YOURSELF QUESTIONS

**Q1** List the New Deal measures which:
**a** restored confidence
**b** provided jobs
**c** improved the USA.

**Q2** Compare 7.8 (p103) and 7.10 (p107). How did the New Deal change the downward spiral in 7.8 to the upward spiral of 7.10?

*Answers are on page 200.*

# UNIT 8: INTERNATIONAL RELATIONS, 1919–1939

REVISION SESSION 1

## The League of Nations

After the mud, death and destruction of the First World War, many ordinary people felt a strong desire to find a peaceful way of solving disputes between nations. US President Woodrow Wilson expressed this in a proposal for a **League of Nations** – the last of his 14 Points (see units 2 and 3).

- But how should it work?
- Who should be members?
- What powers should it have?

At the peace conference in 1919 Wilson was told to come up with the details. Through all the tough bargaining of the treaty negotiations, he clung hard to his idea of a League of Nations. It was written into each Treaty.

The plans were based on what they thought had gone wrong in 1914. One historian has pointed out that the League was really set up to prevent the First World War happening again! Events from 1919 to 1939 proved rather different from 1914, however, which caused problems.

### What was the League supposed to do?

- Bring together all nations in a parliament to discuss and settle disputes peacefully.
- Improve people's living and working conditions; help people to become better off by improving international trade. (The belief was that injustice and poverty were important causes of war.)
- Make war impossible by persuading all nations to disarm.
- If one country was aggressive to another, the League would force the aggressor to back down by:

  1 pressure of world opinion

  2 world trade ban

  3 force, if necessary.

How the League of Nations would work is shown in 8.1.

### What were the problems of membership?

- There were 42 members at the beginning. This rose to a peak of 60 in the 1930s.

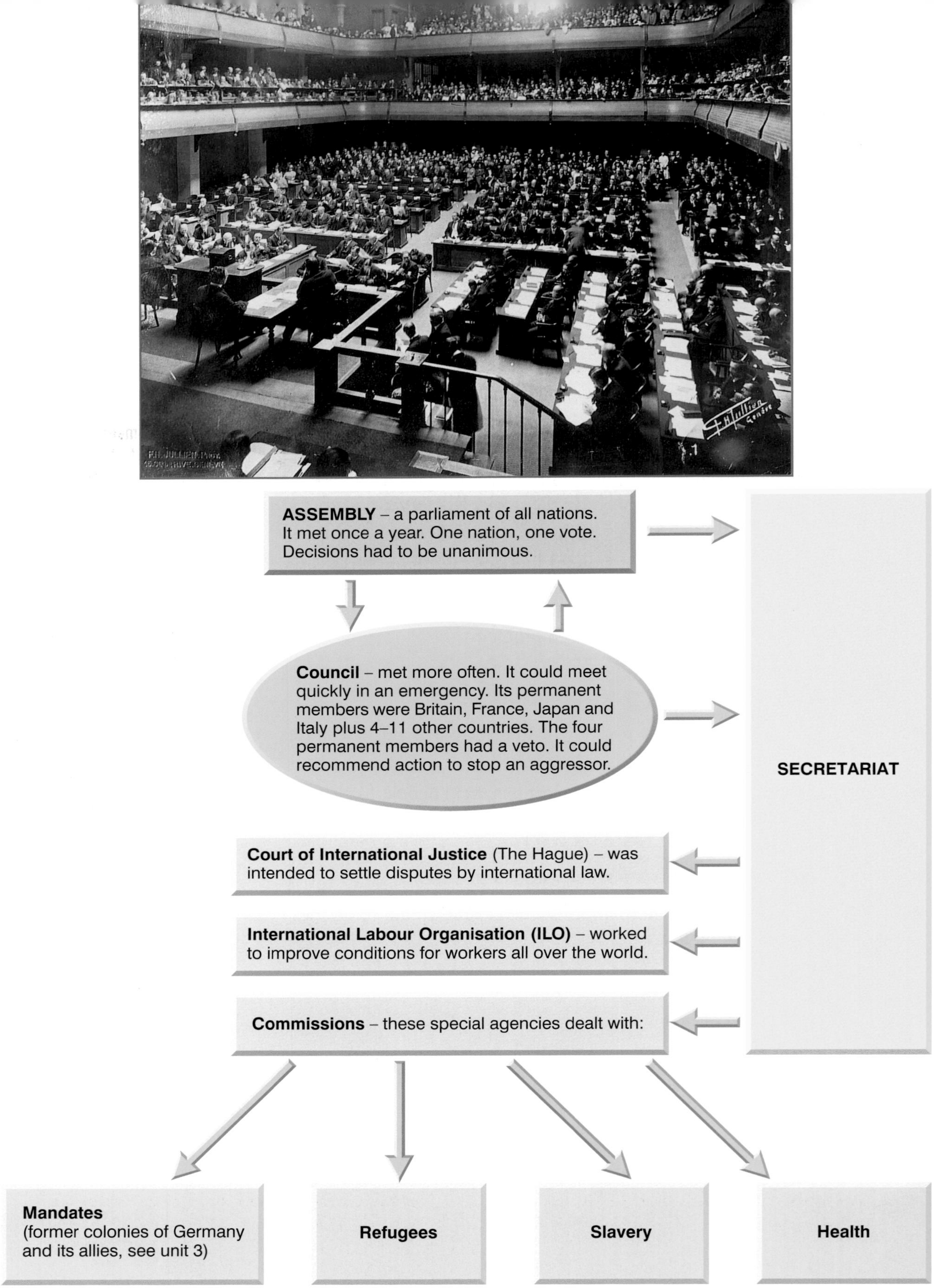
ASSEMBLY – a parliament of all nations. It met once a year. One nation, one vote. Decisions had to be unanimous.
Council – met more often. It could meet quickly in an emergency. Its permanent members were Britain, France, Japan and Italy plus 4–11 other countries. The four permanent members had a veto. It could recommend action to stop an aggressor.
SECRETARIAT
Court of International Justice (The Hague) – was intended to settle disputes by international law.
International Labour Organisation (ILO) – worked to improve conditions for workers all over the world.
Commissions – these special agencies dealt with:
Mandates (former colonies of Germany and its allies, see unit 3)
Refugees
Slavery
Health

**8.1** *The structure of the League of Nations. It met at Geneva in neutral Switzerland.*

### THE USA NEVER JOINED

- When President Wilson returned to the USA, he found that public opinion had turned against him. This change is explained more fully in unit 7, but in summary, many US citizens:
  - feared membership of the League would drag the USA into more wars
  - disagreed with the terms of the Treaty of Versailles, and membership of the League involved signing the Treaty
  - were not keen on joining closely with Britain and France – two imperialist countries
  - did not agree with trade bans as a weapon.

So the country with the greatest power and moral force to make the League work was not a member.

### BRITAIN AND FRANCE

- This threw the weight of making the League work on to Britain and France:
  - Britain wanted to hold on to the Empire, build up its trade again and stay clear of European conflicts.
  - France wanted to keep Germany down.
- Which would Britain and France put first in a conflict: their own aims or the aims of the League? Would Britain and France act on their own, or always work through the League?

### THE USSR

- This other powerful country was not invited to join the League at first. It was regarded as an outsider because it was Communist and because Lenin's government had broken its agreements with its allies in order to get out of the war. (The USSR joined the League in 1934.)

### THE VICTORS OF 1918

- The League was dominated by those who had won the war and were dedicated to enforcing the terms of the Treaties. Germany and other defeated nations were not members at first. They bitterly resented the terms of the Treaties of 1919 (see unit 3) and wanted to change them. They therefore resented the League.

### WHITE IMPERIALISTS

- White European nations dominated the League. Britain refused to build an anti-racist statement into becoming a member of the League.

#### A* EXTRA

The commitment of Britain and France to the League was always a matter of doubt. They had set up a Conference of Ambassadors in 1919 to ensure that the Treaty was kept to. When the League was set up this group was no longer needed, but they found it convenient to keep it going, often bypassing the League.

#### QUESTION SPOTTER

Typical exam questions on this topic:

- What were the aims of the League of Nations?
- What problems did the League of Nations have in achieving its aims?
- What were the attitudes of Britain and France towards the League of Nations?

## CHECK YOURSELF QUESTIONS

**Q1** Where did the League of Nations meet, and why?

**Q2** Which nations were on the Council of the League, and why?

*Answers are on page 201.*

REVISION SESSION 2

# The League in the 1920s

## What were the League's successes?

- The agencies of the League showed the need for an international organisation to solve international problems.

  1 Millions of **refugees** from the First World War were helped to return to their homes.

  2 The **Health Commission** began work to reduce leprosy, yellow fever and malaria worldwide.

  3 An international **highway code** and **shipping signals** were agreed.

  4 Slave labour and the use of dangerous chemicals were stopped.

- Border disputes settled included:

  1 Upper Silesia, 1921 – an area disputed between Poland and Germany. The League held a **plebiscite** (vote) and used the results to split the area according to what its people wanted.

  2 Åland Islands, 1921 (see 8.2) – these islands in the Baltic were disputed by Finland and Sweden. After an enquiry, the League awarded them to Finland, which Sweden accepted.

  3 Greek invasion of Bulgaria, 1925 – the League condemned Greece, which withdrew its troops.

**8.2** *Territorial changes, 1919–1924*

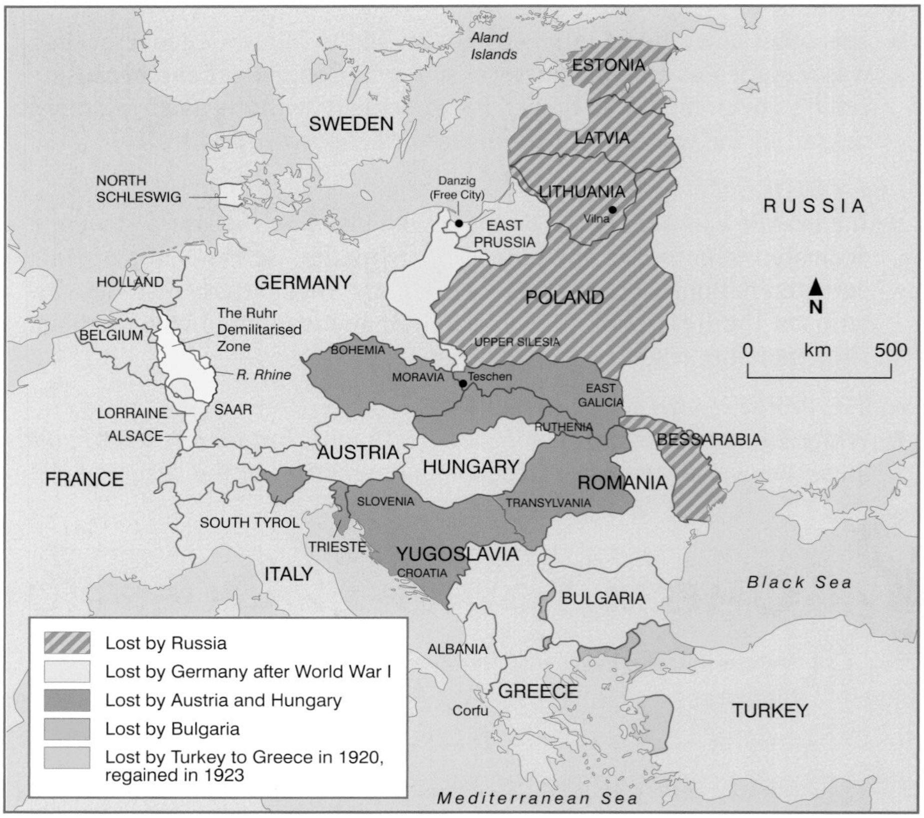

## What were the League's failures?

### VILNA, 1920

- Vilna was the largest city in Lithuania. It was made the capital of the new country. However, the majority of its population were Poles and a Polish army seized the city. France wanted to keep on the right side of Poland and Britain was not prepared to act alone, so the League did nothing.

### GREECE AND TURKEY, 1920–1922

- Turkey refused to accept the terms of the Treaty of Sèvres (see p29). They attacked the Greeks and drove them out of Smyrna. The League failed to stop this war, even though one of its main purposes was to enforce the 1919 peace settlement.

### THE RUHR, 1923

- When Germany stopped **reparation payments**, France and Belgium did not refer their grievance to the League, but acted on their own. They sent troops into the Ruhr to seize German industries (see p32).

### CORFU, 1923

- An Italian general was murdered in Greece. **Mussolini**, dictator of Italy, was furious. He sent Italian forces to shell and then occupy the Greek island of Corfu. Greece appealed to the League. This looked like a serious dispute and the League acted fast: Italian troops had to withdraw and Greece would have to pay compensation when the general's murderers were found. Mussolini then went to Britain and France, behind the League's back, who made Greece pay up at once. Mussolini boasted of his triumph: he had got what he wanted by using aggression – a bad sign for the future.

## What about disarmament and peace?

Several attempts were made in the 1920s to ensure peace in the world. These were often made outside the League. Did this matter?

- **Washington Treaty, 1922** – an agreement signed by the USA, Britain, France, Japan and Italy to limit the size of their navies and not to build any more battleships for 10 years. This seemed a positive step; the fact that the USA was not in the League did not seem to matter.

- **Proposals for a Disarmament Treaty, 1923** were rejected by Britain. Plans for a Disarmament Conference were drawn up in 1926, but not fully agreed until 1931 (see p116).

- **Locarno Pact, 1925** – at a conference held at Locarno (Switzerland), Germany's Foreign Minister, Stresemann, agreed:

  1 to accept the boundaries with France and Belgium laid down at Versailles

  2 to accept that the Rhineland was a de-militarised zone

  3 to refer any disputes to the League.

Germany had apparently accepted the terms of the Treaty of Versailles at last.

### DAWES PLAN, 1924

Under the **Dawes Plan**, the German economy was reviving and reparations were being paid. The British and French economies were also doing better. In this general atmosphere of cooperation – called the 'Locarno Honeymoon' (see p37) – Germany joined the League in 1926.

### KELLOGG–BRIAND PACT, 1928

**Kellogg** (representing the USA) and **Briand** (France) got 15 major nations, including the USSR, and over 30 smaller ones to sign an agreement never to go to war.

## What conclusions can we draw?

By 1928, the prospects for peace looked quite good.

- Business was doing well.
- World leaders had made agreements outlawing war.
- Germany seemed to have put aside its bitterness.
- The League had had some success in solving disputes.

But underlying resentments were unchanged:

- Many Germans were still bitter about the Treaty of Versailles. The Locarno Treaty secured Germany's western boundaries, but made no mention of those on the east: that seemed to suggest that they could be altered.
- If so, where did that leave countries like Poland and Czechoslovakia?
- France was still terrified of Germany. They viewed German economic recovery with alarm and made military alliances in eastern Europe. How did these square with France's support for the League?

### QUESTION SPOTTER

Typical exam questions on this topic:

- In what ways was the League of Nations successful in the 1920s?
- Why did the League of Nations fail to achieve disarmament?

## CHECK YOURSELF QUESTIONS

**Q1** How much disarmament had been achieved by the end of the 1920s?

**Q2** 'Making the League work meant sinking your own interests and putting the League first. Nations were usually reluctant to do this.'

How accurate is this statement? Use examples from the 1920s to illustrate your answer.

*Answers are on page 201.*

# REVISION SESSION 3 The League in the 1930s

## How did the Great Depression affect the League?

- Depressed economies, unemployment and falling trade meant that countries found it hard not to put themselves first. Banning trade with a country that had been aggressive, for example, could hit the trade of those imposing the ban as much as the one they were trying to punish.
- Some countries turned to **dictatorship**, and dictators turned to foreign wars as a way of distracting people from hardships at home. Japan, Italy and Germany all did this.
- Countries became more selfish, clearly putting their own interests first. France, for example, began work on the **Maginot Line** – a huge set of fortifications along the German border (see 8.6, p119).
- In 3 crises – in Manchuria in 1931, over disarmament in 1933, and in Abyssinia in 1935 – the League was seen to fail. In the end, crises like these stopped the League from being an effective peacekeeping organisation.

### MANCHURIA

- Japan had become a successful industrialised nation, but the Depression forced it to find new markets. Many leading Japanese, especially in the powerful army, looked with envy at European empires in the East. They already possessed Korea and had their eyes on the huge provinces of China.

**8.3** *China, Japan and Manchuria*

**A* EXTRA**

After their invasion of Manchuria, the Japanese called it Manchukuo. They put the Chinese Emperor, who had been deposed in 1911, on the throne as a puppet ruler. It was the beginning of the Second World War in the East.

- In 1931, the Japanese army invaded Manchuria, in northern China (see 8.3). All efforts by the Japanese government to stop the army action failed. By 1932, they had taken over Manchuria, and began to move into the rest of China. Although Japan was on the Council of the League, it seemed a classic case of right and wrong. What would the League do?

  1 It took nearly a year to investigate the situation, while Japan completed its conquest.

  2 The report said Japan was wrong. Japan simply left the League.

  3 **Sanctions** were imposed on Japan, but the two nations which did most trade with Japan – the USA and the USSR – were not in the League and so not bound to take part in the trade ban. The nations in the League could not even agree to ban sales of weapons to Japan.

**Conclusion:**

- The League seemed powerless to stop the aggressive actions of a powerful nation (see 8.4).

**THE DOORMAT.**

**8.4** *British cartoon of 1931 called 'The Doormat'. The document the Japanese soldier has trodden on is named 'Honour of Nations'; the elderly man is using a 'face-saving outfit' on the face of the woman who represents the League.*

## DISARMAMENT

- A Disarmament Conference finally got under way in 1932. The problem was: should all nations reduce their armaments to Germany's level, or should Germany be allowed to re-arm up to everyone else's? Both options were very unpopular.

- In 1933, Hitler became Chancellor of Germany and immediately began to re-arm. He rejected disarmament plans from League members and took Germany out of the League in 1933.

Conclusions:

1 The failure of the League to disarm in the 1920s left it in a weak position to argue against Hitler.

2 France and Britain were split over how to treat Germany: France wanted to keep Germany weak; Britain felt Germany had a point. In fact, in 1935, Britain made its own naval agreement with Germany, allowing German naval re-armament up to 35% of British strength.

3 In a depression, re-armament was one way several countries took of helping industry. Several countries began to re-arm from 1933 onwards.

4 The Disarmament Conference failed totally: another war seemed to loom ahead.

## ABYSSINIA

- This country, now called Ethiopia, was one of the few countries left in Africa that was not a colony. In 1896, the Abyssinians had defeated an Italian invasion. The Italian dictator Mussolini wanted a glorious victory to win popularity at home, so he threatened to invade in 1935. **Haile Selassie**, the Emperor of Abyssinia, appealed to the League. Again it seemed a clear-cut case of right and wrong. What would the League do this time?
- The problem this time was that Britain and France did not want to make an enemy of Mussolini; they saw him as an important ally against Hitler. They feared that tough policies against him would push him into friendship with Hitler. For most of 1935 they did nothing. They

### A* EXTRA

Hitler took advantage of the world's attention being focused on Abyssinia in 1936 to send troops in to the Rhineland. France was eager for Italian support against him and all thought of tough sanctions was abandoned. Yet even then the hopes of France and Britain were dashed: Mussolini joined in alliance with Hitler, the **Rome–Berlin Axis**, later in 1936.

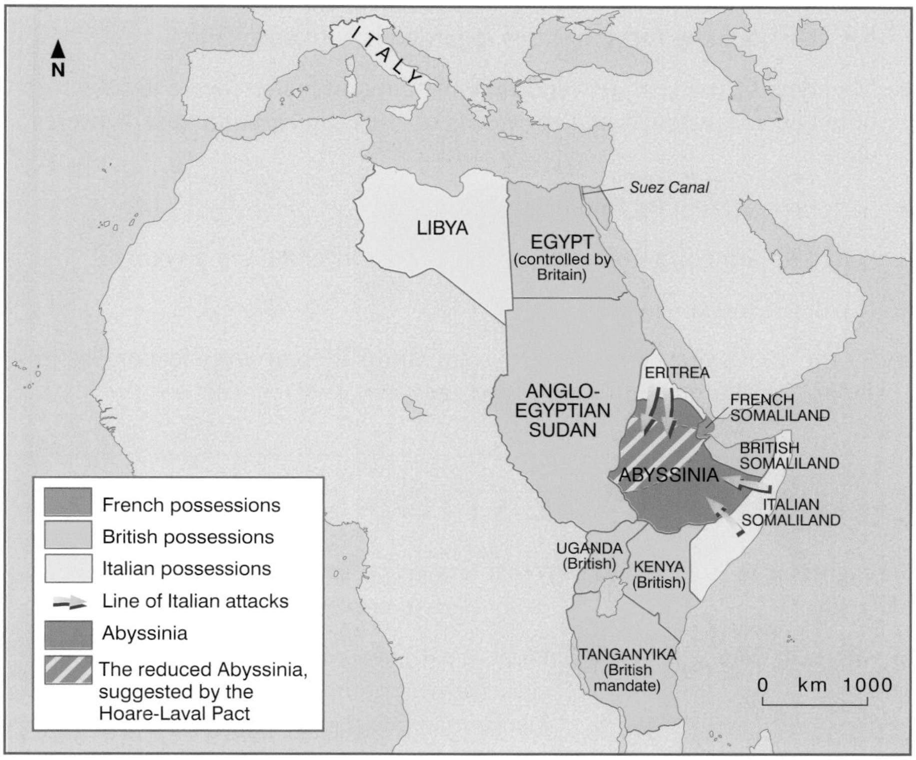


**8.5** *Map of Abyssinia*

even made an alliance with Italy – the Stresa Front – at which Abyssinia was not discussed.

- Thinking he could get away with it, Mussolini invaded Abyssinia, using all the weapons of modern warfare such as gas and flame-throwers. The League called for **sanctions** against him. There were delays for 2 months while they discussed whether to include oil and fuel.
- Britain and France could have stopped all supplies getting to the Italian troops as they controlled the Suez Canal (see 8.5), but kept it open for Italian shipping.
- The dilemma which sanctions produced can be summed up thus: the British government received information that a ban on coal exports to Italy would cost 30,000 coalminers their jobs. Was this too high a price to pay for acting as League police?
- The reluctance of Britain and France to work through the League was shown by the **Hoare–Laval Plan** – a secret plan worked out by the foreign ministers of Britain and France on their own to let Mussolini have most of Abyssinia. There were howls of protest when it was revealed.
- Conclusion: the League was seen to have totally failed. War now seemed likely sooner or later.

**QUESTION SPOTTER**

Typical exam questions on this topic:

- In what ways did the Depression of the 1930s affect the League of Nations?
- Why did the League of Nations fail to stop Japanese aggression in Manchuria?
- Why did the League of Nations fail to stop Italian aggression in Abyssinia?

## So what were the League's problems?

- The absence of the USA in particular, but also the USSR, severely weakened the League.
- It was too closely linked to the Treaties of 1919. This meant those who had lost badly by those treaties regarded it with suspicion.
- Members of the League, especially Britain and France, were always torn between self-interest and the needs of the League. Usually self-interest won.
- Sanctions were hard to put into action.
- It had no armed force to keep the peace or intervene in a war.
- It worked too slowly.
- By the 1930s dictators, like Mussolini and Hitler, or army leaders, as in Japan, were prepared to defy the League.

## CHECK YOURSELF QUESTIONS

**Q1** **a** Which country was the aggressor in (i) Manchuria and (ii) Abyssinia?

**b** Why did they get away with it, in each case?

**Q2** What lessons do you think Hitler learned from the two crises?

**Q3** Look at 8.4. How does the cartoonist make clear his view of the League in the Manchurian crisis?

*Answers are on page 202.*

REVISION SESSION 4

# Hitler and the causes of the Second World War

## Did Hitler plan for the Second World War?

- Historians have argued long over this: it depends what you mean by 'plan'. If you mean did Hitler have a blueprint of events, which would lead, stage by stage to war, then the answer is probably no. If you mean did he expect to have to go to war sometime, then the answer is probably yes.

### HITLER'S IDEAS

- The problem starts with what Hitler said in ***Mein Kampf*** – his long, rambling autobiography. It was written in 1924 when Hitler had time on his hands, serving his prison sentence after the beer-hall putsch (see unit 4). He made several points:
  - The German people are a superior race. All Germans should be in the same country. He criticised the Treaty of Versailles for leaving German-speaking people in Austria, Czechoslovakia and Poland.
  - Once all Germans are united, they will need more land. This will be taken from the land to the East: Poland, Russia. These are lived in by Slavs, whom Hitler believed to be inferior people. Hitler also hated the USSR because it was Communist.
  - This will mean war. Germany should ignore the Treaty of Versailles and re-arm so as to be ready.
- Are these just vague ideas? Or a statement of intentions? Let's see what happened when he got into power, 9 years after he wrote *Mein Kampf*.

> **A* EXTRA**
>
> Historians argue about the **Hossbach Memorandum**. This document came out of a meeting held in 1937 in which Hitler told his generals to be ready for war within 5 years. It gives strength to the idea that Hitler planned for war, but did not necessarily plan when it would happen.

**8.6** *Map of Europe, 1936–38*

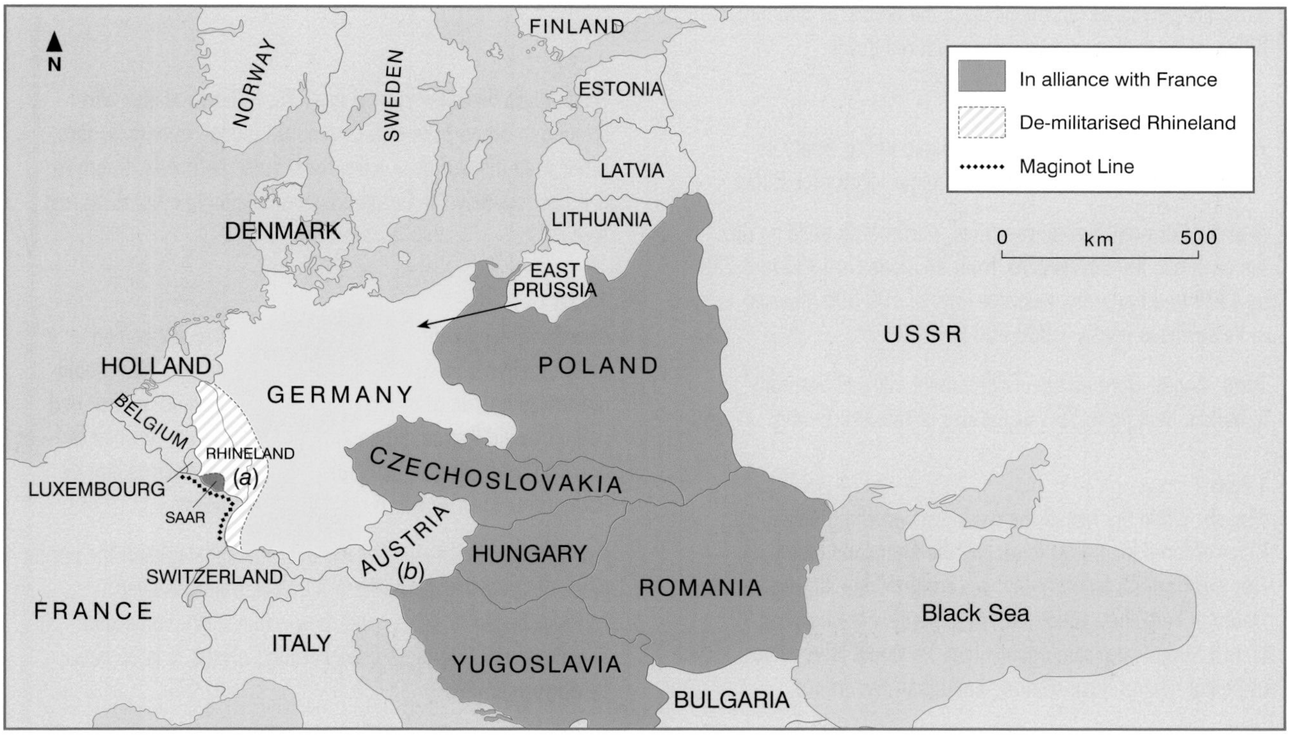

> **A* EXTRA**
>
> Another excuse Hitler could use to defend his re-armament programme was the alliances France had built up with several eastern European countries: Poland, Hungary, Czechoslovakia, Romania. They had looked for France's protection against any attempt by Germany to alter the eastern boundaries laid down by Versailles. Hitler said he was being surrounded and had to defend himself.

## HITLER'S GERMANY

(This section is just a reminder; for more see unit 4).

- Hitler set about building weapons and increasing the size of the German armed forces (see below). This was partly to solve the unemployment problem, but it also made Germany strong again.
- The German economy was put on a war footing. By 1939, more than half the German economy was devoted to war preparations.
- The Hitler Youth movement was designed to prepare young male Germans for war.

This still doesn't mean that Hitler had a plan. Look at the events of 1933–38, below. Notice:

- how cleverly Hitler uses events to get what he wants, choosing his time perfectly
- how ruthless he was – prepared to use force, murder, threats, or whatever suited him.

### 1933

Germany left the League over re-armament. Hitler was indignant that other countries had not disarmed while Germany was forced to do so in 1919. Britain, among others, thought he had a point. Secret re-armament of Germany began.

### 1934

Austrian Nazis, on Hitler's orders, assassinated Austrian Chancellor Dollfuss. Hitler prepared to take over Austria but Mussolini moved Italian troops up to the border to stop him. Hitler, lacking strong armed forces, backed down.

### 1935

**January** Plebiscite in Saar, as arranged at the Treaty of Versailles, voted to join Germany: a minor victory for Hitler.

**March** Germany openly re-armed, particularly building up the air force, the ***Luftwaffe***, from 36 planes in 1932 to 8,250 by 1939 and the army, from the limit of 100,000 imposed at Versailles to nearly 1,000,000 by 1939.

**June** Anglo–German naval agreement allowed Germany to build a fleet up to 35% of the size of the British navy.

### 1936

**March** While the rest of the world was watching Abyssinia, Hitler ordered his troops to occupy the Rhineland (see 8.6). This was German territory but was declared demilitarised at the Treaty of Versailles. Hitler and his generals were nervous. If French troops were sent against him, he would have to back down as he did not yet have a strong enough army. France, in the middle of an election campaign and unsure of British support, did not act. Hitler got away with it.

**November** Mussolini, fed up with the attitude of France and Britain over his Abyssinian invasion, made the Rome–Berlin Axis agreement with Hitler. This was extended in 1937 when Germany, Italy and Japan signed the **Anti-Comintern Pact**, so lining up one of the alliances in the Second World War. (Comintern was the international Communist organisation.)

### 1937

The Spanish Civil War started in 1936. Hitler (and Mussolini) decided to support the anti-Communist leader, General Franco. Hitler used the war as practice for his new *Luftwaffe*. Guernica was destroyed by the German Condor Legion in a bombing raid (see 8.7).

### 1938

**March** Hitler threatened to take over Austria. He bullied Austrian Chancellor Schuschnigg, pointing out that Italy would not rescue Austria as it had in 1934, France would not act, and neither would Britain. Schuschnigg prepared to defy Hitler by holding a plebiscite on the issue, but Hitler forestalled him by taking over Austria. This is called the **Anschluss**.

**April** Hitler threatened to take over the Sudetenland, the border areas of Czechoslovakia where 3 million Germans lived. As Hitler began to move towards new lands, Britain became heavily involved through Chamberlain's efforts to keep peace by **appeasement**.

**8.7** *Guernica, in northern Spain, destroyed by German bombers in April 1937*

## QUESTION SPOTTER

Typical exam questions on this topic:

- What were Hitler's achievements in foreign policy up to 1938?
- Why was Hitler successful in achieving his foreign policy aims without war before 1938?

## CHECK YOURSELF QUESTIONS

**Q1** Look at 8.6.

**a** Describe what action Hitler took over areas (a) and (b) on the map.

**b** What was he trying to do in each case?

**c** Was he: lucky? clever?

**Q2** Was Hitler solely to blame for the drift to war up to 1938?

*Answers are on page 202.*

# Appeasement

> **A* EXTRA**
>
> Other examples of appeasement in action are: the Hoare–Laval plan to carve up Abyssinia in 1935 (p118); the agreement between Britain and Germany allowed Germany to rebuild its navy (p120); the failure to take any action over Hitler's re-occupation of the Rhineland in 1936, and the Anschluss in 1938.

## What was the Sudetenland Crisis?

By the mid-1930s, British and French leaders adopted a policy of **appeasement** towards Hitler (and Mussolini). They felt that the Treaty of Versailles had been too harsh and that some of the dictators' demands were fair. They hoped that if Hitler and Mussolini got most of what they wanted, they would be satisfied and start behaving reasonably – they would be 'appeased'.

- In 1938, some German Nazis in the **Sudetenland** (part of Czechoslovakia) complained that they were being badly treated by the Czech government. Hitler threatened to invade Czechoslovakia to protect them.
- War seemed quite likely: Czechoslovakia had a modern and well-equipped army and was ready to fight. It also had an agreement with France that they would protect each other if either was attacked. The war could spread.
- The British Prime Minister, **Chamberlain**, flew to meet Hitler in Germany in September 1938. He thought he had persuaded Hitler to calm down and allow a plebiscite to be held in the Sudetenland, but at the next meeting Hitler stepped up his demands and threatened war.
- Chamberlain called a conference at Munich, attended by Germany, France, Italy and Britain. They agreed that the Sudetenland should be handed over to Germany.

**8.8** *A Czech woman watches German forces march into Prague, the Czech capital, March 1939*

RESULTS

- The Czechs were furious – they had not been consulted and had lost the Sudetenland and their defences against Germany.
- Hitler was jubilant – he had got what he wanted without a shot being fired. He promised Chamberlain: 'I have no more territorial demands in Europe.'
- Chamberlain was welcomed by the British public as a hero, a peacemaker. 'I believe it is peace in our time,' he said.
- Winston Churchill, out of favour with the government, warned: 'We have suffered a total defeat. You will find that in time Czechoslovakia will be engulfed in the Nazi regime.'
- In March 1939, Hitler's troops invaded **Czechoslovakia** (see 8.8).

## Why did the British adopt an appeasement policy?

1 A majority of the British people hated the idea of another war. Almost all that generation of British leaders had fought in the First World War and never wanted to fight again.

2 Government experts had told Chamberlain that another war would be devastating, based on the wars going on in China and Spain. They estimated 1.8 million British civilians would be killed in bombing raids in the first 60 days of a war.

3 Britain was not ready for war. The armed forces were run down. British military planners had believed German propaganda about re-armament and thought Germany was more prepared for war than Britain was.

4 Many British people were not prepared to go to war over a European crisis. Chamberlain called Czechoslovakia 'a far-off country of whose people we know nothing'. To many British the overseas Empire was far more important. They preferred to buy peace at the price of the Sudetenland.

5 The British feared **Communism** far more than Nazism. Some even admired Hitler for the stand he was taking and felt a strong Nazi Germany was a good defence against the USSR.

### THE DRIFT TO WAR

Hitler and Chamberlain misunderstood one another.

- Chamberlain thought Hitler could be trusted and meant what he said. He had never dealt with anyone who was prepared to lie, bully and break his word as Hitler did. As soon as Hitler invaded Czechoslovakia in March 1939, it was obvious that Poland would be his next target. Chamberlain therefore made an alliance with Poland to support it if it was invaded. France already had such an alliance.
- Hitler thought Chamberlain was so set on peace at all costs that Britain would never go to war. He thought he could go on seizing land to the east while Britain and France did nothing.

### THE NAZI–SOVIET PACT, 1939

- The only country which could interfere in Hitler's planned seizure of Poland was the USSR. To the astonishment of the world the two arch-enemies, Germany and the USSR, signed an agreement in August 1939 not to attack each other. The **Nazi–Soviet Pact** contained secret clauses to divide up Poland between them.
- It was a dishonest deal on both sides: Hitler knew he would attack the USSR sooner or later (it happened less than 2 years later). Stalin hoped it would buy him time while Hitler made war in western Europe first. In September 1939, German forces invaded Poland. Britain and France stood by their alliance with Poland and declared war on Germany. The Second World War had begun.

### A* EXTRA

Appeasement, far from preserving peace as it was intended to do and the mass of the British public hoped it would, may have made war more likely. This is because appeasement may have encouraged Hitler to think he could get away with any kind of aggression.

### QUESTION SPOTTER

Typical exam questions on this topic:

- Explain how Hitler managed to take over most of Czechoslovakia by March 1939 with hardly a shot being fired.
- What were the motives for the British policy of appeasement?
- Why did Chamberlain give way to Hitler's demands at the Munich meeting of September 1938?

## CHECK YOURSELF QUESTIONS

**Q1** Describe what Hitler was up to at each of these four moments:

**a** Sudetenland, April 1938
**b** invasion of Czechoslovakia, March 1939
**c** Nazi–Soviet Pact, August 1939
**d** war with Poland, September 1939.

**Q2** Why did Chamberlain adopt a policy of appeasement?

Look at the 5 reasons given on page 123. They are different types of reasons: some public statements, some private attitudes, some secret information. Sort the reasons into different types; explain your decisions, using these paragraph headings:

'The reasons Chamberlain gave for appeasement were...'

'He also had information which could not be made public. This was...'

'Some people in Britain also thought...'

*Answers are on page 203.*

REVISION SESSION 1

# The origins of the Cold War

- Soldiers from the USA and the USSR were wartime allies in the struggle against Hitler. Yet within a year of the end of the war the two **superpowers** were locked in a new struggle – a **Cold War** – which lasted for 45 years.

**9.1** *US and Soviet soldiers meet in Germany, May 1945*

## SUPERPOWERS

- The most dominant countries in world politics up to 1945 were European: Britain, France and Germany. By 1945, these countries were in ruins or crippled by the Second World War. The world was now dominated by two new countries: the USA and the USSR.
- The statistics about these two new superpowers are shown in table 9.2. They were very different from each other.
  - The USSR was the largest country in the world, with the biggest army.
  - The USA was the richest country in the world, with the **atom bomb**.
- These two were far ahead of their rivals, and their power extended over the whole world.

**Table 9.2 Statistics about the USA and the USSR**

| | USA | USSR |
|---|---|---|
| Size | 9 million sq. km. | 21 million sq. km. |
| Population | 226 million | 262 million (1984) |
| Armed forces | 2 million | 4.8 million (1984) |
| Wealth | $2,100 billion | $1,200 billion (1984) |

### COLD WAR

- This term was first used in 1947. It was a war carried out by every means possible short of the USA and USSR actually fighting each other. Sometimes, the Cold War nearly became a real – 'hot' – war, but one side or the other always held back.

  - An **arms race**: both sides spent large amounts of money on building up stockpiles of weapons, particularly nuclear weapons. Soon they had enough weapons between them to destroy all life on earth. This is why the Cold War is so important.
  - They were rivals in the **space race**: the USSR launched the first satellite, in 1957; the USA made the first moon landing, in 1969.
  - They were also rivals in **sport**.
  - Each side broadcast **propaganda** to their own people and to the rest of the world.
  - Each side had a huge network of **spies** to find out what the other was up to. The USA had the CIA (Central Intelligence Agency); the USSR had the KGB.
  - Each side controlled the countries nearby. Any attempt by one of these countries to break free and follow their own line was crushed.

    1 The USSR in Hungary, 1956 and Czechoslovakia, 1968 (see pp 154–6), Afghanistan, 1979 and Poland, 1980–81 (see p156).

    2 The USA in Cuba, 1962 (see p143), Guatemala, 1954 and Chile, 1973.
  - Both superpowers took part in **substitute (or proxy) wars** (i.e. each helped its allies fight the other superpower or its allies).

    1 The USSR helped North Vietnam in war against the USA, 1961–73.

    2 The USA helped South Korea and the USSR helped North Korea in the Korean War, 1950–53.
  - The USA and the USSR helped rival sides in **civil wars** in the Congo, 1960 and Namibia. The USA helped Israel and the USSR helped several Arab nations in their conflicts in the Middle East.

## What were the long-term causes of the Cold War?

### RUSSIAN FEAR OF THE WEST

- Russia had been invaded 3 times in the 20th century: in 1914, at the start of the First World War (see p14), in 1918, in the Civil War (see p75) and in 1941.
- Stalin felt that some Western leaders wanted to see Communism crushed. They remembered that:

  1 Britain, France and other Western countries sent troops to help the Whites against the new Communist government in 1918.

  2 Western powers had been slow to join with them against Hitler in the 1930s.

**QUESTION SPOTTER**

Typical exam questions on this topic:

- What is meant by the terms 'superpower' and 'Cold War'?
- What were the main differences between the superpowers in 1945?

3 In the Second World War, up to 20 million Soviet citizens had been killed – soldiers as well as civilians. Farmland, industries and cities had been devastated. The Red Army had only driven back the German invasion after a long and bitter struggle. They felt Western countries did not understand how they had suffered and had been too slow to relieve German pressure on the USSR by invading Western Europe.

> **A* EXTRA**
>
> Early Communists, like Marx, Lenin and Trotsky, had tried to spread Communism all over the world. Comintern, set up in 1919, was designed to promote this. Stalin, however, promoted a policy of 'Socialism in one country'.

## US AND WESTERN FEAR OF COMMUNISM

- Some people believed that **Communists** were intent on causing revolutions in other countries. In units 5, 6 and 7 we saw something of the ways the governments and the economies of the USA and the USSR worked. They were very different (see 9.3).

**USA**

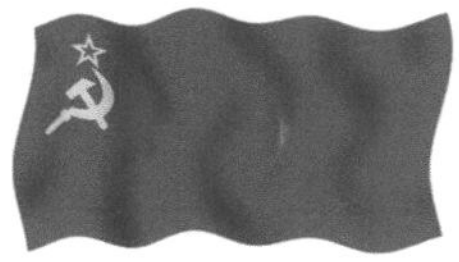

**USSR**

**Government:** a *two-party democracy*, with elections for President and Congress.

**Economy:** a *capitalist country* (i.e. land+industry owned by private individuals who run them for their own profit) – produced great unfairness, with some people very rich and some very poor, but created successful industry and commerce. The average standard of living was higher in the capitalist West.

**Freedom:** more political freedom (e.g. more than one party to vote for, a free press which could criticise the government, no secret police, freedom to travel where you wanted, relaxed censorship in arts and media).

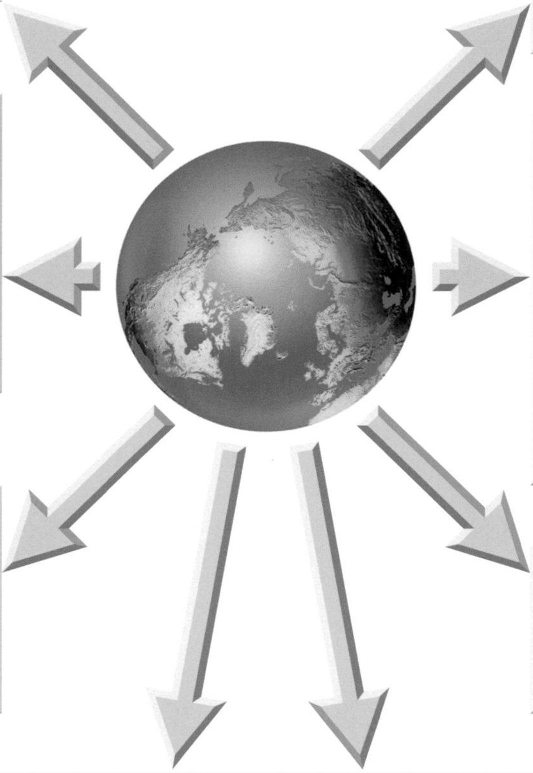

**Government:** a *one-party state*. There were elections, but the Communist Party was the only party allowed. Stalin had ruled as a dictator since 1928.

**Economy:** a *Communist country* (i.e. land+industry owned by the state, which ran them, in theory for the good of every citizen) – security of employment, free education and health, but lack of competition; heavy government control led to inefficiency in industry and business. Result was a shortage of goods, lower quality and less innovation; in general, a lower standard of living.

**Freedom:** strict censorship, criticism of the government could land you in prison, you couldn't travel outside the USSR and the Soviet block.

BOTH SIDES FELT THEY WERE RIGHT
and claimed that the other was trying to extend its system all over the world.

**9.3** *Comparisons between the USA and the USSR*

### THE END OF US ISOLATION

- Americans felt partly to blame for the Second World War because of their **isolationist** policy between the wars (see p91). They felt they could have done more to stop Hitler earlier. Now they were determined to use their power to play a big part in world affairs. For many Americans this meant opposing dictatorship and setting up **multi-party democracies** and **capitalist economies** everywhere. Many were bitterly opposed to Communism.
- President Roosevelt was keen to take up the idea of an international peacekeeping organisation which President Woodrow Wilson had supported in 1919, but which the USA had never joined (see p109). Roosevelt had plans for a new organisation, the **United Nations**, of which he had high hopes (see unit 10).

## CHECK YOURSELF QUESTIONS

**Q1** Use the information on the two different systems in the USA and the USSR (9.2) to fill in the gaps at a, b, c and d on the table:

| | USA | USSR |
|---|---|---|
| Government | Two-party democracy | **a** |
| Economic system | **b** | **c** |
| Freedom | **d** | Censorship, secret police, restrictions on travel |

*Answers are on page 204.*

# REVISION SESSION 2 The beginning of the Cold War

- The short-term causes of the Cold War arose out of the events of 1945–46, as the war ended. The long-term fears and resentments began to surface at two important meetings in 1945:
  - at **Yalta**, in the USSR, in February
  - at **Potsdam**, in Germany, in July.

## Who was at Yalta?

- **Churchill** (the British wartime Prime Minister), **Roosevelt** and **Stalin** met at Yalta (see 9.4). It was clear that Germany was about to be defeated and the three victorious allies met to decide how to manage the peace. There were some disagreements, but the three leaders were able to negotiate to settle them.

**9.4** *Churchill, Roosevelt and Stalin at Yalta (seated)*

- The USSR agreed to join in the war against Japan as soon as Hitler was defeated.
- All 3 agreed to join the new **United Nations** (UN).
- They discussed, in general terms, what should happen in countries liberated from Nazi rule: 'free' elections would be held and Eastern Europe should be a Soviet 'sphere of influence'.
- They agreed that Germany should be divided into 4 zones as their armies advanced. Churchill pressed for a French zone to be added to the other 3 in order to give another anti-Soviet voice to the armies of occupation. The capital city of Berlin was similarly divided, even though it was inside the Soviet zone. So was the country of Austria (see 9.5). These were not intended to be permanent divisions.

- There was disagreement over Poland. Stalin wanted to add some Polish territory to the USSR, compensating Poland with land in the east from Germany. Roosevelt was not keen on this but Churchill was ready to accept it if the USSR accepted British influence in Greece. In the end, Roosevelt agreed as the price for the USSR joining the UN. There was little the Allies could do about anything in Eastern Europe, as the advancing Red Army occupied it all.

**9.5** *Europe in 1945*

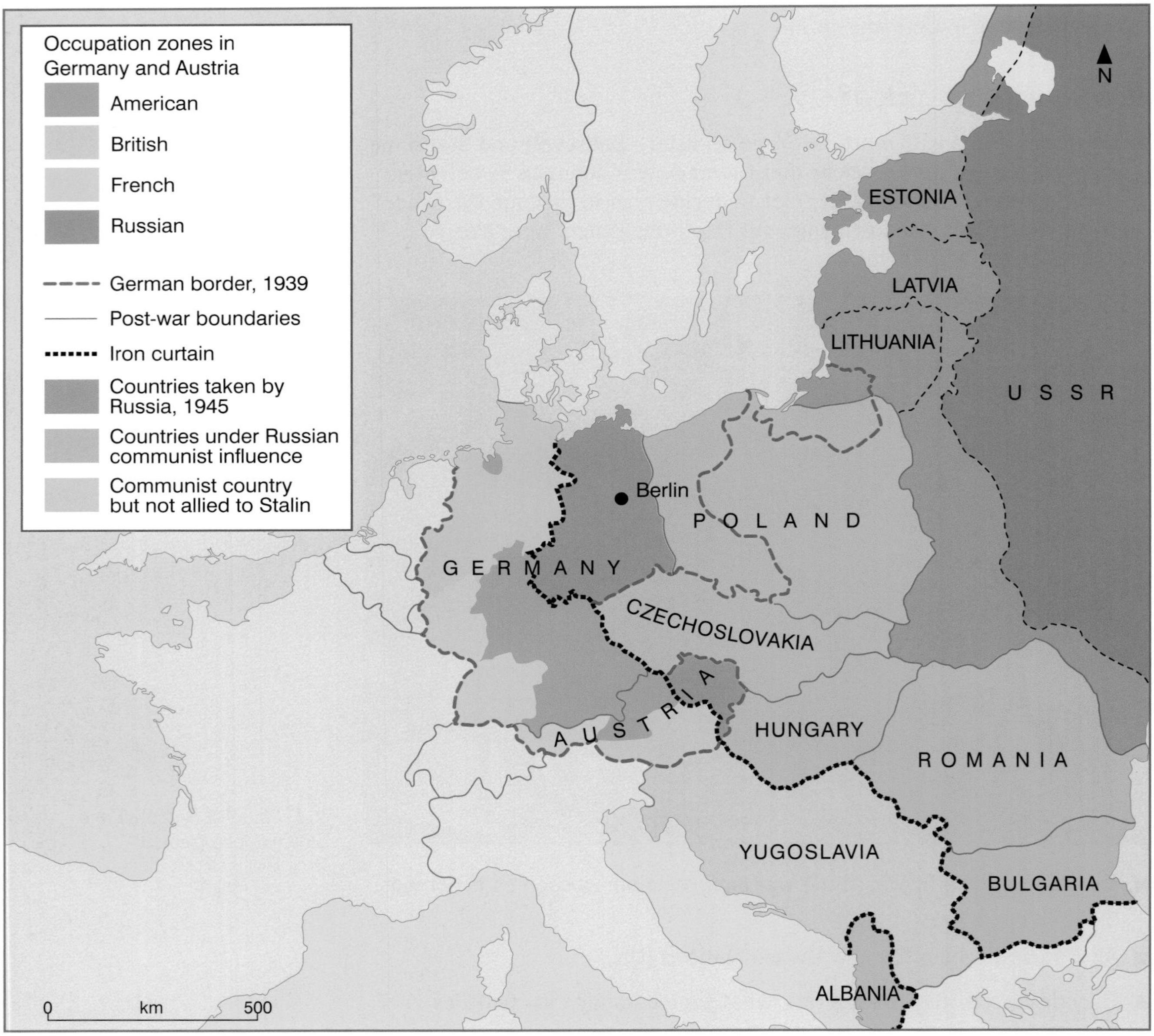


## EVENTS AFTER THE YALTA CONFERENCE

- Roosevelt died of cancer in April 1945 and Harry Truman took over as President of the USA.
- Germany surrendered in May.
- A Communist government was set up in Poland, without democratic elections.

- The next meeting was at Potsdam, just outside Berlin.
- The USA successfully tested an atomic bomb just before the conference. Stalin's spies had already told him that this was going to happen, but he was annoyed that the USA had not shared their knowledge with him, as their ally. This also increased his fear of the USA, which could clearly now destroy the USSR if it wished.

> **A* EXTRA**
>
> Personal relations between the leaders at Yalta and Potsdam played a part in the growing hostility. Roosevelt felt he got on quite well with Stalin and was critical of Churchill's imperialism. Truman was openly hostile to Stalin. Stalin was suspicious of all the Western leaders he had to deal with.

## Who was at Potsdam?

- Churchill was defeated in the British General Election in July 1945, part way through the conference. Discussions therefore took place between **Truman**, **Stalin** and the new Labour Prime Minister **Clement Attlee**. Truman did not get on with Stalin and the Potsdam conference did not go well.
  - The only agreement was to put 21 leading Nazis on trial at **Nuremberg** for war crimes and to round up and punish Nazis in their respective zones.
  - Stalin wanted harsh peace terms for Germany, demanding $20 billion **reparations**, crippling the country and seizing what was left of its industry. Truman disagreed, remembering the effects of the 1919 Versailles Treaty on Germany.
  - Truman was angry at Soviet actions in Poland imposing a one-party Communist state and their seizure of more land (see 9.5). Parts of Finland, Poland, Czechoslovakia, Romania as well as all of Lithuania, Latvia and Estonia were now under Soviet rule. The USSR had expanded 480 kilometres westwards, bringing 22 million people under Soviet rule.

## How did the Soviets take over Eastern Europe?

- Over the next 3 years all of Eastern Europe came under Soviet control.

  1 Communists took over at once in Bulgaria, Hungary and Romania.

  2 In Poland and Czechoslovakia they shared power for a while and then non-Communists were thrown out.

  3 The last to fall was Czechoslovakia, in 1948.
- The next stage was that local Communist leaders were replaced by pro-Soviet, pro-Stalin Communists. In 1947, **'Comiform'** (the Communist Information Bureau) put all Communist parties under the control of Moscow. Secret police began their work, putting an end to freedom. Their economies were run for the USSR's benefit. Soon all 8 countries shown in 9.5 were little more than provinces of the USSR (often called 'satellites' in the West).
- Only Tito, in Yugoslavia, managed to keep a Communist government free of Stalin's control.

What was really going on?

### INTERPRETATIONS

- Stalin said that these measures were purely defensive. He pointed out that anti-Soviet governments in these countries had helped the German invasion of 1941. 'What can there be surprising about the fact that the Soviet Union, anxious for its future safety, is trying to see that governments loyal to the Soviet Union should exist in these countries?'
- People in the West were horrified.

  1 They were angry that undemocratic governments had been set up in these countries, contrary to what they thought Stalin had promised at Yalta. They were opposed to dictatorship.

  2 They did not believe Stalin was acting purely defensively. There were powerful Communist parties in France and Italy; the Red Army had not gone home. Perhaps they would march into Western Europe next.

### THE IRON CURTAIN

- As early as May 1945, Churchill used the phrase **'Iron Curtain'** to describe what was happening in Europe. Speaking at Fulton, Missouri, in 1946, he said: 'An iron curtain has descended across Europe. Behind that line lie all the states of Central and Eastern Europe. This is not the liberated Europe we fought to build. Nor is it one which allows permanent peace.'

**QUESTION SPOTTER**

Typical exam questions on this topic:

- What were the attitudes of the USSR and the West towards each other in 1945?
- Why did the West fear Stalin's USSR in 1945?
- Explain why Churchill said there was an 'Iron Curtain' across Europe.

**Summary of short-term causes of the Cold War**

- Soviet need for secure borders
- Soviet fear of US atomic weapons
- Soviet fear of US attack
- US resentment of Communist takeover of Eastern Europe
- US fear of Communist move into Western Europe
- US fear of Communist plans to expand all over the world.

## CHECK YOURSELF QUESTIONS

**Q1** Which do you think was the strongest superpower in 1945? Give reasons for your choice.

**Q2** List the reasons why Stalin feared the West.

**Q3** Why were relations between the Allies at Potsdam worse than they were at Yalta?

*Answers are on page 204.*

REVISION SESSION 3

# Truman Doctrine, containment and the Berlin Airlift

## What was the Truman Doctrine?

- Truman did not agree at first with Churchill's 'Iron Curtain' speech of 1946. As events unfolded in Eastern Europe, he began to feel that the USA should be taking a tougher line with the USSR. In 1947, he set up the **National Security Council** (NSC) and the CIA.
- After 1945 there was civil war in Greece between the **monarchists**, supported by the British, and Greek **Communists**. In 1947, Britain decided that it could not afford to go on helping the monarchists. Truman decided he could not let another country fall to the Communists and sent money to help the monarchists.
- He said: 'I believe that it must be the policy of the United States to support free peoples who are resisting attempted subjugation by armed minorities or outside pressure.'
- This was called the **'Truman Doctrine'** and began the policy of **containment**. This meant that the USA was not going to allow any more countries to turn Communist: it was going to 'contain' the expansion of Communism.

## What was the purpose of Marshall Aid?

- Truman and his advisers believed that people were turning to Communism because they were desperate. In 1948, Truman sent his Secretary of State, **General George Marshall**, to Europe. He found Europe still in dire difficulties.
  - Fighting in the Second World War had taken place all over Europe.
  - Retreating Nazis had destroyed everything, ripping up railway tracks and burning towns.
  - Allied bombing raids left massive destruction.
  - Refugees were criss-crossing Europe looking for their homes and families or for safety.
  - Europe owed the USA $11.5 billion.
  - Marshall recommended loans totalling $17 billion so that Europe could recover.
- The US Congress was reluctant to agree to such a huge loan. Then came the brutal Communist takeover in Czechoslovakia and Congress voted to find the money for **Marshall Aid**.
- Marshall Aid helped to rebuild Western Europe. Britain alone received $3.1 billion between 1948 and 1952. It was not a selfless gesture: Marshall Aid helped US industry by giving them a market for their goods. Stalin refused to accept any, and would not allow any Eastern block country to accept any. He said it was just part of the US plan to undermine Communism and spread capitalism all over the world.

### A* EXTRA

More of Truman's words from his speech explaining the Truman Doctrine quoted here are worth reading as examples of how the USA thought about the clash of systems at that time:

'At the present moment nearly every nation must choose between alternative ways of life. The choice is too often not a free one. One way of life is based on the will of the majority, freedom of speech and freedom from political oppression. The second way of life is based on the will of a minority forcibly imposed on the majority. It relies on terror and oppression, a controlled press and radio, fixed elections.'

## Why was Berlin a flashpoint in the Cold War?

- At the heart of the problem of reviving Europe was what to do about Germany. The agricultural east was in the Soviet zone while the more industrial west was in the three Allied zones (see 9.6). This split had been agreed at Yalta but they had not allowed for disagreements between the 4 occupying powers.
- 16 million **refugees** from all over Europe swelled the German population. Its economy was in ruins, reduced to barter or using cigarettes as currency. There was not enough food or medical supplies.
- Stalin continued to dismantle German factories and take them off to the USSR. As far as he was concerned, Germany and its people could rot.
- The Allies felt they could not let the German people starve. On the other hand, they could not afford to just hand out food.

INTERPRETATIONS

- The Western Allies decided that the **German economy** should be allowed to recover so that the German people could work and trade and so earn money to feed themselves. In 1946, the 3 Allied zones were united in 1 unit. In 1948, a new currency was introduced to help the German economic revival. The USSR was not consulted over this owing to the mistrust developing between the 2 sides.
- Stalin feared the **revival of Germany**. The USSR had suffered terribly at German hands during the war and he now feared that German revival would lead to a combined attack on the USSR. In June 1948, Stalin closed off all road, rail and canal access to Berlin (see 9.6).

**9.6** *Berlin and Germany, 1948–49*

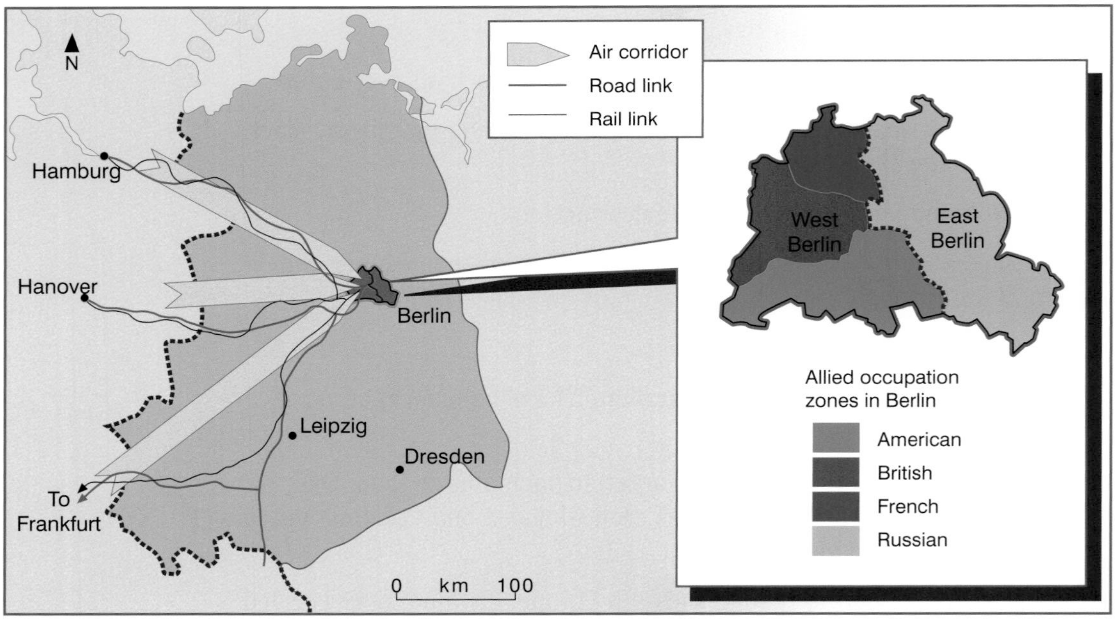

- Stalin hoped the **blockade** would force the Allies out of West Berlin. 2.1 million citizens lived in the Allied Western zones of Berlin. They needed 4,000 tonnes of supplies a day. How were they to be supplied? Should the Allies send tanks down one of the roads and fight their way through? Should they threaten to bomb the USSR in retaliation?
- Either of these alternatives would lead to another war and the Allies chose the least aggressive option: to supply the city by air. For the next 318 days food, fuel and medical supplies were flown in. The aeroplanes made a total of 27,000 flights before the USSR opened the land routes again in May 1949.

### RESULTS OF THE BERLIN CRISIS

1 Germany remained divided (until 1990). In 1949, the Allied zones became **West Germany** (Federal Republic of Germany); the Soviet zone became **East Germany** (Democratic Republic of Germany).

2 West Berlin stayed a western island inside East Germany and a permanent source of tension in the Cold War.

3 The division of Europe – the Iron Curtain – became permanent. By the 1950s, watchtowers, barbed wire and mines had turned it into a real barrier. Travel across it was very difficult. Europe was a divided continent as long as the Cold War lasted.

### QUESTION SPOTTER

Typical exam questions on this topic:
- Why did the USA introduce Marshall Aid?
- Why was there a crisis over Berlin in 1948–49?
- Why did the Western Allies organise an airlift of supplies to Berlin in 1948–49?

## CHECK YOURSELF QUESTIONS

**Q1** What two reasons does Truman give in his speech to explain how Communists were taking over?

**Q2** 'A helping hand to Europe'; 'An attempt to spread US capitalism across the world'. Which of these two views of Marshall Aid do you think is more accurate?

**Q3** In what ways is the Berlin Airlift an example of Cold War, not hot war?

*Answers are on page 205.*

# Containment around the world: Korea

- 1949 was a bad year for the USA in the Cold War:
  - The USSR exploded its own atom bomb. This meant that the USA no longer had a monopoly of nuclear weapons and its whole strategy had to be re-thought.
  - China became Communist after a long civil war in which the USA had backed the losing side, the Nationalists. They had spent $2 billion. Now, despite their efforts, the most populous country in the world was Communist.

### McCARTHYISM

- A kind of anti-Communist hysteria gripped the USA. A US senator, Joseph McCarthy, claimed that things were going wrong for the USA because there were Communists in high places in American society and government. He received lots of publicity by claiming that he had evidence of 57 Communists in the US State Department.
- In the anti-Communist mood of the time no one dared oppose him. To question his charges led to accusations of being a Communist. Many people lost their jobs as a result. Lawyers were afraid to defend those accused.
- In 1952, McCarthy was put in charge of the '**Un-American Activities Committee**'. He turned his attention to the film industry. Charlie Chaplin was among those accused. Some producers and actors could not get work. In 1954, it became clear that McCarthy had no evidence and his lies and bullying were revealed.

**A* EXTRA**

McCarthy's accusations were made just a little more credible because in 1950 two Americans were found guilty of selling US nuclear secrets to the USSR during the war (the USSR was an ally of the USA at that time). Also, some State Department officials had been members of the Communist Party 20 or 30 years earlier.

### NSC 68

- In 1950, the National Security Council sent Truman a document – **NSC 68** – telling him about Communist activities in the world beyond Europe. Was containment intended to apply all over the world? Truman soon had to decide.

## Why was Korea a flashpoint in the Cold War?

- At the end of the Second World War the Japanese in the northern half of Korea surrendered to the USSR and those in the southern half to US forces. A Communist system was set up in the north and a capitalist one in the south. The two countries became bitter enemies.
- Then, in 1950, North Korean troops invaded the South. By September, they had taken most of the country (see 9.7). Truman sent troops and ships to the area and appealed to the United Nations.

**A* EXTRA**

Both North and South Korea were undemocratic countries with more or less dictatorial rulers. US support for the ruler of South Korea was based on little more than his opposition to Communism. In this way US Cold War policy led the USA to support governments in several parts of the world which were far from democratic.

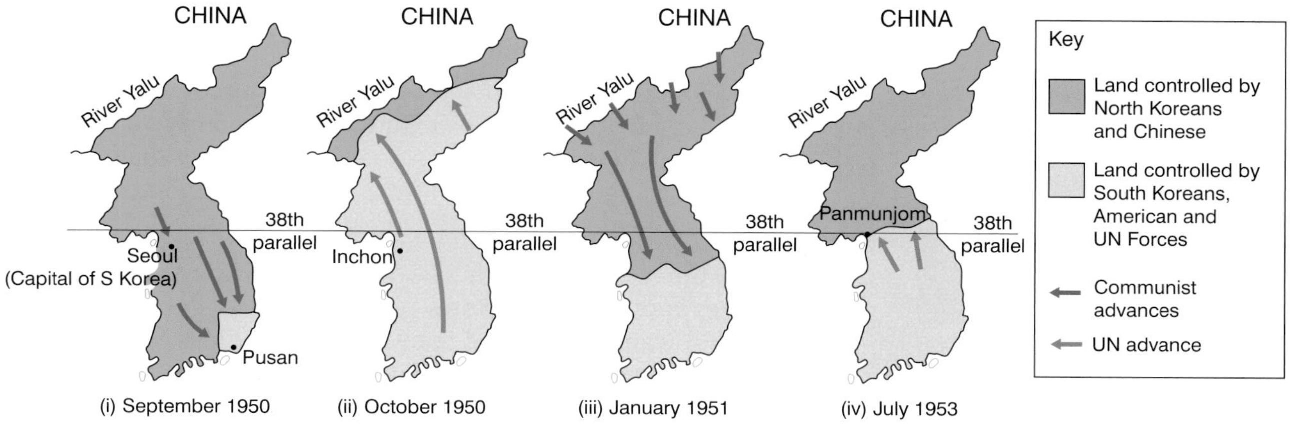


The 38th parallel was the border between North and South Korea from 1945 to June 1950

**9.7** *The Korean War, 1950–1953*

## INTERPRETATIONS

- This was an international crisis like the Manchurian and Abyssinian crises of the 1930s. One country was being invaded by another. The USA believed that their failure to get involved then and the subsequent failure of the League of Nations had helped to cause the Second World War. They were determined to see that the powers of the UN were used to deal with North Korea.
- This was part of the Cold War. North Korea was an aggressive Communist state. Communists had taken over in China in 1949 and were now trying to take South Korea. They were also active in other countries in Asia: Indo-China, Malaya, Indonesia, Burma. The US government believed in the '**domino theory**' (i.e. one country after another would fall to Communism like a line of dominoes) – see page 147. Containment must, therefore, be extended all over the world.

## WHAT HAPPENED NEXT?

- Normally, the USSR would have used its Security Council veto to stop the UN acting. However, the USA had refused to allow the new Communist government of China to take over China's place in the UN. The USSR had withdrawn from the UN in protest, so the veto was not used. The UN condemned the North Korean invasion and authorised the use of force to stop it.
- 18 countries, including Britain, sent troops to join the UN force, but the USA provided most of the armed forces as well as the commander, the Second World War veteran **General MacArthur**.

- The events of the war can be seen on map 9.7:

1 UN forces landed at Inchon and South Korean forces moved north – see 9.7(ii). By October, the North Korean army had been driven back nearly to the Chinese border. This was already further than the UN resolution had agreed. Chinese leader Mao Zedong warned them to stop. They did not.

2 200,000 Chinese troops with Soviet weapons invaded and drove the UN forces back into South Korea by January 1951 – see 9.7(iii). MacArthur wanted to extend the war to attack China, using nuclear weapons. He said the USA should put 'Asia first' in the battle against Communism. Truman could see the dangers of this and stuck to containment. In April 1951, Truman, as President and therefore supreme Commander of US forces, sacked MacArthur.

3 Peace talks began but fighting continued until July 1953 – 9.7(iv). Peace was made with more or less the same boundaries as the 2 countries had had before the war.

**QUESTION SPOTTER**

Typical exam questions on this topic:

- Why was there a crisis over Korea in 1950?
- Explain what happened in the Korean War, 1950–53.

## CHECK YOURSELF QUESTIONS

**Q1** How did the victory of the Communists in China affect US Cold War policy?

**Q2** Why was it so difficult to oppose Senator McCarthy's charges?

**Q3** What did Truman and MacArthur disagree about?

*Answers are on page 205.*

# REVISION SESSION 5 Containment around the world: the arms race

- From 1952 to 1959, **John Foster Dulles** was US Secretary of State. As soon as he took up his post, he spoke of going beyond containment to 'liberating' countries from Communism. This need not be done by force, but by putting pressure on Communism and by propaganda.

## ALLIANCES

- In 1949, **NATO (North Atlantic Treaty Organisation)** was set up. Its 12 members were Britain, France, Belgium, Holland, Luxembourg, Portugal, Denmark, Ireland, Italy, Norway, Canada, USA. It was a military alliance. The USA provided by far the largest part of its forces.
- The Cold War was clearly now a world war and Dulles built up a system of global alliances.
  - **SEATO** (South-East Asia Treaty Organisation), 1954: Thailand, Philippines, Pakistan and USA.
  - **CENTO** (Central Treaty Organisation), 1955: Turkey, Iran, Iraq, Pakistan and USA.
  - The USA also had alliances with Japan (1951) and Australia and New Zealand.

## INTERPRETATIONS

- These were **defensive** alliances, to contain Communism (see 9.8).
- These were **aggressive** alliances, designed to surround the Communist countries of the world (see 9.9). The USSR was particularly concerned that the alliances allowed the USA to set up air bases in member-countries. US bombers or missiles could therefore be stationed on the borders of the USSR.

**9.8** *US cartoon about the USSR*

**9.9** *Soviet cartoon about the USA, 1952. The main caption reads 'Words and Deeds'. It shows a US general sticking a flag in Greece, on the map. Greece had just joined NATO. The US politician holds an olive branch (symbol of peace) and talks of 'Peace, Defence, Disarmament'.*

## What happened in the arms race?

- The **atom bomb** dropped on Hiroshima, on 6 August 1945, killed 45,000 people instantly and reduced the city to rubble.
- The results of dropping the bomb on Hiroshima, and the second one on Nagasaki, were:

  1 Massive death and destruction was now possible. The awesome power of the atomic bomb totally changed the idea of war and made international relations more serious.

  2 The USA had a monopoly of nuclear weapons for the time being. This gave it superiority, but produced great fear in the USSR.

  3 The imbalance was so serious that an **arms race** began between the superpowers. At first, the USSR was racing to develop its own bomb. The arms race continued as each side strove for superiority. By 1987, there were enough nuclear weapons in the world to kill the entire human race several times over.

- Key features of the arms race were:

  1 Each side tried to get ahead of the other – to produce more bombs or better technology. Neither side dared to fall behind or else the other might think it was so far ahead that an attack was worth launching. In fact, the USA was almost always ahead in the race, but they were afraid to think so, and the race continued.

  2 There were several turning-points, where the race changed because of new technology (see below).

  3 It was massively expensive. Even the USA, the richest country in the world, had to divert money from more worthwhile programmes in order to pay for the arms race. For the USSR, not nearly so rich, the expense was crippling. It helped to lead to the collapse of Communism in the 1990s.

### Turning-point 1: USSR explode own atom-bomb, 1949

- The USA began to develop a much more powerful bomb, the **hydrogen bomb**. Their first H-bomb test was in 1952. H-bombs were hundreds of times more powerful than the Hiroshima bomb.

### Turning-point 2: USSR explode own H-bomb, 1953

- US President Eisenhower realised that it was cheaper to build up nuclear weapons than ordinary explosive bombs. He therefore decided to put the USA so far ahead in numbers of bombs that the USSR would not dare attack for fear of **massive retaliation** (i.e. the US counter-attack would be so huge that the USSR dare not act first).
- Eisenhower also thought the USSR had far more bomber aeroplanes than it actually had. He ordered lots of big bombers to deliver US H-bombs.

### Turning-point 3: USSR launch a satellite into space, 1957

- If they could launch a satellite, they could launch a missile carrying a nuclear bomb. At once **ICBMs** (Inter-Continental Ballistic Missiles) made bomber aeroplanes out of date. A new arms race began, to build missiles. In the 1960 presidential election campaign, Kennedy claimed that there was a 'missile gap' – that the USSR had more missiles than the USA. This was not true, but it helped him win the election. When he was in power Kennedy ordered more missiles to be built and, by 1963, the USA had 550 ICBMs to the USSR's 100.

### Turning-point 4: USA launches missile from submarine, 1960

- Submarines could go anywhere, almost undetected, and so be able to launch missiles at any city or military site in the USSR. The race continued and soon the USSR had submarine-launched missiles.

#### PROTEST

- Public opposition to the nuclear arms race began to grow in the 1950s:
  - Information about **Hiroshima** told of the horrible deaths of those who died at once, and the lingering deaths of those who died afterwards. Hiroshima victims were still dying of radiation sickness many years later. Many people did not want their government to possess such immoral weapons.
  - Testing the bombs caused loss of life. We now know that some servicemen were deliberately exposed to radiation. So were some islanders in the Pacific where bombs were tested.
  - Some objected to the enormous cost of this military expense at a time when their countries were not at war.
  - Many felt that possessing nuclear weapons made war more likely, not less. Civilians knew they stood little chance of surviving a nuclear attack.
  - In Britain, the **Campaign for Nuclear Disarmament (CND)** was formed in 1957. By the early 1960s, many thousands joined its Easter marches to the government's Atomic Weapons Research Establishment at Aldermaston.

#### A* EXTRA

The arms race continued as new inventions brought about more changes: anti-ballistic missiles, which could knock out incoming enemy missiles, were developed. For a while they gave one side an advantage, until MIRVs (Multiple Independent-Targeted Re-entry Vehicles) were developed in the 1970s. These were missiles that carried lots of warheads (bombs). Each was separately targeted, so if just one missile got through, lots of places would be destroyed. And so the race went on.

#### QUESTION SPOTTER

Typical exam questions on this topic:

- Describe what the nuclear arms race was.
- Why was there a nuclear arms race?
- Did the nuclear arms race make war more, or less, likely?

## CHECK YOURSELF QUESTIONS

**Q1** Look again at the 2 cartoons (9.8 and 9.9).

**a** What does cartoon 9.8 tell you about the US views of the USSR?

**b** What does cartoon 9.9 tell you about Soviet views of: US military power? Air bases? Marshall Aid? US politicians?

**c** Use these 2 cartoons and your own knowledge to explain why the Cold War went on so long.

**Q2** Use the account of the arms race to give examples of policy being motivated by: money; US politics; mistakes; military issues.

*Answers are on page 206.*

REVISION SESSION 6

# Khrushchev, Kennedy and Cuba

> **A* EXTRA**
>
> Khrushchev was sincere about trying to develop better relations with the West, particularly when he first came to power. Soviet forces withdrew from Austria. Khrushchev travelled to Western countries and met their leaders.

Stalin died in 1953. There was a power struggle at the top but, in 1955, **Nikita Khrushchev** emerged as leader. He was the son of a miner who had worked under Stalin. Khrushchev was premier of the USSR, 1955–64.

## PEACEFUL CO-EXISTENCE

- Khrushchev wanted to improve the **standard of living** of the ordinary Russian people. He could see that the Cold War was enormously expensive and proposed a policy of 'peaceful co-existence' with the West: rivalry in trade and industry, not weapons.

In fact, this did not happen and the arms race continued.

## DE-STALINISATION

- Khrushchev tried to make Soviet society freer than it had been under Stalin. In a speech to the 20th Communist Party Congress in 1956, he denounced Stalin for his intolerance, brutality and abuse of power in killing and imprisoning millions of Soviet citizens (see unit 6).

## THE EASTERN BLOCK

- In 1955, Khrushchev formed the **Warsaw Pact**, a defensive alliance of the USSR and all Eastern block countries (a NATO of the east). In spite of peaceful co-existence and de-Stalinisation, he was not prepared to let Eastern block countries cut their links with the USSR: he sent tanks to crush the rising in Hungary in 1956 (see p155).

## U2 SPY-PLANES, 1960

- The USA used special U2 spy-planes to fly at high altitude over the USSR taking photographs. In 1960, one was shot down. Khrushchev claimed it proved that the USA was not sincere in talking about peaceful co-existence. A proposed peace conference in Paris broke up and Cold War hostilities continued.

## BERLIN WALL, 1961

- By this time the contrast between West and East Berlin was enormous.
  - The West's shops were full of goods as part of the economic recovery West Germany was having.
  - East Berlin was still poor and dowdy.
- 15,000–20,000 people left East Germany for the West through Berlin every year, draining the country of its best workers.
- Most Russians of Khrushchev's generation still hated Germany because of the war and resented West Germany's prosperity. In 1961, a wall was built around West Berlin. No one was allowed to cross it and anyone who tried to escape was shot.
- Many people expected US President Kennedy to react, as Truman had done in 1948 over the Berlin airlift, but Kennedy did nothing. Khrushchev took this as a sign of Kennedy's weakness.

## Why did Cuba become a flashpoint?

- The island of Cuba is only 150 km from the US coast. For many years the USA had supported the corrupt and brutal dictatorship of Batista. US companies owned much of Cuban business and most of Cuba's main export, sugar, was sold to the USA.
- In 1959, Batista was overthrown during a rising led by **Fidel Castro**. Castro said he wanted to run Cuba independently and meant no harm to the USA. However, he took over US businesses on Cuba. When the USA refused to buy the sugar crop, Castro sold it to the USSR.
- In 1961, the USA backed an attempt to overthrow Castro. The force landed at the Bay of Pigs and was defeated by Castro's men. From then on, relations grew steadily worse between Castro and the USA. The Cuban army received large amounts of weapons from the USSR.

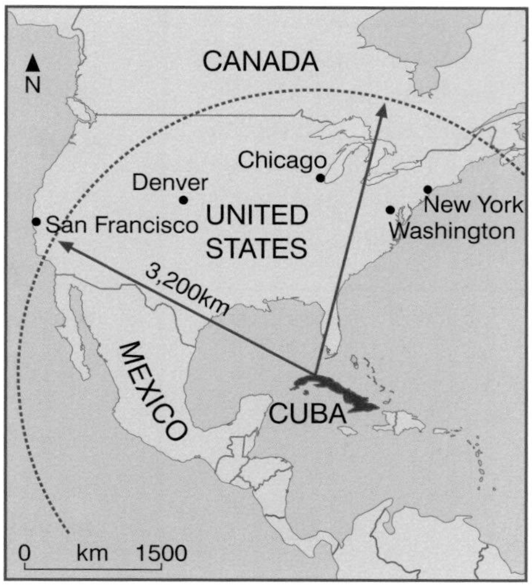


**9.10** *The Cuban missile crisis*

- On 16 October 1962, a US spy-plane came back from flying over Cuba with photographs showing that Soviet missile bases were being built there (see 9.11). As map 9.10 shows, Soviet bases on Cuba would put nearly all of the USA within reach of their missiles. US spy-planes also reported that the missiles were not yet installed but were on Soviet ships on their way to Cuba.

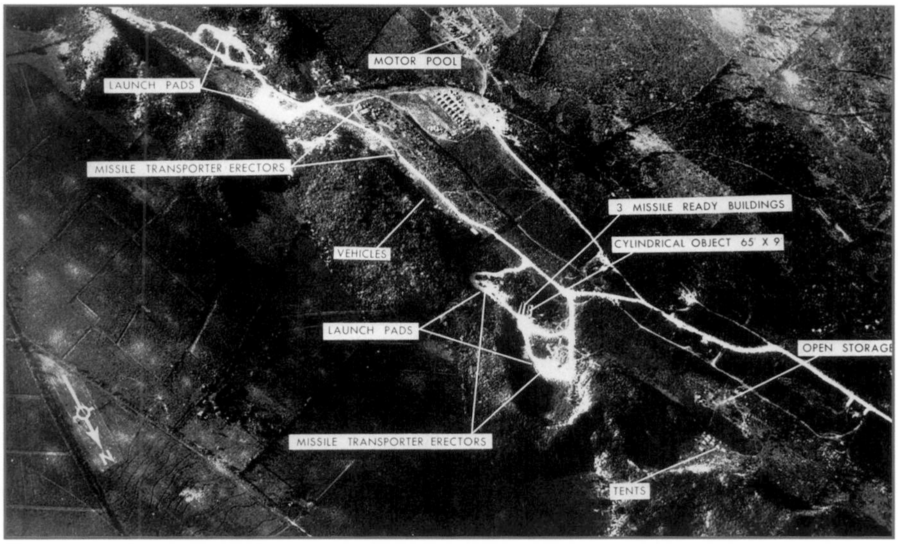


**9.11** *Spy-plane photographs of Soviet missile bases on Cuba*

## Why did Khrushchev put missile bases on Cuba?

This was very provocative. Why did Khrushchev do it?

- The USA was far ahead of the USSR in long-range missiles. Short-range Soviet missiles on Cuba would make up for this.
- Perhaps Khrushchev thought he could get away with it. Kennedy had done nothing about the Berlin Wall and had failed over the Bay of Pigs: Khrushchev had a low opinion of Kennedy.
- Perhaps Khrushchev intended them as a bargaining point: he would remove them in return for some concession by the USA. For example, there were US missiles in Turkey that could hit any city in western USSR in 6 minutes.

**A* EXTRA**

The Soviet presence on Cuba was large: there were 9 missile sites, with capacity for 64 missiles. There were also 43,000 Soviet soldiers on the island.

## What should Kennedy do?

1 He could do nothing. US cities were already within reach of Soviet long-range missiles so nothing much had changed. However, this would look weak. Kennedy had already been criticised over his reaction to the Berlin Wall and did not want to lose the support of the US public.

2 He could invade Cuba, or bomb the bases, or send troops into Berlin. This was risky. Soviet soldiers would almost certainly be killed, the USSR could retaliate and nuclear war could break out.

3 He could find a strong but non-violent response. This is what he did:

- On 20 October, Kennedy ordered US warships to intercept the Soviet ships carrying the missiles reaching Cuba. At the same time, he ordered his forces to be ready for nuclear war. The world waited anxiously: it was the closest to nuclear war – and perhaps total annihilation – that the world had come.

WHAT HAPPENED?

| | |
|---|---|
| *24 October* | *Soviet ships stopped* |
| *26 October* | *Letter from Khrushchev to Kennedy offering to think about withdrawing the missiles if Kennedy promised not to attack Cuba.* |
| *27 October* | *Second letter from Khrushchev, under pressure from his military advisers, saying he would only withdraw his missiles if US missiles were withdrawn from Turkey.* |
| *28 October* | *Kennedy ignores second letter; agrees to first. Khrushchev orders missile sites to be dismantled and missiles to be sent back to USSR.* |

**A* EXTRA**

President Kennedy's brother Robert played a big part in the crisis. It was he who suggested answering Khrushchev's first letter. He also secretly told the USSR that the USA would withdraw their missiles from Turkey.

### RESULTS OF CUBAN MISSILE CRISIS

- Both leaders felt they had taken their countries and the world too close to nuclear war. They made efforts to improve relations:

  1 A telephone **hotline** link between the White House and the Kremlin, 1963.

  2 **Test Ban Treaty, 1963**: a ban on testing nuclear weapons. This was one of the things the anti-nuclear protestors wanted.

- Kennedy came out of it well. US public opinion felt he had stood up to Khrushchev, but also avoided war.
- Khrushchev did not come out so well. Opinion in the USSR condemned him for putting the missiles there in the first place, and then for giving way. The Cuban crisis was a factor in his fall from power in 1964. Later historians are puzzled by his initial decision to place the missiles in Cuba but feel he acted bravely in agreeing to withdraw them rather than push Kennedy any further.

**QUESTION SPOTTER**

Typical exam questions on this topic:

- Why did US President Kennedy decide to take action over Cuba in 1962?
- Why did Khrushchev set up missile bases on Cuba?
- Who was the winner of the Cuban missile crisis of 1962?

## CHECK YOURSELF QUESTIONS

**Q1** Look at 9.11 again.

**a** How was this picture obtained?

**b** Why did the picture alarm President Kennedy and the US government?

**Q2** Who won the Cuban missile crisis?

Start your answer to this question by writing a sentence each about Kennedy and Khrushchev. Then decide what factual information you are going to use to support your opinion.

Then write an answer, beginning each paragraph as follows:

'Kennedy could claim that he won because ...'

'However, he had not succeeded in ...'

'Khrushchev could claim that he won because ...'

'However, he had not succeeded in ...'

'My conclusion is ...'

*Answers are on page 207.*

REVISION SESSION 7

# Vietnam and the end of containment

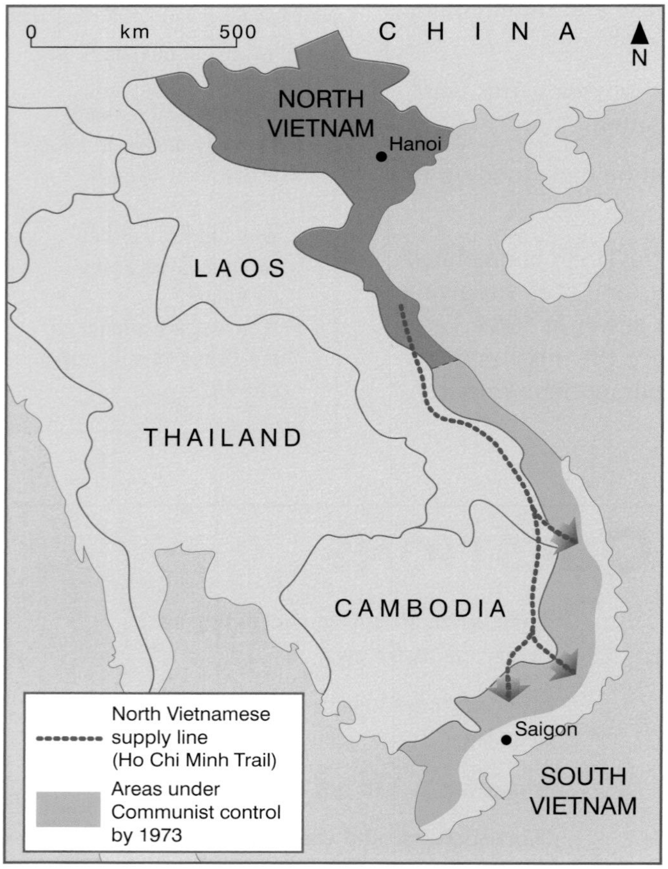


**9.12** *Vietnam after 1954*

## Why did Vietnam become a flashpoint in the Cold War?

- Vietnam, in South-East Asia, was part of the old French colony called Indo-China. When the Japanese captured it from the French in the Second World War, a Vietnamese resistance organisation, the **Vietminh**, was formed. Its leader was **Ho Chi Minh**, a Communist, but the Vietminh was supported by most Vietnamese.
- The Vietminh fought a successful **guerrilla** war against the Japanese. When the Japanese surrendered in 1945, the Vietminh were ready to take power. The French, however, wanted their colony back. The Vietminh then began a new guerrilla war against the French.

## How did the USA get involved?

- At first the USA disapproved of the French, but from 1949 Communist China began to support the Vietminh. The USA – by now deep into their Cold War fear of Communism – began to help the French. Soon they were bearing a third of the cost of the war.
- Despite US support, the French were heavily defeated in 1954 at **Dien Bien Phu** by the Vietnamese General Giap. At the Treaty of Geneva, 1954:
  - Indo-China was divided into 4 countries: Laos, Cambodia, North Vietnam and South Vietnam (see 9.12).
  - Free elections were to be held in the two Vietnams as soon as possible in order to reunite the country.
  - No foreign power was to intervene in their affairs.
- A Vietminh Communist government took over North Vietnam under Ho Chi Minh. The rulers of South Vietnam were from the 'landlord class' – rich, Christian (while most of the population was Buddhist), undemocratic and often corrupt. Soon war started again.
- A resistance movement, called the **'Vietcong'**, began to attack the South Vietnamese government. It consisted of South Vietnamese Communists, supplied by North Vietnam down the Ho Chi Minh trail. The USSR began to send weapons to North Vietnam.

- The USA sent CIA 'advisers' and weapons to South Vietnam. They opposed holding elections there because they feared that the Vietcong would win.
- By 1962, President Kennedy had increased the number of US advisers to 16,500 and spent $3 billion. In spite of this, more than half South Vietnam was in Vietcong hands and the unpopular South Vietnamese government was collapsing.

## How did the USA join in the war?

- **President Johnson** committed the USA to the Vietnam war. On his election in 1964 he declared: 'I am not going to be the President who saw South-East Asia go the way China went.' US policy was still based on:

  1 'containment'

  2 the 'Domino Theory' (see 9.13), that Communism was taking over the world country by country, like a line of dominoes falling.

  - Congress passed the **Tonkin Resolution** in 1964, allowing Johnson to take what military action he thought necessary.
  - In 1965, he began **Operation Rolling Thunder**, a massive bombing campaign against North Vietnam.
  - He sent in US forces. By 1969, there were half a million US soldiers in Vietnam.
- Yet the USA could not win the war.

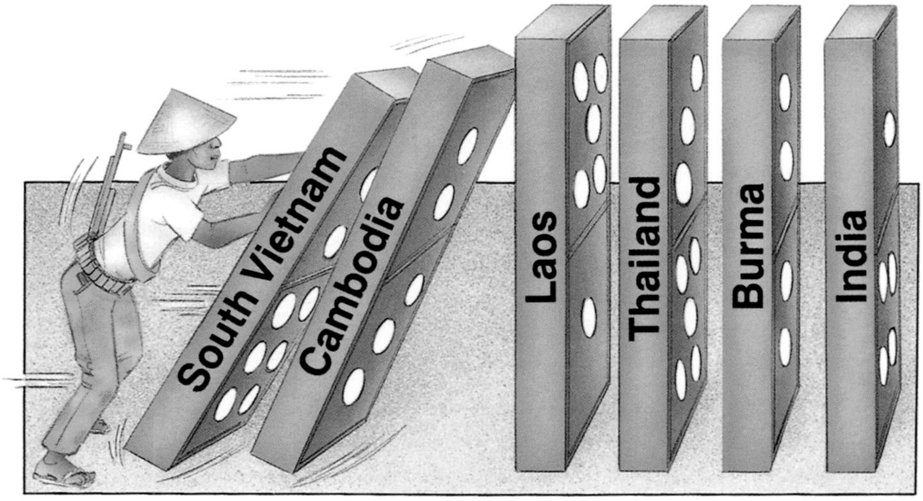


**9.13** *The Domino Theory*

## Why did the USA lose the Vietnam war?

### GUERRILLA WAR

- After over 20 years of fighting against the Japanese, the French, the South Vietnamese and now the Americans, the North Vietnamese were experts in **guerrilla warfare**. They also learned from the successful guerrilla war waged by **Mao Zedong** in China.
- They used their knowledge of the land, its jungles, mountains and paddy fields. They would stay hidden by day, and move about the jungle trails by night. Supplies were carried on bicycles. Guerrilla soldiers lived rough, sometimes underground.
- They had the support of Vietnamese peasants – or, in some cases, forced them to give support. Wearing ordinary clothes, the soldiers could mingle with the villagers. Mao Zedong had described the same tactics in China: 'The people are the water and we are the fish.'
- They specialised in **ambushes** – surprise attacks on isolated groups of US soldiers. Occasionally they massed their soldiers for a big attack, but only if they were sure of winning.

### US MORALE

- It was very difficult to counter this kind of guerrilla warfare. US troops did not know the landscape. Unlike the Vietcong soldiers, most of them were inexperienced recruits. While US soldiers were highly visible among the Vietnamese people, they never knew who was an innocent peasant going about his/her daily life and who was a Vietcong guerrilla about to lob a grenade at them. The Vietcong had no fixed positions to be captured. The danger of ambush was wearing on the morale of US troops.

### US TACTICS

- One thing the USA did possess was technological superiority. They used it to launch massive **bombing** raids on North Vietnam and Vietcong-held areas of South Vietnam. More bombs were dropped on North Vietnam in 3 years than were used by all sides in the Second World War. Inevitably, South Vietnamese civilians were killed too, and their villages destroyed.
- The bombing was extended into Cambodia and Laos, as the Vietcong were using them as bases. The effect was to stir up opposition to the USA in those countries. The people there turned their support to the Communists.
- The USA developed chemical **defoliant sprays**, like Agent Orange, to remove the leaves from jungle trees. This was to deprive the Vietcong of cover, but defoliants also affected the peasants' crops.
- **Napalm bombs** were used. These were inflammable jelly which sticks to human beings. Inevitably, civilians were sometimes horribly burnt and killed.

- The hardest thing for US troops to deal with was identifying the enemy. In '**search and destroy**' tactics, soldiers were sent into areas where all the villagers had been ordered to leave. They were told that anyone left there must be a Vietcong. However, mistakes were made and innocent villagers were also killed.
- This was supposed to be a war of ideals, of **freedom versus Communism**. Each side was trying to win the 'hearts and minds' of the South Vietnamese people. Clearly, US tactics prevented them from winning the battle for 'hearts and minds' any more than the military conflict.

### PUBLIC OPINION IN THE USA

- By 1969, the war was costing $30 billion a year. It was also costing 300 US lives a week. Yet the USA was not winning.
- The war was covered by television so that war pictures were seen in homes every night. People saw:

  1 villagers' huts being burnt

  2 Vietcong suspects being tortured

  3 US soldiers dying.

- Reporters revealed even more shaming deeds, such as events at **My Lai**:

  1 In 1968 a company of soldiers was sent on a 'search and destroy' mission into the village of My Lai in South Vietnam. They had been told that all the villagers would be at market and that it was a Vietcong headquarters. They killed 300–400 villagers, including women, children and old men, and burnt their houses.

  2 A year later a soldier told the press what had happened. Reporters followed it up and one of the officers, **William Calley**, was put on trial for murder. He was found guilty and sentenced to 20 years, of which he served only 5. Many people felt he was the scapegoat for what had happened and that such events had often happened in the war.

- A strong **anti-war movement** began, in the USA and across the world, including among US allies in Europe.

**A* EXTRA**

Low morale, and the difficulties of fighting a guerrilla war in unfamiliar territory, among unfamiliar people, produced a sort of racism among many soldiers. They ceased to distinguish between Vietnamese and regarded all of them as potential enemies. In this situation, ordinary Americans could carry out massacres like My Lai and the battle to win 'hearts and minds' could never be won.

## When did the USA pull out of Vietnam?

- In 1968, in spite of US presence in Vietnam, the Vietcong launched the **Tet Offensive**, capturing many towns in South Vietnam. Clearly, the USA could not win this war.
- In the same year, Johnson announced he would not be standing for President again and called a halt to the bombing.

## A* EXTRA

The chief negotiators at the Paris peace talks were Henry Kissinger, for the USA, and Le Duc Tho, for North Vietnam. They were awarded the Nobel Peace Prize for their efforts.

## QUESTION SPOTTER

Typical exam questions on this topic:

- Why did the USA decide to get involved in the war in Vietnam?
- Why couldn't the USA win the war in Vietnam?
- How important was US public opinion in ending the war in Vietnam?

- Johnson's successor, President Nixon, tried to find a way of getting out of the war without the USA losing face. He came up with **'Vietnamisation'**: opposition to the Communists would be handed over to the South Vietnam government, helped by US money, but 'the boys would come home'.
- Peace talks with North Vietnam began in Paris and ended in 1973.
- In fact the war continued and Saigon, capital of South Vietnam, fell in 1975. Vietnam was united under Communist government.

### What were the results of the war?

- Containment had failed. A policy devised for Europe in the 1940s was not right for Asia in the 1960s.
- Communism had advanced. This had not happened 'by armed minorities or outside pressure', but by the wish of the people of Vietnam.
- Communism had also made progress in Laos and Cambodia as a direct result of US actions.
- The USA had presented its Cold War strategy as a moral crusade against the evil of Communism. After their actions in Vietnam – atrocities, napalming, chemical warfare, support for an unpopular and undemocratic government – the USA had lost its moral superiority.

## ? CHECK YOURSELF QUESTIONS

**Q1 Source 1**

'For Hanoi (capital of North Vietnam), the immediate aim is the conquest of the south. But for Beijing (capital of China), however, Hanoi's victory would only be the first step towards eventual Chinese rule over the two Vietnams and South-East Asia.'

*Robert MacNamara, US Defence Secretary, 1964*

**a** What does the speaker in Source 1 think is happening in Vietnam?

**b** Use this source and your own knowledge to describe what is meant by the 'Domino Theory'.

**Q2 Source 2**

'In sending US troops to South Vietnam, the US imperialists have met a people's war. The people's war has succeeded in gathering all the people to fight their attackers in all ways and with all kinds of weapons.'

*General Giap, 1967*

**a** Who was General Giap?

**b** Use this source to explain what he means by 'a people's war'.

**Q3** Use both sources and your own knowledge to explain why the USA lost the war for the 'hearts and minds' of the Vietnamese people.

*Answers are on page 208.*

# REVISION SESSION 8 Détente

**Détente** means an easing of tension. What did this mean in the Cold War?

- A halt to the arms race
- Not interfering in each other's affairs
- Meetings of leaders (called 'summit' meetings)
- Contacts between citizens on each side, in sport, the arts, science etc.

## Why did détente happen?

### FOR BOTH SUPERPOWERS

- The arms race was tremendously expensive, and getting more expensive all the time. Both the USA and the USSR could see that there were better things on which they could spend their money.
- The Cuban missile crisis (see p143) had brought the world to the edge of nuclear destruction. It could happen again while relations between the two superpowers were so strained. War could happen by accident: a missile could be launched in error. There was also the danger of other countries acquiring nuclear weapons (apart from USA, USSR, Britain and France). Israel, China, South Africa and India were developing nuclear weapons. The more countries which had them, the more the likelihood of nuclear war.
- There was opposition to nuclear weapons, mainly in the West, but also in the Communist block.

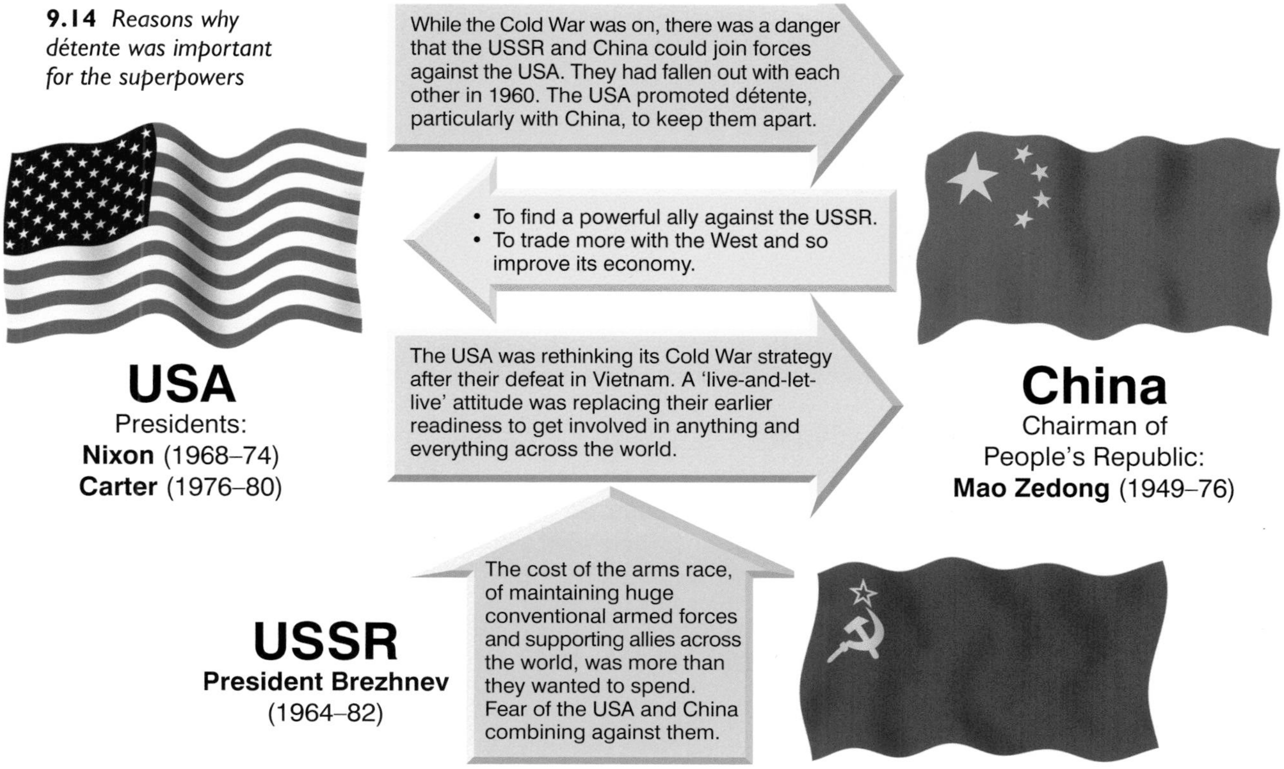
While the Cold War was on, there was a danger that the USSR and China could join forces against the USA. They had fallen out with each other in 1960. The USA promoted détente, particularly with China, to keep them apart.
• To find a powerful ally against the USSR.
• To trade more with the West and so improve its economy.
The USA was rethinking its Cold War strategy after their defeat in Vietnam. A 'live-and-let-live' attitude was replacing their earlier readiness to get involved in anything and everything across the world.
USA
Presidents:
Nixon (1968–74)
Carter (1976–80)
China
Chairman of People's Republic:
Mao Zedong (1949–76)
USSR
President Brezhnev
(1964–82)
The cost of the arms race, of maintaining huge conventional armed forces and supporting allies across the world, was more than they wanted to spend.
Fear of the USA and China combining against them.

**9.14** *Reasons why détente was important for the superpowers*

## When was détente?

- In some ways the first example of détente was the '**hotline**', established in 1963 after the Cuban missile crisis. The main years, though, were from the late 1960s to 1980.

### MAIN EVENTS

**1968** Nuclear Non-Proliferation Treaty: USA, USSR and Britain agreed not to supply any other countries with nuclear technology. Unfortunately, France, China, Israel and South Africa refused to sign the treaty.

**1971** Table-tennis players from the USA went to play in China: first contact of any sort between the 2 countries since Mao and the Communists came to power in 1949. China joined the United Nations later, in 1971.

**1972** US President Nixon visited Mao Zedong in China (see 9.15).
SALT (Strategic Arms Limitation Talks) between USA and USSR ended in a treaty to limit the numbers of long-range missiles each side had.

**1975** Helsinki agreement between the USA, USSR and 35 other countries. Each side recognised the boundaries of countries in Europe reached in 1945. At US President Carter's insistence, each side agreed to observe human rights. US and Soviet astronauts met up in space.

**1979** SALT 2, covering other sorts of nuclear weapons as well as long-range missiles, was prepared after long and difficult negotiation. Then the USSR invaded Afghanistan and the USA refused to sign the Treaty.

**9.15** *Nixon and Mao Zedong in China, 1972*

### QUESTION SPOTTER

Typical exam questions on this topic:

- Give examples to explain what is meant by détente.
- How successful was détente in lowering tension in the Cold War?

### WHAT WERE THE LIMITS OF DÉTENTE?

- The arms race went on. Despite the SALT treaty, both sides had large stockpiles of weapons. They put a lot of effort into getting round the SALT restrictions. There was also the problem of verification: how did you tell what weapons the other side actually had?
- Wars still happened (e.g. the 1973 war in the Middle East, with the USA supplying Israel and the USSR supplying Egypt and Syria).

- Human rights violations continued. The USSR made little effort to observe the terms of the Helsinki Agreement.
- In 1980, this period of détente came to an end as Ronald Reagan became President of the USA and returned to Cold War attitudes and policies.

## CHECK YOURSELF QUESTIONS

**Q1** **Source 1**

'We shall pay any price, bear any burden, meet any hardship, support any friend, oppose any foe, to ensure the survival and success of liberty.'

*President Kennedy, speaking in 1961*

**Source 2**

'America cannot, and will not, conceive all the plans, design all the programmes, execute all the decisions and undertake all the defence of free nations around the world.'

*President Nixon, speaking in 1972*

**a** What are the differences between the policies in these two speeches?

**b** Why had US policy changed in the 11 years between these two speeches?

**Q2** Why did the USA make such an effort to improve relations with China in the 1970s?

**Q3** What did détente achieve?

*Answers are on page 209.*

# The USSR in Eastern Europe

- In 1945, the **Red Army** occupied much of Eastern Europe as it pursued the retreating Nazis into Germany. For the next 44 years, these countries were totally controlled by the USSR. Several attempts were made to break free, but they were all crushed.
- As Europe began to recover after the war, the people of Eastern Europe compared themselves with the people of Western Europe. They saw that people in Western Europe had:
  - more freedom – e.g. more than one party to vote for, a free press which could criticise the government, no secret police, freedom to travel where you wanted, relaxed censorship in the arts and media
  - a higher standard of living.

**A* EXTRA**

Nagy, the Communist who took over Hungary in the 1956 revolt, had been Minister of Agriculture after the war. He had ordered the sharing out of land among Hungary's 640,000 peasants. This had made him very popular, but there was no place for him under Rakosi.

## What did the people of Hungary want in 1956?

- Hungary had been hostile to the USSR before the war. The Communist Party had never been popular and in the first elections after the war it only gained 17% of the vote. Nevertheless, **Stalin** insisted on it taking part in government and then the other parties were eased out. By 1948, Hungary was ruled by a Communist dictator, **Rakosi**. He was hated for the following reasons:
  - He was pro-Soviet: he did exactly what Stalin told him. The Red Army continued to occupy Hungary.
  - Hungary is a prosperous agricultural country but under **COMECON** (Stalin's system of uniting all the economies of Eastern Europe together) it had to develop industry, mainly to serve the needs of the USSR. The Stalinist system of Five-Year Plans was introduced. Workers' hours were long and pay low.
  - Collective farms – also on the Soviet model – were forced on the Hungarian peasants. They did not cooperate and there were food shortages.
  - The standard of living actually fell by 5%, 1949–55.
  - There were 100,000 in the secret police (**AVOs**). 200,000 Hungarians were in prison and torture was common.
- Khrushchev's speech to the 20th Communist Party Congress in 1956, denouncing Stalin, brought a ray of hope in Eastern Europe. There were anti-Soviet demonstrations in Germany and Poland. Soviet troops were sent in to crush them. Many people were killed.

- In Hungary, Rakosi was forced to resign following massive demonstrations. He was replaced by **Nagy**, a more popular Communist. However, Nagy was no longer in control of events. On the streets of Budapest, people attacked and killed AVOs. They demanded:
  - free elections, with other parties apart from the Communists allowed to take part
  - the Red Army should leave
  - Hungary should leave the Warsaw Pact (see p142), and become part of the group of neutral nations.
- Some Hungarians took US anti-Communist propaganda at face value, and expected the USA to support them.
- Khrushchev decided that he could not have Hungary pulling out of the Soviet block. He sent in a thousand tanks to crush the revolt (see 9.16). There was bitter fighting in the streets and 30,000 Hungarians were killed. 180,000 fled the country. Another Communist, **Kadar**, took over the country. Many Hungarians felt betrayed by the West.

### A* EXTRA

The man who put forward the ideas for economic reform in Czechoslovakia in 1967 was called Otto Sik. He proposed that factories and businesses should run their own affairs, instead of being controlled by the state planning office. They should each have boards of management, with elected worker representatives.

Sik realised that economic freedom and political freedom were linked: people will not have enterprising attitudes and ideas to make businesses prosper unless they have freedom to think for themselves. It was these ideas which led to the 'Prague Spring' of 1968. 20 years later they appealed to Mikhail Gorbachev when he was trying to convert the USSR to 'Communism with a human face'.

**9.16** *Soviet tank commander advances angrily on Western cameraman, Budapest, 1956*

## What did the people of Czechoslovakia want in 1968?

- Before the war Czechoslovakia had a more developed democracy and manufacturing economy than Hungary. However, the situation 20 years after the war was much the same as in Hungary in 1956 (and indeed throughout Eastern Europe):
  - Stalinist rule under **Novotny**
  - Soviet control of the economy
  - strict censorship
  - stagnant economy and a low standard of living.

### QUESTION SPOTTER

Typical exam questions on this topic:
- Compare the motives of the rising in Hungary in 1956 with the protest in Czechoslovakia in 1968.
- Why did the USSR crush the protests of 1956 in Hungary and that of 1968 in Czechoslovakia?

### SOCIALISM WITH A HUMAN FACE

- In 1968, a different group of Communists led by **Alexander Dubcek** removed Novotny and took over the government. They put forward alternative plans. In order to achieve more growth and competitiveness in the economy, there should be more freedom. More economic freedom needed more political freedom. They called it '**Socialism with a human face**'.
  - They reduced censorship.
  - Allowed more free discussion on television and in the newspapers.
  - Weakened the powers of the secret police.
- Writers and artists supported them. This exciting time in Czechoslovakia was called the 'Prague Spring'.
- The authorities were careful to stress that they:
  - were Communists
  - did not intend allowing other parties to take part in politics
  - had no intention of leaving the Warsaw Pact or **COMECON**.
- Soviet leader **Leonid Brezhnev** did not like it, but did not act at once. He threatened Dubcek and Czechoslovakia. Eventually, the other Communist leaders of Eastern Europe feared for their own positions if 'Socialism with a human face' spread, and tanks were sent in to crush the Prague Spring. The Czech people reacted with **passive resistance**, but Dubcek was removed and gradually the old system was restored.
- Again the West did nothing. Western leaders were trying to get détente going and did not want direct confrontation with the USSR.
- Brezhnev announced that:
  - no member of the Soviet block was allowed to leave the Warsaw Pact
  - no multi-party systems would be tolerated.
- These two principles became known as the **Brezhnev Doctrine**.

## What did the people of Poland want in 1980?

- Protest in Poland had always been purely economic: demanding higher wages, or lower prices, or the right to 'free' trade unions. (There were official trade unions but the government and the Communist Party controlled these. Strikes were forbidden by law.)
- The government had usually met their demands. Polish workers did quite well in the 1970s, but by 1980 depression had set in.
- In July 1980, **Lech Walesa**, an electrician in the Gdansk shipyards, led a strike for higher wages. He set up a free trade union, called **Solidarity**. By January 1981, Solidarity had 9.4 million members – 60% of all non-agricultural workers in Poland. It was recognised by the government and campaigned for all kinds of workers' rights, including the right to join the free unions and to strike.

## WHY DIDN'T THE GOVERNMENT CRUSH SOLIDARITY?

1 It had massive support, including many Communists.

2 It had lots of members in vital Polish industries.

3 Walesa was careful not to criticise the Communist Party or make any proposals for political change.

4 Walesa and Solidarity had close links with the powerful and popular Roman Catholic Church.

5 Half of all journalists, writers and film-makers had joined it.

6 Walesa was well known in the West – appearing on Western television and in the media.

- The Solidarity protest lasted longer than the revolts in Hungary and Czechoslovakia. However, it was too much of a threat to the government to be allowed to continue. Poland was in chaos, with massive inflation and unofficial strikes. Walesa could not hold Solidarity together. Splits occurred and some members called for changes which were against the Brezhnev Doctrine.
- Early in 1981, **General Jaruzelski**, head of the Army, became Prime Minister of Poland. In December 1981, he arrested Walesa and 10,000 Solidarity members. Solidarity was suspended. 150,000 members were hauled in by the police for 'cautionary talks'.
- Poland remained in a state of unrest for the next few years. By 1986, Solidarity was reviving and Walesa was again a leading figure. But by then events all over Eastern Europe were changing fast (see p160).

### QUESTION SPOTTER

**Typical exam question on this topic:**

- **How did Solidarity protests in Poland differ from the revolts in Hungary in 1956 and Czechoslovakia in 1968?**

## CHECK YOURSELF QUESTIONS

**Q1** At the beginning of this revision section you read that people in Eastern Europe felt that they had less freedom and a worse standard of living than people in Western Europe. Which of these two motives was uppermost in the three protests described here?

**Q2** Did the Czech protesters break the Brezhnev Doctrine?

**Q3** In what ways did each revolt try to learn from the one before?

*Answers are on page 209.*

# The end of the Cold War

## Why did Reagan start a new arms race?

- The Cold War was over by the end of the 1980s, yet the decade began with a new arms race. This was almost entirely due to **Ronald Reagan** (President of the USA, 1980–88). Reagan was a determined anti-Communist. He criticised his predecessors for their détente policies, which had allowed the USA to fall behind in the arms race. He was encouraged in his new arms race by **Mrs Thatcher** (Prime Minister of Britain, 1979–90).
- Reagan dropped the détente language of friendship with the USSR. Instead, he returned to the 1950s language of a moral crusade against Communism, calling it the 'evil empire'.
- He increased US arms spending from $178 billion in 1981 to $367 billion in 1986.
- He developed lots of new weapons:
  1. the neutron bomb, which killed people by radiation but left buildings intact
  2. the MX bomb
  3. Cruise missiles
  4. the 'Star Wars' defence system, in which laser satellites in space would destroy all incoming missiles from the USSR.
- The USSR responded to this arms race with new weapons of its own, like the SS-20 missile. New weapons and a new arms race seemed to make nuclear war more likely.
- The deployment of Cruise missiles at US bases in Europe led to a revival of **anti-nuclear protest**. CND membership increased. Women protesters set up peace camps (e.g. at the US base at Greenham Common, Berkshire).
- START (Strategic Arms Reduction Talks) between USA and USSR in 1985 failed.
- The USA boycotted the Moscow Olympics in 1980 and the USSR boycotted the Los Angeles Olympics in 1984.

> **A* EXTRA**
>
> Andropov, ruler of the USSR briefly (1982–83), was a reformer but did not have time to put his reforms into practice. Gorbachev was his deputy.

## What was happening in the USSR at this time?

- In 1985 the USSR had a new leader, **Mikhail Gorbachev**. He was only 54 in 1985 (Reagan was 74). Gorbachev was charming, intelligent, with an equally charming and intelligent wife, Raisa. He was a lifelong Communist, but was determined to bring about radical reforms in the USSR.

### STANDARD OF LIVING

- The people of the USSR continued to have a low standard of living. Although the USSR is rich in raw materials and with fertile agriculture, they could not seem to make household goods that worked, or to supply the shops with food.

### THE BREZHNEV YEARS

- **Brezhnev** had ruled the USSR from 1964–82. He was followed by two more old men – **Andropov** (1982–83) and **Chernenko** (1983–85). Little had changed in the USSR since Stalin's days. But people did not work hard, as they had under Stalin, because there was no point.
- Alcoholism and corruption were rife. Party members had too many privileges, including their own shops, where food and imported luxuries were on sale, and dachas (country cottages where they retired to at weekends and holidays).

### COST OF WAR AND WEAPONS

- The USSR was locked into:
  - the arms race, which probably took 25% of its spending, compared with 7% of that of the USA
  - a war in Afghanistan, which began in 1979 but which the USSR could not win.

### LACK OF FREEDOM

- As there was no freedom of speech, discussion of the problems of the USSR could not take place.
- Intellectuals sent round **samizdat** (self-published, or duplicated newssheets or other writing), but this was illegal.
- Government secrecy was a habit (e.g. parents had difficulty finding out what had happened to their sons who were killed fighting in Afghanistan).
- So strict and secretive was government control of censorship that when the **Chernobyl** nuclear accident took place in 1986, no news was released until Western observers noticed it. The result was greatly increased loss of life in the USSR.
- Managers of factories, farms and other economic enterprises had no freedom to take their own decisions. Everything was decided in Moscow. This was the main reason for the lack of economic success.

### THE ENVIRONMENT

- Lack of a free press to criticise the government, and lack of government self-control resulted in some of the worst pollution and environmental disasters in the world:
  - Chernobyl (see above)
  - the Aral Sea disappeared because of river diversions
  - Lake Baikal and many of Russia's great rivers were terribly polluted.

#### A* EXTRA

A sign of how the Cold War distorted the Soviet economy was pointed out by Gorbachev: their scientists could launch a rocket to put a cosmonaut (Russian term for astronaut) into space with pinpoint accuracy, but the USSR did not seem to be able to make good, cheap fridges. Although Communism was supposed to provide for the needs of working people, the Soviet state had become better at weapons technology.

## What could Gorbachev do?

- Gorbachev could see that all these problems were linked. If he was going to improve people's standard of living he had to change the way the economy worked. This meant:
  - getting out of expensive and unnecessary military expenditure
  - more freedom to create a more enterprising economy
  - more freedom of the press and debate to make industry more responsible.
- He had to tackle the Cold War, Eastern Europe, and all aspects of life inside the USSR. He was trying to change 40 years of Cold War and 70 years of Communism. It was a huge gamble.

**9.17** *Soviet missiles being dismantled*

**May, 1989** Free elections in Poland lead to victory for Solidarity. Lech Walesa becomes Prime Minister.
**June, 1989** Hungarian border guards dismantle the 'Iron Curtain' border with Austria, allowing free movement. Thousands of Eastern Europeans, especially East Germans, cross to the West.
**October, 1989** Huge demonstrations in East Germany.
**November, 1989** Demonstrators march to the Berlin Wall. Guards throw down their weapons. Berlin Wall demolished. Czechoslovakia sets up multi-party state.
**December, 1989** Anti-Communist demonstrations in Hungary, Bulgaria and Romania. Ceaucescu, Communist dictator of Romania, executed.
**March, 1990** Germany reunited.

### THE COLD WAR

- Gorbachev met Reagan at Reykjavik in 1986 and in Washington a year later. They declared their friendship and Gorbachev offered to make such concessions in the arms race that Reagan could only agree.

1. **INF (Intermediate Nuclear Force) Treaty, 1987**: both sides agreed to remove all medium-range missiles from Europe within 3 years.
2. **START (Strategic Arms Reduction Treaty), 1991**: this promised further reductions in long-range nuclear missiles at once and more over the next 12 years (see 9.17).
3. Soviet forces left Afghanistan, removing a major cause of US–Soviet tension and an unpopular and expensive war.

### EASTERN EUROPE

- Gorbachev realised that Eastern Europe was not as essential to the security of the USSR as it had seemed to Stalin in 1945. Besides, by the 1980s missiles could attack the USSR from any direction, without the 'buffer' of Eastern Europe.
- He also wanted the changes he was bringing to the USSR to benefit the peoples of Eastern Europe too. The old Stalinist rulers of the Eastern European countries were horrified when Gorbachev told them that he would no longer send Soviet troops to support them. The Soviet empire in Eastern Europe rapidly collapsed.

THE USSR

- All these events made Gorbachev immensely popular in the West and in Eastern Europe, but he was not so popular inside the USSR.
- In most of Eastern Europe, which had been Communist only since the late 1940s, democracy and capitalism were soon restored. It was more difficult in the USSR, which had been Communist since 1917, had little experience of democracy and was a backward economy even then.
- Gorbachev proposed two new policies:

  1 **glasnost** – openness, more democracy, freedom of speech

  2 **perestroika** – restructuring, introducing a free market in which goods were produced that people wanted at prices they were prepared to pay, not produced and priced by a government department.
- In fact, glasnost undermined the success of perestroika: the only people who could make the economy work were removed by the free elections. By 1990, the USSR was suffering from rising prices, falling value of wages, crime and black marketeering.
- Powerful anti-Russian nationalist feelings were released.
  - In 1990, Latvia left the USSR. The other 2 Baltic states – Lithuania and Estonia – soon followed.
  - By 1991, the USSR had collapsed, leaving 15 new independent states. They formed a loose group called the '**Commonwealth of Independent States (CIS)**' but this was not what Gorbachev wanted.
- Russia was by far the most powerful of these new states and its Prime Minister was Gorbachev's enemy, **Boris Yeltsin**. In 1992, the old Communists tried to seize power. They failed, but Gorbachev was forced to resign. Yeltsin declared the Communist Party illegal. He also brought in many other changes, including changing the name of Leningrad back to St Petersburg.
- With the arms race over, independent countries in Eastern Europe and the USSR collapsed, the Cold War was definitely over.

## QUESTION SPOTTER

Typical exam questions on this topic:

- Describe why and how Ronald Reagan changed the Cold War when he became President of the USA in 1980.
- Why did Soviet leader Gorbachev want to end the Cold War?
- Describe how the Cold War ended.

## A* EXTRA

Although the INF Treaty and START reduced the numbers of nuclear weapons, there are still thousands of them. Since the break-up of the USSR, these have become the possession of many of the states that make up the CIS. There are now, therefore, more nuclear states than there were during the Cold War, which some see as a more dangerous situation.

## CHECK YOURSELF QUESTIONS

**Q1** How did Gorbachev and Reagan end the arms race so rapidly?

**Q2** How were glasnost and perestroika designed to solve the problems of the USSR?

**Q3** Why was Gorbachev so popular in the West?

*Answers are on page 210.*

Revision Session 1

# Source-based questions: comprehending sources

**1** Look at this photo and read the caption.

What does this source tell us about the United Nations? (3 marks)

*United Nations (UN) soldiers in the Congo, 1961*

- When you look at the **photograph**, what can you see?

  At a glance you can see that there is a queue of black people on the right and some soldiers on the left.

- Now read the **caption**.

  This information helps in pinning down what we are actually looking at. But this is not a 'spot-the-ball' competition, it is a historical source.

- Historians find out about the past by studying **sources** to obtain evidence. The obvious historical question – What does this source tell us about the United Nations? – is in the simple style that often starts off a source paper in a GCSE History exam.

  Even this simple opening question needs some thought.

- Look closely at the source.

  Take your time. Go beyond first impressions. For example, in this case most of the people queueing are black women or children; they appear to be holding containers – buckets or bowls; the soldiers are armed and there is an armoured car on which some of them are riding. You can just see the olive branch badge of the UN on the front of the armoured car.

  Most of the soldiers appear to be white. It is all happening on a road, with thick trees in the background. Not all this information may be useful, but it goes far beyond that 'first glance' impression.

- Read the caption carefully.

  It gives three essential bits of information, without which the picture is only a guessing game:

  1 the place – the Congo

  2 the time – 1961

  3 confirmation that these are UN soldiers.

  The caption gives no information about the people on the right.

- How does the question focus your answer?

  One thing to remember when tackling exams is **always answer the question**. Here, you are asked to act as a historian finding out about the United Nations. This helps to focus the bits of information you have put together from your close scrutiny of the picture.

- This simple question requires 2 stages of thinking:

  1 What is there **on view** which tells you something about the UN?

  2 What can you **infer** from the picture about the UN?

  (To *inf*er means to work out something that is not actually shown in the picture.)

  Under 1, you could say that it shows that the UN took part in active operations in the Congo in 1961. Soldiers were sent, and some were armed.

  Under 2, you can infer that these people needed food supplies and that the UN is probably arranging the distribution of food aid. You can tell that the UN was prepared to use armed strength, making up an army with soldiers from member-countries.

Putting these two together, a short answer might read:

*This picture tells us that the UN was prepared to use armed force to intervene in crisis areas such as the Congo in 1961. It used soldiers from member-countries, in UN uniform, to keep the peace and look after the basic needs of the people.*

## How do you place sources in context?

- The photo in **1** was looked at in isolation – we only considered what you could see and what the caption told you. Historians hardly ever work like that – in complete ignorance of the **context of a source**. They study sources in the light of what they already know about a topic. GCSE questions are more realistic. They are more like the questions historians ask.

  Look at the words used in this question and compare it with those in the previous section:

**2** Use this source and your own knowledge to explain why the USA became involved in war in Vietnam.

'The threat to the free nations of South-East Asia has long been clear. The North Vietnamese government has constantly sought to take over South Vietnam and Laos ... The USA will continue its basic policy of assisting free nations of the area to defend their freedom.'

From *President Johnson's message to the US Congress, 1964*

- This kind of question is asking for two things: to understand the source in its own right and to use recalled information to explain it further. Because of this double request, it is probably better to tackle the answer in two stages:

  1 **What does the source say?**
  It is telling us what President Johnson put forward in 1964 as his reasons for sending more US forces to Vietnam. He sees it as assistance to free South Vietnam from North Vietnamese invasion. This is an important speech, as the caption tells us: the President speaking to the US Congress.

  2 **How does our knowledge of the history help us understand this extract better?**

  There are lots of bits of information we could use:

  - The USA had been determined to halt the advance of Communism as part of its Cold War strategy since the Truman Doctrine of 1947.
  - Johnson was extending this by seeking to prevent South Vietnam from becoming Communist.

- In fact, Vietnam had been split, supposedly temporarily, at the Peace of Geneva in 1954.
- The USA had resisted free elections in South Vietnam as they feared the Communists would win.
- Although Johnson calls South Vietnam 'free' it was not a democratic country.

We also know that the date – 1964 – is crucial, because in that year Johnson began to increase US presence in Vietnam enormously. This speech gives the justification for this escalation.

A short answer might therefore read:

In this speech President Johnson is setting out his reasons for increasing US participation in the Vietnam War. He is explaining to Congress that he sees it as a war to protect free South Vietnam from invasion by North Vietnam. This was part of US Cold War strategy from the Truman Doctrine of 1947 onwards. The US Congress supported him and the number of US soldiers in Vietnam increased dramatically from 1964 onwards.

Now let's look at another example.

**3** Use this source and your own knowledge to explain one of the problems of the League of Nations.

*A British cartoon from December 1919 called 'The Gap in the Bridge'.*

- **Cartoons** are popular with examiners as they often sum up a situation, covering quite a lot of points in a single picture. However, they are not as easy as they may look!
- Start by remembering that this simple drawing has taken the cartoonist many hours of thought and work. Every detail is significant, so the first task – observing – is quite demanding.

1 The cartoonist has drawn a bridge. We can tell from the noticeboard that the bridge represents the League of Nations and that it was designed by the President of the USA. Four nations on the bridge are named: Belgium, France, England and Italy. There is a man sitting nearby: 'Uncle Sam' representing the USA (you will have to learn some of these national symbols: John Bull for Britain, a bear for Russia, etc.). Uncle Sam is leaning on a keystone labelled 'USA'. The keystone is missing from the bridge and the cartoonist draws our attention to it by the title: 'The Gap in the Bridge'.

2 The League of Nations had been designed by US President Woodrow Wilson as a better way of conducting world affairs after the First World War. Its charter was written into the terms of all the treaties at the end of the war. The US Senate, reluctant to get entangled with European and world affairs, would not ratify the treaties. In 1919 – the year this cartoon was drawn – the USA had not joined the League, and in fact it never did. The organisation was always without its 'keystone', its most important member, the USA.

3 Note that the question does not ask for all of this. It asks you to focus on explaining why the situation shown here was a problem.

- As we have seen, not all the details we have listed here need be included in the answer. A good short answer, using the wording of the question to give a sharp focus, would say:

*One of the problems of the League of Nations was that some important nations were never in it. The USA, whose President, Woodrow Wilson, had given the idea of a League of Nations such prominence, never joined because the US Senate refused to ratify the Treaty setting up the League. The League was therefore always without what was intended to be its most important member.*

## Is the evidence enough?

- Sometimes the question asks you to use your own knowledge to comment on whether the evidence is enough to supply a good answer to some historical question. (These are sometimes called **'sufficiency' questions.**)

  Look at this example.

**4** Is this map enough to explain why the Cuban missile crisis took place?

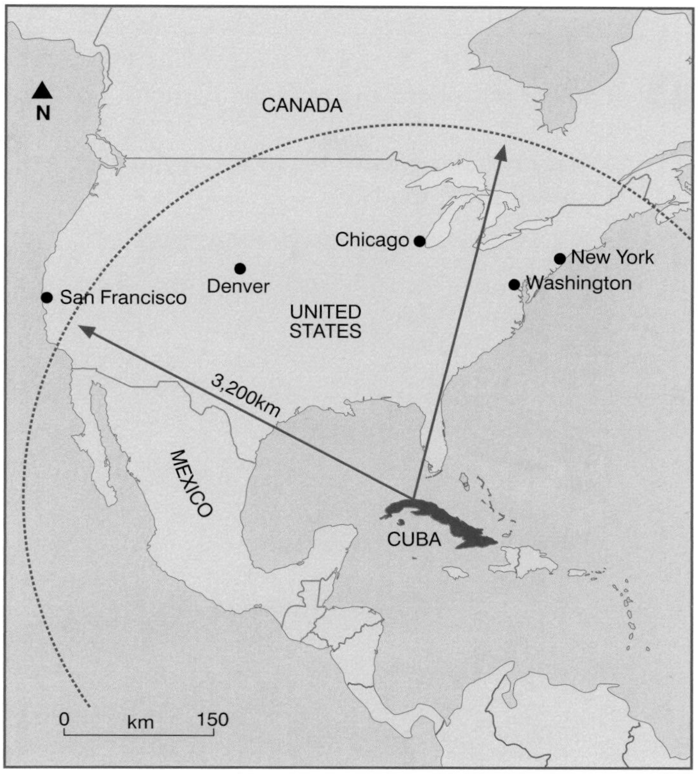


*Map showing parts of the USA within range of missiles based in Cuba, 1962.*

- You can almost always guarantee that the answer to this kind of question will be 'up to a point only'. Your answer is likely to consist of 2 paragraphs:

1 outlining the ways the source *does* fit the question

2 laying out the other factors *not* dealt with in the source.

The two paragraphs below show a full answer.

In this case, the map explains more clearly than any words that missiles based in Cuba would be able to hit almost any part of the USA. The speed of these missiles would mean that these areas would have only a few minutes warning of a nuclear attack. This explains why, when his spy-planes showed photographs of these missile sites being erected, President Kennedy acted fast and strongly. He even considered an attack on Cuba, but decided to blockade the island. He told Soviet leader Khrushchev that he must not install the missiles on Cuba.

However [as you saw on p143 of this book], that is not the whole story – the map only explains the reasons for the crisis 'up to a point'. There were longer-term factors involved. For example, the USA opposed the regime of Cuba's revolutionary leader, Castro, and Kennedy had already tried to remove him with the 'Bay of Pigs' invasion, 1961. Long-range Soviet missiles could already hit the USA anyway. Khrushchev placed his intermediate range missiles in Cuba by way of retaliation for US missiles on the borders of the USSR in Turkey. And at the most general level, there was an arms race on between the USA and the USSR and Kennedy could not afford to let the USSR get ahead.

# Questions to try

**5** Look at this photo and read the caption.

What does this picture tell us about the effects of the Great Depression on the USA? (4 marks)

*Unemployed workers in New York queueing for bread, 1930*

**EXAMINER'S HINTS**

- Look closely at the picture – go beyond first impressions.
- Don't forget the caption. When was this photo taken? Where?
- Now focus on the question. It asks you to relate the source to the 'effects of the Great Depression' – quite a wide topic. You start with what's there and relate the information to this wider issue.
- Be sure to go beyond just what you can see. What can you infer? What things must be true from the source but are not on view?

*Answers are on page 211.*

**6** Use this poster and your own knowledge to explain why the Nazis gained support during the Great Depression in Germany. (6 marks)

*Nazi election poster, 1932. The wording reads: 'Our Last Hope: Hitler'.*

## EXAMINER'S HINTS

- Remember to do both the things asked for by the question: examine the source AND use what you can remember. It is probably best to do these two things in that order.
- Don't forget to do the basic skills in relation to using the source, as in question 5. That is, look at it thoroughly; use the caption.
- The question asks you to use the source and your own knowledge to explain why the Nazis gained support. It does not ask you to tell them every single thing you can remember about Hitler and the Nazis! Note the number of marks – 6 – so this requires only a medium-length answer.

*Answers are on page 211.*

# Source-based questions: using sources

## How useful are sources?

- Historians use sources to find out about the past. It seems fair, then, to ask questions about **how useful** a particular source would be **for finding out about some historical topic**.
- Note the last 7 words: sources are never useful or useless regardless, they are only useful, or useless, depending what you want to know.
- There are a number of issues involved in this idea of **usefulness**:

  **1 Is it relevant?**
  This means studying the source to see if it is about the topic in which you are interested. In an exam it is unlikely that you would be given an irrelevant source. However, you must not forget the **attribution** – the caption or description of the source. This will tell you who said or wrote it, when, where etc.

  **2 Is it reliable?**
  Is it absolutely accurate and truthful? Again, study not only the source itself but also the attribution.

  It is important to realise that the **absolutely reliable source** *is very rare*. It is therefore not very clever simply to dismiss some source as 'unreliable' or 'biased' and leave it at that. You should think about *how* unreliable it is, *why* it is unreliable and **in what ways**.

  You then go on to think about how you could use it **even though it is unreliable in the ways you have described**.

  **3 How does it increase my understanding of this topic?**
  Even though it may be biased, a source can nevertheless help you to find out more about a topic: the important thing is to keep that topic in mind.

- It is time to look at an example.

**7** How useful is this source as evidence about the storming of the Winter Palace in 1917?

*A still picture from the film 'Oktober', made by Sergei Eisenstein in 1927.*

- This picture shows the storming of the Winter Palace by the Bolsheviks in October 1917. The film was made using the actual buildings and streets where the events it shows took place.
- Let's use the three checklist points given above:

1 It is *relevant*: it is about the event in question; but, as we can see by using the attribution, it was made 10 years later, and is from a film. Then again, Eisenstein did use the actual buildings and streets where it all happened.

2 It may not be very *reliable*. It is a film and films are made to hold an audience's attention. Events may be altered to make them more dramatic, more interesting. The actual storming of the Winter Palace, for example, took place at night. This still picture shows a daylight attack because film-cameras at that time could not film at night. Even though Eisenstein used the same buildings and streets, these may have changed in 10 years.

On the positive side, Eisenstein was quite close in time to these events, so he could easily have spoken to people who were there and so got an accurate impression of events. It may be more accurate than if, for example, we were making the film now, beyond living memory.

3 Finally, the film may be *accurate* in showing streets and buildings. It *may* be accurate in terms of what happened, although it will be seen as if it had happened by day. Most of all, however, the film is a better record of how people like Eisenstein, supporters of the Bolshevik Revolution, felt about these events 10 years later. It is more accurate in telling us about 1927 than about 1917. (For example, although you cannot see it here and so could not be expected to say this in an exam, Trotsky played a large part in events in 1917, but was becoming disgraced in 1927, so his role was played down in the film.)

## How should you compare sources?

- Further into the exam paper, you will find **comparison questions**. These extend the issues raised in the last section, where we looked at the usefulness of a source, to comparing usefulness. For example:

**8** Which of these two sources do you think is more useful for finding out about collectivisation in the USSR in the 1930s?

**Source A**

'Men began slaughtering their cattle every night. Both peasants who had joined the collective and individual farmers killed off their stock. "Kill, it's not ours now", "Kill, the State butchers will take it anyway", "Kill, they won't give you any meat on the collective", the rumours spread around.'

From a novel, *Virgin Soil Upturned* by Mikhail Sholokhov, published in 1938

**Source B**

*Government propaganda photograph showing tractors on a collective farm, 1935.*

- The most sensible way of tackling this kind of question is to take the sources one at a time and so lead up to the comparison at the end.
- **Source A** is about peasants' reactions to collectivisation, but is from a novel. It is therefore a **work of fiction** – Sholokhov's view of what happened. As it was published close to the time when Stalin was forcibly collectivising farms in the USSR, it was therefore possible for the author to find out about the events he puts in his novel.
- As with any biased source, novels are not necessarily useless; they may not be total fantasy just because the novelist chooses to make a story out of events. You could mention that other sources would help to verify whether the incidents described here actually happened (after all, a historian does not write a book on the basis of one source). If these incidents did take place (and they did), then *Virgin Soil Upturned* is quite a useful source.

- **Source B** is a photograph. There is a tendency to believe that 'the camera cannot lie'. In fact the camera *can lie*. Photographs can be unreliable evidence because:

  - the photo can be cut up, re-made and re-printed;
  - the subject can be 'set up' so that the photo shows something that only existed for the camera;
  - the camera can select. The photographer can point the camera only at parts of the scene, perhaps untypical parts. We thus see a real photograph, but not helpful evidence.

- In the 20th century, governments learned how to use photography to get across the message they wanted, using all of the techniques above. For these reasons, photographs in 20th-century history should be used with extreme caution.

- In this case we are told that the photo is propaganda. The scene it shows did happen but it has been set up to look as if the collectives were full of tractors. Source B is therefore **relevant, but biased**. It probably does not show what really happened on the average collective. It is, however, extremely useful evidence of what the government wanted people to think was happening on collectives. One of Stalin's motives for collectivisation was to mechanise Soviet agriculture to make it more efficient. Source B seems to show just what he said was going to happen, and so prove that collectivisation was a success.

- Having analysed each source separately, we can now compare them.

- There are two golden rules for all sorts of comparison questions:

  1 Don't say one is all good and one is all bad.

  2 Discuss both.

  An answer to the last part of this question could therefore say:

> *Source A needs checking to see if it is typical, but if it was then it is useful for describing and explaining peasant hostility to collectivisation. Source B is only useful as a propaganda picture of the impression Stalin wanted to create of the success of collectivisation. Both have limited uses, but Source A is probably more useful as we have little evidence of how ordinary Soviet people thought at this time.*

- There is no right answer to these comparison questions. The marks are awarded for how you argue your choice.

## Questions to try

**9** **Source A**

*New boys join the Hitler Youth at a special swearing-in ceremony.*

**Source B**

'I think one of the worst effects is that our children no longer get any peace and quiet. I dread to think the kind of people they will grow up to be with all this endless propaganda.'

*A German woman's comments on the Hitler Youth, published in 1985 but made earlier.*

(8 marks)

Which of Sources A and B is more useful for finding about the Hitler Youth?

**EXAMINER'S HINTS**

- Be sure to address the reliability issue. It is obvious that both these sources are relevant, but you must comment on their reliability. This means thinking about what each source is, who made it and why. Look especially at the date Source B was published and think about the implications of this.
- You have to make a comparison, so don't forget to write about both sources.
- Don't worry about trying to guess the 'right answer'. The examiner just wants to see if you can make sensible comments, and a judgement, about each.
- Don't waste time telling the examiner what is in the sources: s/he can see that for her/himself.

*Answers are on page 211.*

REVISION SESSION 3

# Source-based questions: analysing interpretations

- People make statements about the past all the time: 'Bad King John', 'Good Queen Bess', 'The Roman Empire was the greatest empire the world has ever seen', and so on. Different people make different statements about the same topic. This is because many of these issues are matters of judgement and not matters of fact. New information comes up which throws new light on old certainties or different priorities require old judgements to be revised. Beyond a few certain facts, it is difficult to have the last word in History.
- These judgements about the past are called **interpretations**. One of the tasks of historians is to analyse them, to comment on how accurate they are. Some GCSE questions, usually towards the end of the paper, ask you to comment on interpretations. For example:

**10** 'The New Deal was a great success.' Use this source and your own knowledge to comment on this interpretation of the New Deal.

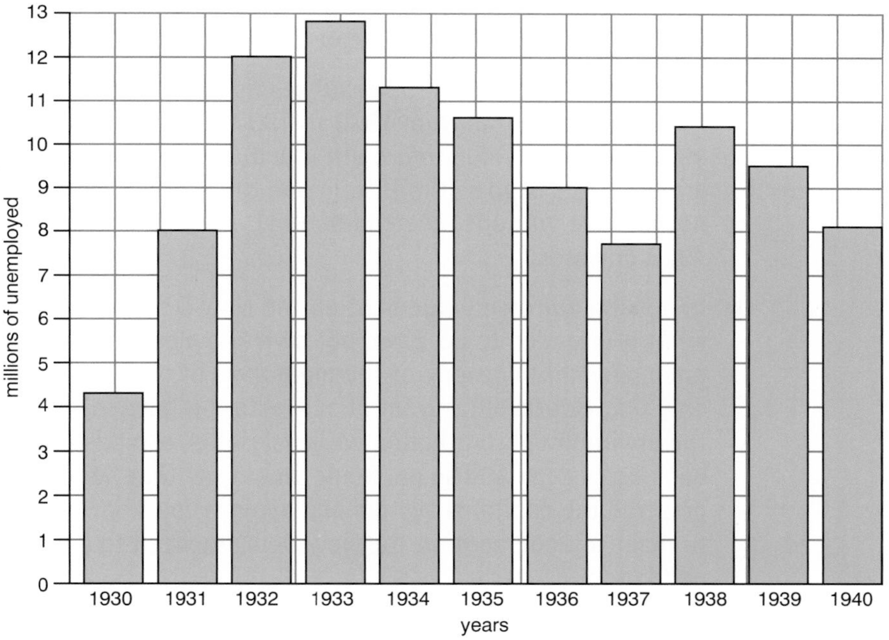


*Graph showing the number of people unemployed in the USA, 1930–40*

- All sorts of thoughts may rush into your mind as you face this question: the graph, the statement, your own views, those you have read. What you need is a plan to sort it all out:

  1 Comment on the source and how far it proves the given judgement.

  2 Use your own knowledge to talk about other issues.

### A* EXTRA

Don't be frightened by statistical sources like this graph. As you should with any source, take time to come to grips with it. Look first at the 'axes' – the horizontal line along the bottom and the vertical line up the side. These tell you what the graph is about.

Try to get an idea of the general trend of the graph – in this case, it shows unemployment rising sharply to a peak and then falling. Don't stop there! Look for the extra bits of information: the extremely low unemployment of 1930, the second rise in 1938. Like any source, a graph can often be 'squeezed' for information beyond what is obvious.

3 Come to your own conclusion which does not totally agree or totally disagree with the judgement.

- The graph shows that unemployment fell during the New Deal period. It was 12.8 million in 1933, when Roosevelt came to power and the New Deal started. It was 7.7 million by 1937.
- However, some points need to be made before saying that the graph proves that the judgement is correct:

  1 Unemployment never fell to what it was before the Depression: 4.3 million.

  2 We need to show that it was the New Deal that caused the fall from 1933 to 1937.

  3 We need to comment on the rise in unemployment in 1938 and 1939, which were when Roosevelt was still in office and most New Deal laws still operative.
- Critics of the New Deal had said that many unemployed had simply been removed from the register because they were working on government contracts or directly for one of the 'alphabet agencies' – such as the Works Project Administration (WPA), the Tennessee Valley Authority (TVA), the Public Works Administration (PWA), or the Civilian Conservation Corps (CCC). Roosevelt therefore tried to cut government spending in 1937. The result can be seen in the graph.
- The 'blip' in the graph (1938–39) seems to prove that the New Deal was the cause of the fall from 1933 to 1937. The fall in unemployment after 1937 was mainly due to growth in industry to make weapons for the US armed forces or to sell to Britain and other Allies. (Although the USA did not join the war until the end of 1941, it was heavily involved from 1939 onwards.)
- In making our own judgement on the New Deal, we need to judge it by what it intended to do. From our own knowledge we know that solving unemployment was one of the main aims of the New Deal, but not the only one. Roosevelt also set about restoring faith in the USA, improving the environment, protecting workers' rights, establishing a sound banking system, and so on. Some would say that he also wanted to preserve the capitalist system and avoid revolution. If we are going to make a judgement on the New Deal, we need to look at these points too.
- In conclusion, we can say that the New Deal was successful in many of its aims. In cutting unemployment it was only partially successful. There were still 10.4 million unemployed in 1937 and the fall in the years after that is more due to military contracts for armaments for the Second World War than to New Deal measures.

# Questions to try

**11** **Source A**

'The situation in Petrograd is serious. The government can do nothing. Food and fuel are running out. Troops are firing at each other. Someone who is trusted by the country must form a new government.'

*Telegram from Rodzianko, President of the Duma (Parliament) to Tsar Nicholas II, who was away at the Front, 11 March 1917*

**Source B**

'That fat Rodzianko has sent me some nonsense. I shall not even reply.'

*Letter from the Tsar to a friend, 12 March 1917*

'Tsar Nicholas II was responsible for his own downfall.'

Use Sources A and B and your own knowledge to comment on the accuracy of this statement.

(12 marks)

**EXAMINER'S HINTS**

- Be sure to use the sources (both of them, in this case) and your own knowledge in your answer.
- Remember that the statement is unlikely to be entirely correct, or entirely wrong. You are going to have to say something on each side.
- Find a plan for your answer that does this, arranging the sources as you go. Then end the answer with your own conclusion.

*Answers are on page 211.*

# REVISION SESSION 4 Writing essays

- The majority of the marks in a GCSE History exam – normally about 60% – are awarded for recalling, selecting and organising knowledge in answer to questions which ask you to describe, explain or analyse historical events. That is why the bulk of this book is given over to laying out the History you have to know in a way that will make it easy for you to recall it for the exam.
- Shorter questions, say for **3–6 marks**, usually require a paragraph of information. Here is an example:

> Choose two items from this list:
>
> Hotline between Washington and Moscow
>
> Strategic Arms Limitation Talks
>
> Helsinki Agreement
>
> and show how they contributed to better relations between the superpowers.

To answer this, you will have to do only two simple things:

1 **describe** two of the items

2 **explain** how it made relations between the superpowers better.

- More demanding, however, are questions which:
  - cover a wider range of History
  - ask you to think about a more serious question
  - carry more marks
  - require a longer answer.
- This book is written to help you tackle these big questions. The units are:
  - organised around questions, so that you are used to the idea of History being about answering questions
  - laid out in lists of points. These give the basis of an essay-plan.
- An **essay** is:
  - extended writing. In an exam you will be expected to write two to three sides.
  - organised so as to answer a question. You will never be asked to 'write all you know about...'. You will always have to organise your answer. Hence the need for a plan.

Think about this example:

> Why were the people of Germany angry about the Treaty of Versailles?

If you know this topic well, this is an easy question. Lots of ideas will rush into your mind: loss of colonies, war-guilt, reparations – and the Rhineland.

Stop! Don't start the essay yet!

- Take a piece of paper and jot down these ideas. Where is the pattern? Is an order emerging?

  Note that this essay does not say: Write all you know about the terms of the Treaty of Versailles. It has a clear question: Why were the German people angry? History is full of 'why?' questions: they are the most common kind of GCSE essay question.

- Here are three tips to help you form your plan:

  1 **Make a list.** Very few historical events had only one cause. You will get yourself above the 'ground floor' of marks at once if you can present several reasons.

  2 **Think of a logical pattern for your list**; it shouldn't just be one thing after another. Often 'why?' questions divide into long-term/short-term causes. Another possible distinction is more important/less important causes. When you have done this, number the items on your list – it is unlikely that the final essay will deal with items in the order you first thought of.

  3 **Make up your mind what you think about the whole question.** In this case: were the German people justified in feeling angry? Be ready to make comments to support your general view as you write the essay, both in an opening statement, and as comments on the items on the list/plan as you go through it.

- You will find the details for this question on p30, but a plan might look like this:

PARA 1 Introduction (brief). Germans v. angry when terms of T of V announced: had expected negotiated peace between near-equals. Despite German anger terms not in fact that bad.

PARA 2 Diktat: a dictated peace. Describe situation of 1918: German army surrenders on basis of Fourteen Points, expecting lenient settlement. German people unaware of depth of defeat. Terms actually worked out by WW, LLoyd G. & Cl. Last two much more revengeful.

PARA 3 Territorial terms: loss of land (give as many details as you can remember). Colonies.

PARA 4 Other restrictions: armed forces; Rhineland.

PARA 5 War guilt clause, leading to reparations

PARA 6 Seen as unfair – e.g. self-determination applied to others, not Germans, many left living under non-German governments. Reparations punished the German people, not their rulers, and carried on well into future. Failure of Allies to disarm as promised.

PARA 7 Conclusion. Up to you: could mention harsh German treatment of Russia at Brest-Litovsk; could point out rapid German recovery as evidence of underlying strength. Probably need to repeat German people's ignorance of events of 1918.

- Some essay questions are **double questions**, the first usually being quite straightforward but moving on to a judgement in the second. For example:

> How did Hitler try to solve Germany's unemployment problems between 1933 and 1939? How successful was he?

- The simplest plan deals with these two questions in the order given, although you might like to refer to the second question in your introduction, as below. (Details of this topic are on p54.)

PARA 1 Introduction. Situation in Germany in 1933: 6m unemployed. Hitler's election promises to cure unemployment. By 1939 a labour shortage. Apparently his greatest success.
PARA 2 National Labour Service (started before he came to power). Forced labour for six months from 1935.
PARA 3 Big public schemes: e.g. autobahns. Good propaganda. Some of Hitler's policies, e.g. road building, began under Weimar.
PARA 4 Rearmament. Growth of armed forces + contracts to rebuild armaments against terms of T of V.
PARA 5 Conclusion. A success and source of popularity. Unemployment was cured, unlike many other countries. In a dictatorship workers are tools of the state: cost to workers – loss of freedoms, low wages, etc.

# Questions to try

**12** In September 1938 Britain and France were ready to make an agreement with Germany. In September 1939 Britain and France declared war on Germany. Explain why this change came about.

(5 marks)

**EXAMINER'S HINTS**

- This is really a double 'why' question: why agree with Hitler in 1938? Why go to war with him in 1939? You will have to explain both.
- Remember that this is an explanation essay: to say what happened is not enough – you need to say why things happened that way.
- Think of a logical order for the points you want to make, tying them into the question. The chronology will be important and will provide the basis of the plan, in this case.

*Answers are on page 212.*

## What about coursework?

You will normally be asked to do **two pieces of coursework**, each targeted on one objective. These objectives are the same as those on which the examination is based. The only differences are:

- that you will not be writing them against the clock
- that you do not have to commit all the information to memory but will be writing with access to whatever books or other information you need.

The temptation, given these circumstances, is to spend too much time telling the story and not enough on analysis. Here is some simple advice to think about before tackling coursework:

- Are you clear which objective is being targeted?
- When you are, read about that objective in the appropriate section of this unit.
- Plan your answer.

Normally, each piece of coursework consists of between 2 and 6 questions. Each one will need some planning.

- **Make sure you answer the question.**

  This advice applies to exam questions too, but in coursework you must produce a well-focused answer. Do not be led astray by the fact that you have ready access to all kinds of resources. When you have finished your answer, read the question again and then read your answer again. This is a luxury you will not have time for in the exam, but you can check that you have answered the question.

- **Write enough to answer the question properly**, but not so much that you exceed the word-limit.

  Word-limits are not absolute rules – you won't fail if you go over it – but the moderator won't be very pleased. If you have written too much, chances are you have not answered the question and not met the analytical requirements of the objective.

## UNIT 1: BRITAIN 1906–1914

### 1 The Liberal Reforms (page 4)

**Q1** Rowntree's survey, published in 1901, was important because he tried to define poverty. This would mean that the numbers of people who could be called 'poor' could be measured accurately.

**Comments** Other writers had only described poverty: some exaggerating how many poor there were, some playing it down. Rowntree's survey drew a line (at a very severe level) which everyone could see. It also allowed him to show the reasons why people became poor.

**Q2** The worker paid 4 pence (2p) a week into an insurance scheme. The employer and the government also paid in. If he was too ill to work, he could claim 50p a week for up to 26 weeks. Unemployment insurance worked the same way: the worker, the employer and the government paid into the scheme and a worker could claim 35p a week for up to 15 weeks if unemployed.

**Comments** Note that it was an insurance scheme, to which workers had to contribute – not a flat rate paid out of taxes which is what the Labour Party wanted.

It only looked after the breadwinner, not the whole family, so was little or no help to women. It also only paid out for a fixed number of weeks: what if the worker was sick, or unemployed, for longer than that?

### 2 Women and the vote (page 7)

**Q1** Suffragettes interrupted political meetings, by shouting out 'Votes for women!'. They did minor acts of violence against property in order to get arrested. They held marches, demonstrations and rallies.

**Comments** The suffragettes' aim was to ensure that 'Votes for women' was always in the news. That way those who opposed them could never be allowed to forget the issue. Their example of non-violent action, including a readiness to get arrested, has been copied by many other protest groups since.

**Q2** Both groups wanted votes for women, but while suffragists believed in peaceful methods of protest, suffragettes did not.

**Comments** The suffragists were a larger, long-established, organisation. Suffragettes were a newer and smaller organisation. Both had the difficult task of trying to persuade those with power to give some of it up to those who didn't have it.

## UNIT 2: THE FIRST WORLD WAR

### 1 The beginning of the war (page 10)

**Q1** On the left, south of Metz, German forces would keep the French army occupied. North of Metz, the German right would advance into northern France, through Belgium. Moving fast, they could capture Paris from the west and south. France would surrender and Germany could then attack Russia.

**Comments** The French expected the Germans to advance south of Metz, not to strike through Belgium. Remember that the planned German advance had to be fast as they calculated they only had 3–4 weeks before the huge Russian army ('the Russian steamroller') was ready. As far as possible, they used railway trains to carry their troops.

**Q2** The German army invaded Belgium as planned. The Belgians and the British held up the German advance a bit. Some German forces had to be diverted to the east to deal with an expected Russian invasion. The German forces arrived near Paris in an exhausted condition. The Allies counter-attacked at the Battle of the Marne and the Schlieffen Plan had failed.

**Comments** Try not to give the impression that the Schlieffen Plan was bound to fail: it nearly succeeded. On the other hand, try not to give the impression that the German army was as good then as it was in spring 1940, in the Second World War, when they really did defeat France in 6 weeks. Back in 1914 it still depended on horse-drawn waggons for its food supply, and hundreds of tonnes of fodder for the horses.

**Q3a** There was little to choose between the two sides: neither had the edge over the other.

**Comments** Once the Schlieffen Plan had failed, the war could not be over by Christmas. A quick victory comes when one side is far superior to the other in numbers or weapons or tactics. This was not the case in 1914.

**Q3b** The weapons of 1914 were better in defensive fighting than in attacking.

**Comments** The machine-gun, for example, was the big killer of the Western Front. With this new, industrial weapon a few men could mow down much larger numbers of attacking soldiers.

**Q3c** It was a new kind of warfare and the generals did not know how to win victories in this situation.

**Comments** It is common to criticise the generals for this. (For more on this issue see p12.)

## 2 Stalemate on the Western Front (page 13)

**Q1** Horses used for carrying supplies. Trees with their branches shot away by artillery fire. Mud. Pools of water. Shell-craters. Soldiers. A rough track.

**Comments** Take your time looking at historical photographs. There are often details to be picked out which you do not see at first glance. In this case, note the ropes used to mark off deep craters.

**Q2** The diagram gives you more factual information, more details. However, it looks quite clean and organised.

The photograph gives a better idea of what it was really like. However, it does not give precise information.

**Comments** This kind of question is common in exams. Always try to give a balanced answer: no source is perfect, or perfectly useless. Try to think of the pros and cons of each as you have done here.

**Q3** The weapons – machine-guns and heavy artillery – were very efficient.

**Comments** The British estimated that, of the 20,000 killed on the first day of the battle of the Somme, most had been killed by just 100 machine-gun positions.

The armies were very large – lots of people to kill.

The generals seemed prepared to throw lots of men into battle, knowing that many would be killed.

**Comments** Some have accused the generals of waging 'a war of attrition'. That is, expecting lots of your own men to be killed in return for lots of the enemy, hoping that you can last out longer – see, for example, German tactics at Verdun. Haig never admitted that he was waging a war of attrition, saying that he always fought to win outright.

## 3 The war on other fronts (page 16)

**Q1** The Eastern Front kept German forces split. Germany could not put all its effort into the Western Front.

**Comments** Look at page 22 for what did happen when Russia dropped out of the war in 1917.

**Q2** It was more boring than big battles fought between impressive battleships. It was vitally important because the naval blockade was gradually starving Germany of essential food and other supplies.

**Comments** Before the war both Britain and Germany had been building up their navies with the latest battleships. Popular opinion in both countries expected there to be exciting naval battles, using these new ships.

**Q3** Because it was risky: a whole fleet could be lost in a day. Also, it was unnecessary: Britain and Germany were fighting a war of blockades and U-boats.

**Comments** As on the Western Front, the stalemate was caused by the near equality of the two sides.

## 4 The Home Front: the government (page 19)

**Q1** The poster 2.9 tells men that women wanted them to join the army. Men would feel ashamed if they didn't.

The poster 2.10 stirs up hatred against the Germans.

The poster 2.11 is intended to make women feel that if they were not working in a munitions factory they were not 'doing their bit' for Britain.

**Comments** With an army dependent on volunteers, as the British army was up to 1916, all kinds of propaganda skills were used. You will study different kinds of propaganda in this period of History. Analysis of propaganda often forms part of an exam question.

Poster 2.9 claims to speak for women. Certainly many women, including suffragette leaders, encouraged volunteers to join up. However, not all women relished the thought of their menfolk going off, perhaps to be killed. Poster 2.10 seems to be directed at women, but in fact the message is aimed just as much at men. Poster 2.11 appeals to women's patriotism.

**Q2a** At first most people were enthusiastic about the war and felt very patriotic. Very little criticism was heard.

**Comments** Some of the Labour Party, including its leader, Ramsay MacDonald, were against the war from the start.

**Q2b** In 1915, the government was criticised over the 'shell shortage'. COs refused to fight after conscription was introduced in 1916. People became more realistic from about 1916: they knew millions were being killed and that the war wasn't going to be an easy victory.

**Comments** The simple patriotism of the early years faded from about 1916. Some say that the child-like optimism of the pre-war years died too. Life was now more realistic, more of a struggle, both in the war and in the years afterwards.

**Q3** Censorship of the news; taking over control of the mines; taking over land for food production; directing women into factory jobs.

**Comments** People accepted that the government was going to have more control over your life as they began to realise that this was total war and needed special measures..

## 5 The Home Front: the people (page 21)

**Q1** The biggest increase was in industry. Munitions employed lots of women. The number of servants actually fell.

**Comments** Don't be frightened of statistics. You don't have to do complicated maths with them. Start by making some simple comparisons like those given here.

**Q2** With so many men in the armed forces, the government had to persuade industry to take women workers on.

**Comments** The government had to break down the resistance of trade unions and employers to taking on women to do jobs that they had not been allowed to do in peace.

**Q3a** It showed men that women were not weak, or incapable of working hard, or unable to do skilled work.

**Q3b** It made everyone think that if every citizen, whatever class they belonged to, could be called up to fight and die for Britain, then the country owed them something in peace too.

**Comments** In both cases the change was not dramatic. Women were discriminated against from the end of the war until it was made illegal 50 years later; class differences were still great. But the absolute barriers that existed before 1914 were broken. The war was the turning-point.

## 6 The ending of the war (page 23)

**Q1** By April 1917 the Allies had been fighting for over two and a half years. They had lost millions of men. Their industries were running at bursting-point. The USA offered industrial supplies and fighting men in almost limitless quantities.

**Comments** By 1917 it had become a war of attrition: who could last out longer? US support meant that the Allies could now go on, if necessary for years more.

**Q2** By early 1918 Germany was in a bad way. It had lost millions of soldiers. The blockade had brought their people to the edge of starvation and morale was falling. By the middle of 1918 US support for the Allies would begin to make a difference. On the other hand, Lenin's determination to take Russia out of the war closed the Eastern Front and permitted Germany to do what it had not been able to do since August 1914: fight on one front only. The Germans only had a few months to take advantage of this before the odds against them increased again.

**Q3** By the end of 1917 the USA had joined the war on the Allied side. This was good news because of the huge reserves of men and resources that the USA possessed. Germany could not bring such resources to the war.

However, the prospects for the next year were not all good. Russia had pulled out of the war following the Russian Revolution in October and was now seeking peace. This meant that the Germans could concentrate all their efforts on the Western Front.

Further, fighting on the Western Front was still in deadlock. The Allies seemed as unable as ever to break out of the stalemate and thousands more soldiers had died at the battle of Passchendaele.

In conclusion, I think that at the end of 1917 it was not obvious that the Allies would win the war. I think this because Germany was now free to put all its efforts into the Western Front. The Allies had not found a way of breaking out of the deadlock. The advantage of US support was a long-term thing and the Allies could be defeated before it could make a difference.

**Comments** It is worth remembering that we always know how the story ends, but people at the time did not. We know that 1918 was the last year of the war and that it was over by November; in January 1918 they did not know that. They certainly could not be sure that Germany would be defeated.

1917 was not a good year for the Allies at all. A further cause of concern was a serious mutiny in the French army which, miraculously, Germany did not seem to know about.

# Unit 3: The Peace Treaties

## 1 The problems faced in 1919 (page 26)

**Q1a** Points 6, 7, 8, 9, 11, 13

**Q1b** Points 5, 10, 12

**Q1c** Points 1, 2, 3, 4, 14

**Comments** These were quite mild terms compared with what Clemenceau and even Lloyd George wanted. It was on the understanding that the 14 Points would form the basis of the peace settlement that Germany asked for a ceasefire in 1918.

**Q2** Britain had lost over a million dead. Most families had lost somebody. Fifteen hundred civilians had been killed and property destroyed in air raids. The British had had to sell off foreign investments and borrow money. As a result, its economy was in ruins.

**Comments** Four years of anti-German propaganda had also had an effect. Most British people believed that Germany had caused the war and many actively hated Germans.

**Q3** Lloyd George could see the dangers of revenge. He feared that a shattered Germany would not rest content until it had put things right in another war. He also knew that for Britain's economy to pick up there would have to be a revival of trade and that included trade with Germany.

**Comments** Politicians in democratic countries have to pay attention to public opinion. But they do not necessarily have to follow it. Lloyd George could perhaps see further than the immediate desire for revenge, and events proved him right.

## 2 The terms of the treaties (page 29)

**Q1a** This is a strip of land running 50 kilometres east of the River Rhine in which Germany was not allowed to have anything military – no soldiers, weapons, bases or forts.

**Comments** The purpose of this was, with the Allied troops on the left bank of the Rhine, to keep German armed forces at least 100 kilometres away from the French frontier.

**Q1b** These were the former German and Turkish colonies, taken over by the League of Nations and then handed to victorious Allied powers. The mandated power was responsible to the League of Nations for looking after the colony on behalf of its people.

**Comments** This did mean that the mandated powers had to make some moves towards independence for the colony by providing, for example, education for its people. Much later there was a real clash over South Africa's rule over South-West Africa (Namibia).

**Q1c** This said that Germany was solely and entirely to blame for the war.

**Comments** This article was the basis for reparations: only if Germany was solely and entirely to blame could reparations be justified.

**Q1d** This is the money that Germany was ordered to pay to the Allies for all the damage caused by the war.

**Comments** Germany never paid anything like all the £6,600 million demanded.

**Q1e** This was the new international peacekeeping organisation which Woodrow Wilson hoped would prevent future wars by settling disputes before they got as far as fighting.

**Comments** See unit 8 for how effective the League actually was.

**Q2a** Finland, Estonia, Latvia, Lithuania, Poland, Czechoslovakia, Yugoslavia.

**Comments** With Austria and Hungary, both effectively new countries created out of the former Austria-Hungarian Empire, they make a continuous strip of countries down the centre of Europe from the Baltic to the Mediterranean.

**Q2b** They all existed until 1990, when Czechoslovakia split into two parts and Yugoslavia collapsed into civil war.

**Comments** Austria was in fact taken over by Germany and ceased to exist from 1938 to 1945 (see unit 4). Estonia, Latvia and Lithuania were part of the USSR from 1940 to 1990 (see units 6 and 9). Poland, Czechoslovakia and Hungary were satellites of the USSR from 1945 to 1989 (see units 6 and 9).

## 3 Reactions to the treaties (page 33)

**Q1a** It was a dictated peace because they were not present at the Versailles peace talks and could not negotiate any of it.

**Comments** A starting-point in answering many questions about Hitler is his criticism of the Treaty of Versailles. Some of the things he said were untrue (for example, that the German Army was 'stabbed in the back' by the politicians in 1918). However, it is true that this was not a negotiated peace. The terms were worked out by the victors and handed to the Germans as the defeated power.

**Q1b** The Allies gave Germany only two alternatives: sign or renew the war. Although the truth was hidden from the people, the generals knew that a renewal of the fighting would lead to further defeats and casualties.

Comments Germany was in a terrible state in 1919. The Kaiser had built up huge debts expecting to win the war. The British naval blockade had reduced the entire population to near-starvation. Some generals wanted to go down fighting but Ebert decided to sign the Treaty.

**Q2** Hatred of Germany did not subside in France as it did in Britain as life returned to normal after the war. The French expected to enforce the terms of 1919 to the letter. They were also in deep financial trouble and needed reparations to pay off war-debts. When Germany tried to stop payments, they sent in troops to seize German economic assets.

Comments By 1923 the differences between the former Allies were enormous. With the USA uninvolved and Britain wanting to get on a better footing with Germany, France was isolated. The failure of the French occupation of the Ruhr showed that, only 4 years later, the mood of Versailles was over.

## Unit 4: Weimar and Nazi Germany 1918–1945

### 1 Germany after the War, 1918–1923 (page 36)

**Q1a** The Communists hated the Social Democrats because the Social Democrats had formed the Freikorps, which had ruthlessly crushed their attempted revolution of January 1919.

**Q1b** Many patriotic Germans hated the Social Democrats for making the armistice of November 1918 and for signing the Treaty of Versailles. They regarded the armistice as 'stabbing the army in the back' and the Treaty as a humiliation for Germany.

Comments The Communists also hated the Weimar Republic because they did not believe in parliamentary democracy. Many patriotic Germans did not believe in democracy either and wanted the return of the Kaiser. You need to remember for later both groups' hatred of Weimar in general and their hatred of the Social Democrats in particular. When the Nazis threatened the end of democracy in Germany (see p46) too few Germans cared enough to stop them.

**Q2a** A coalition is a government made up of more than one party.

**Q2b** Coalitions were hard to operate partly because there was so much hatred between parties. Coalitions also need experienced politicians to make them work. The Weimar Republic was Germany's first experience of real democracy.

Comments Unlike the Weimar Republic, Britain does not have proportional representation. This usually brings single party governments. Coalitions have only been formed in wartime and in the crisis of the 1930s Depression. All the governments of the Weimar Republic from 1919 to 1933 were coalitions.

**Q3** People could not run their daily lives with prices rising by the hour. Even wage-earners could not keep up: at the height of the inflation in autumn 1923, a good wage in one week would not buy a loaf of bread the next. The world seemed topsy-turvy: respectable people on fixed incomes were really starving. People who had spent a lifetime saving up their money, found it was all suddenly worth virtually nothing. Debtors, normally looked down on, were the only ones to benefit.

Comments Paper money is based on trust: people expect to be able to exchange a note for what it cost them. During the period of hyper-inflation, the paper money carried enormous values, like '100 billion marks', but was actually worthless. In some areas people stopped using money and bartered for goods. Germany's trade, and international banking system, failed too.

## 2 The Weimar Republic, 1923–1930 (page 39)

**Q1** This was the period when Stresemann built up good relations with other countries, following the Locarno Conference of 1925.

**Comments** The good mood of the Locarno Honeymoon also reflects a change in the attitudes of the Allies too: France had seen that invading the Ruhr had achieved nothing. It now turned to other tactics to preserve its security.

**Q2** Because the German economy was so dependent on loans from abroad. When these were called in, the boom collapsed and millions were thrown out of work.

**Comments** The precarious nature of Germany's economy meant that the depression, when it came, was more severe than in other countries.

**Q2** It may seem that it was doomed from the start. The Kaiser's Germany had not been democratic, so people and politicians lacked experience in making real democracy work. The Weimar constitution led to coalition government. Coalition governments tend to be weak governments, unable to act decisively in a crisis. The Weimar Republic was created in a crisis and faced several serious crises, 1918–23 and again in 1929–33. Furthermore, several parties and people did not want democracy and hated all that the Weimar Republic stood for.

However, the Weimar constitution was a brave attempt to set up real democracy in Germany and might have worked. The achievements of Weimar in the 1920s, in industry and the arts, showed what German democracy was capable of. If it had not been for the Wall Street Crash, which was not Germany's fault, Weimar could have survived. Also, it eventually fell because of Hitler. No one could have foreseen Hitler, so it was not inevitable that Weimar would fall.

**Comments** This is a good, balanced answer. The two paragraphs sum up the arguments on each side. It is important to remember that nothing in History is inevitable: just because we know that Hitler rapidly dismantled the Weimar Republic in 1933–34 does not mean it was doomed.

Another prejudice we have is to see things from a British point of view: Britain does not like coalitions, but that does not mean they are automatically a bad thing. From 1923 to 1930, the 'golden years', coalition governments ran Germany.

However, it is important to note that, in fact, proper parliamentary government was already dead by the time Hitler had become Chancellor. Ministers had ruled by presidential decree, by-passing the Reichstag, for some time (see p43). The ageing President Hindenburg had spent most of his life under the undemocratic government of the Kaisers. Most of the people around him had little belief in democracy. Weimar collapsed because not enough people believed in making democracy work.

One further point: Weimar was important training for the democratic politicians who were to run the Federal Republic of Germany so effectively after it was set up in 1949.

## 3 Hitler and the Nazis, 1918–1930 (page 42)

**Q1** The Nazis were the National Socialist German Workers Party. Nazi takes two letters from NAtional and (in German) SoZIalist.

**Comments** For many early Nazis, like Drexler and Roehm, socialism was as important as nationalism. Hitler was not really interested in socialism: he believed in the German people, but as a racist, not as a socialist.

**Q2a** He has abandoned the idea of seizing power by force and is going to concentrate on elections to the Reichstag.

**Q2b** Because the beer-hall putsch had failed.

**Comments** The idea of seizing power by force was widespread in Germany and Europe in these years. The Bolsheviks had taken power in Russia. In Germany there had been the Spartacists and the Kapp putsch and in 1922 Mussolini had seized power in Italy.

However, the armed forces in Munich had not supported his beer-hall putsch.

**Q2c** Hitler hates democracy: he says 'we will have to hold our noses' as if democracy and the democratic parties smell.

**Comments** It is a good idea in source questions to quote from the source to support your answer. Be sure to make it a short, selected, quote – don't write most of the source. Note Hitler's last words in the source: going into the Reichstag is, for him, just a better way of seizing power, as you will see (Revision Session 4). After he has won the election he will 'have Germany'. Notice also his supreme confidence that one day he will be successful. This is what carried him and his followers through the next 6 years.

## 4 How Hitler won power in 1933 (page 45)

**Q1** The worldwide depression hit Germany hard. Its effects were a massive increase in unemployment, which reached 6 million in 1933. The economy had been dependent on US loans. When these were called in, business collapsed.

The Nazi Party had little support when the Depression started. But in the 1930 elections it won 107 seats. By 1933 Hitler was in power.

People rejected Weimar because they blamed it for all that had gone wrong in 1919–23. Its coalition government now seemed unable to deal with the crisis. From 1930 President Hindenburg ceased to work through the Reichstag, which was deadlocked, but instead ruled by decree. Democracy was therefore already in difficulties.

People turned to the Nazis because they looked impressive and businesslike. They offered solutions to the problems of the country – powerful leadership by Hitler to replace the weak compromises of Weimar leaders; full employment by building up the army; scapegoats to blame for the mess they were in. These messages were forcefully put across by skilled propaganda and exciting political meetings.

**Comments** Many Germans were desperate, and desperate times led people to consider the desperate remedies Hitler was offering. Don't forget, however, that not all Germans thought like this: Hitler never got a majority of the votes of the German people in a free election.

**Q2a** They offered jobs in the army or a revived armaments industry.

**Q2b** They wanted to see Versailles rejected and the army rebuilt.

**Q2c** They were worried by the increasing support for the Communists and the Nazis were violently anti-Communist.

**Comments** Although these divisions help us to understand the appeal of Nazism, people are more complicated than this: there were, for example, patriotic unemployed people, or anti-Semitic ex-soldiers.

## 5 Hitler's dictatorship (page 49)

**Q1a** The Enabling Act was passed in 1933 and gave Hitler the power to pass laws without consulting the Reichstag.

**Comments** The Enabling Act carried out just what Hitler had promised back in 1924: to use democratic methods to take over Germany and then destroy democracy (see p46). At a stroke, it made both President Hindenburg and the elected Reichstag powerless.

**Q1b** The Night of the Long Knives, 1934, was Hitler's attack on the SA, killing their leaders and removing their threat to his supremacy.

**Comments** The Night of the Long Knives – as opposed to the Enabling Act – shows Hitler's readiness to use brute force.

**Q1c** The Reich Church was a Nazi church of Protestants who supported the Nazis.

**Q2a** Hitler had become dictator by removing all democratic opposition by July 1933 – only 5 months after winning the election.

Comments The speed with which democracy collapsed in Germany is quite shocking, but Hitler was helped by the widespread disillusionment with Weimar and Hindenburg's use of dictator-like powers since 1930.

**Q2b** Hitler could use legal methods: the Acts abolishing trade unions and other parties and local elections were all legally passed. The judges agreed to swear a Nazi oath. The only major act of illegal force – the Night of the Long Knives – was used against his own supporters.

Comments This kind of question - putting up a sentence and asking if you agree with it - is often used. It is better to try to find a way of partly agreeing and partly disagreeing.

In this case, although Hitler won elections and passed laws, these were not done fairly. The elections were carried out with massive violence and intimidation of opponents; the Enabling Act, ending the power of the Reichstag, was passed after elected members had been jostled by Nazis outside and with SA and SS members all over the building. This kind of intimidation is not democratic.

**Q3** By not allowing German people access to books by authors of which the Nazis disapproved (4.7), the Nazis were trying to control the thoughts of ordinary people. The mass rallies (4.8) made it look as if everyone supported the Nazis. People therefore felt isolated, afraid to confide in others and afraid that they were the only ones who doubted that the Nazis were a good thing.

Comments The Nazis were very successful at suppressing opposition by a mixture of fear and propaganda. The two factors help to explain why there was so little opposition to them (see p55).

## 6 Women and children (page 53)

**Q1** Women in Nazi Germany were directly encouraged to get married by the offer of marriage loans. There were also medals for having lots of children. Indirectly, Nazi propaganda at school, in youth movements (which young people had little choice about joining) and everywhere on posters, books, art, films did the same. It always showed desirable images of women at home, with children.

Comments It was almost impossible for women to develop a career. Women state employees (doctors, civil servants etc.) were sacked and job discrimination encouraged. There was also pressure from Nazi busybodies: women in make-up, or smoking in public, would be told off in public and your local 'Block Leader' would speak to you if you were of marriageable age and unmarried or married with no children.

**Q2** Hitler was more concerned to develop fit young people than well-educated ones. Education included lots of PE. The other main purpose of Nazi education policy was to turn out young people who supported the Nazis unquestioningly. Hitler wanted young people to be fit, but says nothing about the rest of their education. He also wants them to be 'masterful, cruel etc.' He wanted to develop these qualities because the most important role he had for young Germans was as soldiers.

Comments This is a good answer to the 'Use the source and your own knowledge' type of question. It starts from the wider information in the text and uses it as a context for the ideas in the source. The quotes are well-chosen and short.

Hitler in this source seems only to be talking about boys: clearly, when he thought about young people he thought about boys. The mention of them overcoming the 'fear of death' is another item proving that war is his ultimate aim for German boys. Boys in the Hitler Youth learnt to overcome their fear by doing slightly dangerous things like jumping over fires and out of first-floor windows.

## 7 The Nazi economy/resistance to Hitler (page 57)

**Q1** Young men aged 18–25 had to join the National Labour Service, working on public works schemes, like building autobahns, planting forests, building houses etc. Re-armament of Germany created jobs in factories building battleships, aeroplanes etc. and all the supply industries they needed. Increasing the size of the army took many men off the unemployment register. Women had to give up their jobs. Jews were not allowed to claim unemployment benefit so disappeared from the figures.

**Comments** The public works schemes were strikingly like the New Deal being carried out by President Roosevelt in the USA as the same time (see p105). Hitler took all the credit for them, but they were started under the Weimar government, not the Nazis.

**Q2** Men in the Labour Front were treated a bit like soldiers. As you can see in the photograph, they are wearing a uniform and carrying their shovels like rifles.

**Comments** Much of the work they did was deliberately done with simple hand tools like shovels, rather then using machines, in order to employ as many men as possible.

**Q3** Communists and Social Democrats were Hitler's old enemies. The Communists hated him because the Nazis were nationalist, not international. The Social Democrats hated him for destroying democracy.

Some church leaders hated Hitler because he cut down the power of their Church. But many hated him because his ideas were anti-Christian.

Army officers and upper-class Germans may have looked down their noses at Hitler at first for having risen from the streets, but he pleased them by getting rid of the SA in the Night of the Long Knives and by expanding the armed forces. Only when his interference in the army and his determination to fight to the bitter end looked like ruining Germany did some people in the army turn against him.

Young people disliked the endless propaganda, which, by the later 1930s, had lost the excitement of the early years. The White Rose group was quite different and were supporters of proper democracy in Germany.

**Comments** Both Communists and Social Democrats hated Hitler for removing workers' rights, but they would not work together against him. Nor were any of these groups in contact with one another. You can see they all had very different motives: the splits that had dogged Germany before 1933 continued to make the opposition to Hitler weak.

## 8 Hitler and racism (page 60)

**Q1a** Kristallnacht means the 'night of broken glass' and took place in 1938. It was a Nazi attack on Jews, their homes, property, businesses and synagogues, following the murder of a German diplomat in France by a young Jew.

**Comments** Kristallnacht was marked by utter lawlessness. The ordinary police did nothing as SS and other Nazis carried out these raids, often stealing from Jews' homes and doing exactly what they liked.

**Q1b** Euthanasia was the policy of killing off mentally ill Germans. About 72,000 were killed between 1939 and 1941. The Nazis believed that people who were not physically and psychologically fit Germans were a burden on the state and should not be kept alive.

**Comments** It was part of Hitler's beliefs that the people were there to serve the state, not the state to serve the people. Therefore, if people were not contributing to the state they were no use and could be put to death.

**Q1c** The Final Solution was the Nazi policy of killing all the Jews in Europe. It was agreed in 1941 and led to the building of gas chambers, first at Auschwitz concentration camp and then at 5 others. Jews were transported by train from all over Europe to these death camps, run by the SS. Altogether about 6 million Jews and 5 million others were killed in this way.

Comments The Final Solution was industrialised death. Anti-Semitism had existed for a long time in Europe. Jews had been driven out of England from 1290 to 1655. There had been attacks on Jews in Russia in the late 19th and early 20th centuries, encouraged by the Tsars, in which hundreds died. But only 20th-century technology made the Final Solution possible.

## UNIT 5: THE RUSSIAN REVOLUTION 1900–1924

### 1 Russia before the Revolution (page 65)

**Q1a** The peasants were poor, with large debts to pay off for the land they had received in 1861. Each person's share of land was getting smaller as population was rising, and their farming methods were old-fashioned. Disease was common and bad harvests brought death from starvation.

Comments A better way of putting this is to say that the peasants' real grievance was hunger for land: they could see that the Tsar, the Church and the nobles had lots of land, while they were struggling. They thought that if only they had more land their lives would improve.

**Q1b** Industrial workers were badly paid, for long hours, with unsafe factories and overcrowded living conditions.

Comments These features were common enough in the early stages of industrialisation. What was special to Russia was the size of industrial enterprises – half of them had over a thousand workers. This was unlike Britain in the 18th and 19th centuries.

**Q2** The Tsar was an autocrat. This meant that his word was law. There were ministers and other advisers, but they were chosen by the Tsar, not according to democratic control. His government was carried out by a large number of officials who were often lazy and corrupt. Nicholas did not have strong views of his own, except an unwillingness to change anything. He was therefore very hostile to any form of opposition and fierce in his crushing of it, using his secret police, censorship and exile.

Comments The Church's view helps to explain Russian autocracy: he was chosen by God to rule Russia and so his word was law. You may remember from when you did 17th-century History, that English monarchs of that time held the same views. Nicholas did care for his people in a way, but from a distance: he was hopelessly out of touch with them. His attitude to opponents meant that many turned to violence, as all other doors were closed to them. His uncompromising attitude to reform brought about his own downfall in the end.

**Q3** These four pictures reveal huge differences between the lifestyles of different classes in Russia. The peasants in 5.2 are very poor: the clues to this are the fact that most, perhaps all, of the children are barefoot, because they cannot afford shoes; their houses, in the background, are thatched huts; the clothes they are wearing are not too bad, although the second child from the right is ragged. They seem happy and adults and children are together.

The men in 5.4 are living in a workers' hostel, away from their homes, in a room that just has lots of beds in it. They are unsmiling, perhaps because they are tired from their long hours at work, and the man on the right is lying down. They have cheap, but adequate clothes.

The nobility in 5.3 are wearing fine clothes and the women are wearing jewels. Most men are in military uniform. Both men and women have well-groomed hairstyles. The countess who is holding the party where the photograph was taken must be very rich to have such a huge room in her palace. There are lots of servants at the back. The plates, glasses, tablecloths, and large table decorations infer wealth beyond the dreams of any of the people in 5.2 or 5.4.

The Tsar and his family in 5.5 are not elaborately dressed, but still show many clues as to their wealth. Their clothes are fine, embroidered or fringed with lace; the Tsarina is wearing strings of pearls, a tiara, earrings and other jewellery; so are all the daughters. The Tsar is plainly-dressed, but all of them are clean, well-fed, with expensive hairstyles.

**Comments** This is a very good answer, giving excellent examples of the skills needed in answering this kind of question. First it picks up lots of details from the pictures – it doesn't stay with first impressions only, but examines the photographs minutely, finding clues or examples of the general points made in the answer.

Secondly, it infers from the sources: that is, it draws conclusions about these people's lives which are not explicitly stated but which can be worked out from the clues. For example, the wealth of the princess, the easy lives of the Tsar's family, the fatique of the workers and the cheery looks on the peasants' faces.

The result is a longer, more thoughtful answer than you might expect from an apparently easy question.

## 2 Russia 1905–1914 (page 68)

**Q1** *Long-term:* poverty of the peasantry; bad conditions, low wages suffered by city workers; weaknesses and corruption of the Tsar's government and lack of democracy.

*Short-term:* bad harvests 1903–5; depression in industry; defeat in Russo–Japanese War revealed incompetence of Tsarist rulers and officials. Tsar's troops fired on peaceful demonstration, Bloody Sunday.

**Comments** A few additional points:
*Long-term:* peasants wanted more land and were ready to seize it themselves if they were pushed to the limit.
*Short-term:* workers could be thrown out of work if trade slumped, with nothing to live on – there was no welfare system at all. The war brought food shortages and high prices, as in 1914–17. Conditions in the towns are important, as that is where revolution starts.

**Q2** He survived by making concessions – the October Manifesto, offering relaxation of censorship and a Duma. This won over some of his opponents. He then used force to crush the rest.

**Comments** He then broke his word over the October Manifesto: censorship was restored in 1906 and the Duma was not really democratically elected. In the long run, this probably sealed his death warrant. It shows, however, that if he could have made concessions earlier, and stuck to them, he might have survived longer. What do you think?

**Q3** These figures show the massive number of strikes during the 1905 Revolution dying down afterwards. It shows things were quite peaceful from about 1908–11. It then shows growing dissatisfaction in the years just before the First World War broke out.

**Comments** This answer is good on describing, but does not really explain the decline from 1905 to 1910. It was partly that industry picked up, so there were fewer grievances, but also that Stolypin crushed strike organisers so effectively. The rise from 1911 is ominous for the Tsar. It shows that things were not looking too good even before war broke out.

## 3 The revolution of 1917 (page 73)

**Q1** The war went badly for Russia from the first. The soldiers could see that some of the reasons for their defeats were the fault of the Tsar's government, so they mutinied. Rasputin had more influence on Alexandra because Nicholas was away at the War Front from August 1915; he had also left her in charge of the government, so her influence was more serious. Shortages of food were brought about because of lack of peasants to till the fields and because much of the transport system was tied up with supplying the army.

**Comments** At first the Russian peasants who made up most of the army went off to war willingly. Defeat and death demoralised them, but, as in France in 1916 (see p14), it was the stupidity of high command which tipped them into mutiny.

To sum up, war imposed a stress on Tsarism which it was too weak to take.

**Q2** The Provisional Government failed to meet the hopes of the Russian people in 1917. They were popular at first, but the decision to carry on the war lost them support. They used force to stop peasants seizing land and they failed to halt the shortages of food in the cities: both these failures lost them support. They failed to call a general election. They were also faced with Lenin, determined to bring about a Bolshevik revolution against them.

**Comments** The Provisional Government failed to realise that they were in the middle of both a war and a revolution. They had had no experience of running a government and tried to behave like the British or French parliamentary politicians they admired: sticking by Russia's treaties with France and Britain and going on fighting; stopping the peasants from seizing land. They were ill-prepared for Kornilov's attempt at a counter-revolution. But most of all, they did not give the people what they wanted. After all, it was the people in the streets who had caused the abdication of the Tsar and so brought them to power.

## 4 The Communists and the Civil War, 1917–1921 (page 76)

**Q1a** To get peace. The Germans had been victorious for 4 years and demanded their reward.

**Comments** Lenin had to buy peace. The terms make the German complaints about Versailles, in 1919 (see p30), seem unjustified.

**Q1b** Because the Communists believed that the workers did the work and so should control the business. The capitalists, who owned the factories, simply exploited the workers.

**Q1c** Because the Communist State was acting on behalf of the workers.

**Comments** See the panel on p65 for all the theory behind this. We would say Lenin 'nationalised' the banks and foreign trade by taking them into state ownership. Workers' control had rarely happened outside Communist countries – and did not last long in Russia (see p77).

**Q1d** Because the Bolsheviks were in a minority, with lots of enemies, and they were determined to succeed.

**Comments** This is very controversial. What do you think? Was Lenin justified? Did the situation of 1917–21 justify the 'Red Terror'? He certainly gave Stalin plenty of examples to follow for his use of Secret Police in the 1930s.

**Q2** He was organiser of the Red Army. He inspired the troops. He frightened them, if he thought they might change sides, or retreat. He made use of Tsarist officers, but kept political control of them.

**Comments** He showed brilliant skills as an organiser, as he had already shown in the November Revolution. He made brilliant use of the train, rushing through the countryside with guns, boots, uniform, alcohol, a printing press for pamphlets as well as his own living accommodation for weeks at a time.

**Q3** Communists supported the Reds wholeheartedly. Peasants supported them because they had given them land. Patriots supported them because the Whites had foreign support. Some supported them because their families were held hostage. Some were terrorised.

**Comments** Although the motives were different, and some obviously not whole-hearted, the Communists did have considerably more support by 1921 than they had had at the time of the November 1917 Revolution.

## 5 Lenin's rule, 1917–1924 (page 78)

**Q1** The Kronstadt Mutiny was serious because the sailors had been important loyal Bolsheviks from the early days in mid-1917. They had played a big part in the November Revolution. Now they had turned against the Communist leadership.

**Comments** The Communists had plenty of enemies and did not care what they did to them, but were concerned when their supporters turned against them. Note that the mutineers of 1921 were not the same sailors as had been involved in 1917: those men had gone off to fight in the Civil War.

**Q2** It was not that new: just a return to the situation of free enterprise which had existed under Tsarism only four years previously. However, several things were 'new' compared to the system the Communists had set up in 1917. All kinds of private trade were allowed: in food especially, but also in all consumer goods.

**Comments** It was only partial privatisation. All major industries remained under government control. However, the amount of private trade that arose annoyed many Communists. It abandoned (Lenin said temporarily) the state control and workers control of the early decrees of 1917 and restored capitalism.

**Q3** By Soviet power, he meant the power of the new Soviet government to get things done. In 1921 electric power was only laid on in Russian cities. Electrification was supplying electricity to the hundreds of villages all over Russia. Communism was the ideal state which Lenin was trying to set up.

**Comments** This electrification only began under Lenin and was put into effect under Stalin (see p82), but it was Lenin's idea and it linked the Communist government with the idea of modernity and progress. He hoped, as this slogan says, that people would be converted to Communism by the benefits it brought, such as electricity.

## Unit 6: Stalin and Russia

### 1 How Stalin became leader (page 81)

**Q1** **For:** skilled organiser; well known; good speaker; clever thinker.

**Against:** arrogant; not prepared to get involved in building up groups of supporters among the Communists; late convert from Mensheviks to Bolsheviks.

**Comments** Trotsky was probably shy and so found it difficult to make contact with what ordinary Communists felt. To be fair, the old Bolshevik Party had not been democratically run: the leaders had made all the decisions. He completely misjudged the new situation and his policy of 'World Revolution' was easily defeated by Stalin and his many supporters.

**Q2a** Stalin tricked Trotsky over the date of Lenin's funeral.

**Comments** This enabled Stalin to manipulate a large-scale cult of Lenin, much to the scorn of Trotsky and Lenin's widow, but which promoted Stalin as the one true heir of Lenin.

**Q2b** Stalin used the rivalry other leading Communists felt towards Trotsky in lining up massive opposition to him in 1924.

**Q2c** Stalin had lots of supporters in the Communist Party and used their votes against his enemies in all three stages of the leadership battle.

**Comments** Stalin used his position as General Secretary to keep in contact with Party members everywhere. Thus there were many people who owed debts of gratitude to him for little favours done over the years and would repay him with their votes. Members who supported his rivals found their careers in the Party did not go so well.

**Q2d** Over 'World Revolution' versus 'Socialism in One Country' Stalin's policy was more in touch with rank-and-file Communists. Over when and how to industrialise the USSR, Stalin took up and put down policies as his tactics in the leadership contest demanded. Thus in 1927 he supported the right-wingers, who wanted to continue with NEP, against the Left, who wanted to force the pace. In 1928 he changed policies to force the fall of the Right.

**Q3** Stalin was tough, physically and emotionally. He was a hard worker and wanted power; this drove him on to overcome more talented men than him. Perhaps because he was an outsider (as a Georgian not a Russian) and perhaps because the others were rude about him because he was not such a good talker and thinker as they were, he carried personal rivalry to the limits, even having his former enemies killed.

**Comments** Stalin did have some positive qualities – he showed personal bravery in the Second World War – but, as you will see in the rest of this unit, he was a ruthless monster, with little regard for human life or human feelings.

## 2 Stalin and industry (page 85)

**Q1a** The Five-Year Plans were Stalin's method of industrialising the USSR completely and rapidly. The first started in 1928 and concentrated on heavy industry.

**Comments** Heavy industry – coal, iron, oil and power – had to be the starting-point, because all other industries needed them. The USSR continued with Five-Year Plans after the Second World War and other countries, such as India, also used them as a way of coordinating development.

**Q1b** The plans set targets for each industry. These were then turned into production targets which each region, factory, shift and even each worker had to meet.

**Comments** The point of such centralised planning was that each industry was linked to each other. For example, new ironworks needed lots more coal: the Plans were there to ensure it was produced.

**Q2** There were punishments for those who slacked or who did bad work. These included fines, being held up in front of everyone in the factory and, for serious cases, being sent to a labour camp. Specially good workers – called Stakhanovites – received rewards and were used to set standards for all the others.

All workers were subject to government propaganda telling them to work harder.

**Comments** Think of it as 'the stick and the carrot': the sticks were punishments, the carrots were incentives for fulfilling the targets.

The workers in the new industries often came straight from peasant farms and were totally unused to the discipline of factory work. Some have argued that the strict controls were necessary to get these new workers to fit into the factory system.

Note also that Stalin emphasised the 'danger from abroad', even though there was no real threat to the USSR until well into the 1930s. This reflects Stalin's own paranoia (see p88), but it built up an atmosphere of fear, in which superhuman efforts had to be made to save the country.

**Q3** At work, the Soviet people had to work very hard for long hours. They learned new skills and many millions left the land to become industrial workers. In comparison with other countries, where this was a period of high unemployment, Soviet workers had jobs and job security.

Women's lives changed because they were expected to join the workforce. Crèches and nurseries were provided and Soviet women were probably the most equally treated in the world at that time. However, few reached positions of responsibility, either at work or in government.

People's home life was changed because many moved to new industrial towns and cities. Many of these were inadequate at first as cities were built from scratch in the middle of nowhere. Flats were often very small and badly built and there was a shortage of consumer goods, from clothes to household items.

There were some improvements: free health care was provided. Education was available for all, which it had never been before. In time, the new towns and cities had good, free leisure and cultural facilities.

**Comments** You could add a conclusion weighing all these things up.

## 3 Stalin and agriculture (page 87)

**Q1a** food

**Comments** This is the obvious one. Stalin did not want to be dependent on the kulaks for getting enough food at a cheap enough price.

**Q1b** workers

**Comments** Stalin was short of workers. Remember that only 20% of Soviet citizens were industrial workers. Stalin needed a much bigger labour force in industry so he had to draw on the peasants and at the same time put up agricultural production.

**Q1c** export

**Comments** Don't forget this one. Food was all the USSR had to sell.

**Q1d** machines

**Comments** When your industry is as backward as the USSR's was, you need machines to make machines. The only way Stalin could get hold of them was by buying them from abroad.

**Q2** They would not be making decisions about how to farm, but would be told by someone else.

They feared that government targets for crop production would leave them starving.

They resented interference from the Communist Party.

**Comments** The main reason was that their whole way of life, which they and their forefathers had led for generations, looked like being utterly changed. The land they worked would not be theirs (apart from the little plots around their houses). The animals they tended would not be theirs. They would be expected to grow crops that the country needed, like flax, cotton or sugar-beet, but which were no use to them.

In fact, the government did seize the crops it wanted and the result was famine.

**Q3** He was ruthless. He was prepared to overthrow centuries of traditional peasant farming in the USSR. He was prepared to send kulaks to almost certain death. He was prepared to face famine by forcing collectivisation on the peasants. He did all these things to get his industrialisation carried out.

**Comments** Compare these actions of Stalin's with others: his seizure of power in 1924–9, the industrialisation programme, the purges. Yet he did succeed in modernising the USSR: it survived the German invasion of 1941, it was victorious in the Second World War, and became one of the two superpowers afterwards.

Are these achievements worth the cost?

## 4 Stalin's dictatorship (page 90)

**Q1** 1, 2, 3 and 4 are examples of terror under Stalin; 5, 6, 7 and 8 are examples of indoctrination.

**Comments** There was some overlap, of course: the purges had a propaganda side, that the USSR was being attacked by enemies inside the country. Artists were terrorised into putting up with censorship.

**Q2** It is a piece of propaganda art about Stalin. Stalin looks gentle, friendly, fatherly, getting on well with a group of ordinary Russians. This fitted his propaganda image of the guide of his country and his people.

**Comments** It also shows the dam: a demonstration of the new and spectacular achievements of the Communist regime. Stalin, incidentally, never went out on trips around the USSR looking at the country and meeting people. He stayed in Moscow, speaking only to his dedicated followers and viewing his country through newsreel films.

# UNIT 7: THE USA, 1919–1941

## 1 Isolationism (page 92)

**Q1a** Isolationism is a feeling of wanting to keep isolated from the rest of the world. It meant not joining any alliances, not getting involved in commitment to other countries, cutting off trade and immigration.

**Comments** *It is right to describe isolationism as a feeling, rather than a policy. It was a mood, an attitude, which led to all kinds of policies: refusal to join alliances, economic policy (tariffs), immigration policy. It also had a racist and intolerant side.*

**Q1b** WASPs are White Anglo-Saxon Protestants.

**Comments** *WASPs, as early arrivals in the USA, were more powerful than other national groups.*

**Q1c** Tariffs are duties which foreign-made goods had to pay on entering the USA.

**Comments** *High tariffs were intended to help US industry by removing foreign competition.*

**Q2** The USA did not join the League of Nations because the US Senate refused to ratify (agree) the Treaty of Versailles. The Senate was dominated by isolationist views and they feared that membership of the League would lead the USA into all kinds of foreign wars and obligations.

**Comments** *This US isolation is an important moment in 20th-century history. You will see that it was one of the factors in the weakness and failure of the League (see unit 8). You will also see how the USA tried to reverse the isolationism of 1919 by adopting the opposite policy after the Second World War (see unit 9).*

## 2 The US economy in the 1920s (page 96)

**Q1a** An assembly line is a way of making complicated industrial goods by splitting up the whole process into lots of little tasks. One worker can then just do one task, over and over again, as the car (or whatever) goes past on a conveyor-belt.

**Comments** *The answer could refer more closely to the picture: it is not just a stimulus to get you started. So, you could point out that this is one of the big moments in the assembly line, where the body is put on the chassis, the bodywork is lowered on to the chassis under its own weight.*

**Q1b** Assembly-line methods changed industry by enabling goods to be made in huge quantities, more cheaply.

**Comments** *You could also say that assembly lines are expensive to set up: lots more capital is needed than for building a car in a workshop. It also means that workers do not have to be skilled, and so do not have to be paid high wages.*

**Q2** The boom was really confined to well-off, city-dwelling Americans. This meant that over half the American people did not share it.

**Comments** *It is hard to be exact of course – see A3.*

**Q3** The groups which did not take part in the boom were rural Americans, unemployed, those on low wages.

**Comments** *A disproportionate number of these were black or recent immigrants in the USA.*

## 3 The Roaring Twenties (page 100)

**Q1a** Skyscrapers were very tall buildings put up in US cities in the 1920s.

**Comments** Skyscrapers began in New York, where there was a shortage of space for offices on Manhattan Island, so they built upwards. Other cities were so impressed that they copied the style. New techniques of steel construction were needed.

**Q1b** Flappers was the name given to young women of the 1920s who broke the rules about how women were supposed to behave by, for example, smoking in public, going out alone with men.

**Q1c** Speakeasies were bars, made illegal by Prohibition.

**Comments** Speakeasies usually had to pay the local police to leave them alone; if you didn't pay enough the police would 'raid' them.

**Q1d** Jazz is a kind of popular music invented by black Americans.

**Q2** Prohibition was an experiment because it was an attempt to change people's habits, to make them more 'moral', by law. It was something no other country had tried – hence an experiment, something new.

The main reason it failed was because people were not willing to change their habits. The result was that ordinary people doing ordinary things were now breaking the law. Even after 10 years, they were not willing to change. Millions of people, including the police, found ways of getting round the law, which brought it into widespread disrespect.

Other reasons for the failure of Prohibition were that it opened the way for gangsters to move into the drink business. In this way it did more harm than good. It also cost the country lots of money in trying to enforce the law.

**Comments** See how the writing plan makes a nice, organised case of a few basic ideas taken from this unit.

What other ways can you think of in which governments have tried to make people better by law? Did it work?

**Q3** The main problem is that we are dealing with a large number of people. It is hard to generalise: *some* women may have gained more freedom, but many didn't. *Some* black Americans benefited by moving north, but still 10.5 million stayed in poverty and segregation in the South.

**Comments** This answer has got the main point, which is that the focus of the question is on problems of finding out, not on describing what happened. Apart from the problem of making generalisations about the lives of millions of people, there is a problem of definition: what is improvement? Was a black American in an overcrowded apartment in a ghetto in a northern city on low, casual wages, but able to walk down the street and go into any café or cinema, better or worse off than a relative who stayed in the south?

There is also the problem of the sources: we may need to use more diaries and personal reminiscences to see how people really felt, rather than relying on secondary sources.

## 4 The Wall Street Crash and the Great Depression (page 104)

**Q1a** The Wall Street Crash was a rapid fall in the value of shares in October 1929.

**Q1b** The Great Depression was the mass unemployment and hardship in the USA which began in 1929.

**Comments** It is useful sometimes to get your thoughts together into one sentence: sometimes this is harder than writing several descriptive sentences! In **A1a** it is worth saying what Wall Street is: the New York Stock Exchange. In **A1b** the unemployment was the result of a decline in economic activity, both in industry and agriculture: this was the real Depression.

**Q2** Industry was over-producing, so production was cut. If you were producing less you did not need so many workers, so some were sacked, some worked part-time on lower wages. People who were unemployed or on lower pay had less money to spend. This meant less demand for goods. So industry made less and needed less workers, and so on.

**Comments** The Wall Street Crash made this situation worse by cutting investment in industry and undermining people's confidence. It was very hard for the USA to break out of this cycle, once it was locked into it. Trying to sell abroad was no answer as most of the world was in depression at this time. This is why the Depression lasted so long.

**Q3** Hoover believed what nearly everyone believed in the 1920s: that if you leave the capitalist economy alone, if you let business look after itself and keep government interference to a minimum, everything will go well. And up to 1929 it did. Like everyone else in the 1920s, too, he believed in 'rugged individualism': people should not be coddled, supported by government welfare because that made people weak and dependent. The trouble was that these views were no longer appropriate for the Depression years.

**Comments** Hoover was not a nasty man, but too rigid in his ideas. Individuals were unable to deal with the Depression because the forces at work were beyond their control. It may be that the economy would right itself again: but what was the starving family going to eat tonight?

A new President was coming along (see p105) with very different answers and a more understanding outlook.

## 5 Roosevelt and the New Deal (page 108)

**Q1a** Emergency Banking Act

**Q1b** CCC, PWA, TVA, WPA

**Q1c** CCC, TVA, WPA.

**Comments** This list is worth doing to get you thinking about the New Deal, but really several of the agencies had overlapping aims. Job-creation, through the PWA, for example, helped to restore confidence that the USA was on the road to recovery. The TVA certainly achieved all three aims.

**Q2** When unemployed people got jobs, they got money in their pockets. This meant they could buy goods, so there was some revival of demand. Factories felt it was worthwhile taking on workers, or putting their staff on full pay again, because someone wanted their goods. This meant more money to spend, and so on.

**Comments** The key difference, which reversed the spiral, was government intervention: spending money to create jobs. FDR was prepared to do this, to spend money, even money the government did not have, to achieve this reversal.

**Q3** The New Deal was clearly only a partial success. With unemployment still high even when the USA entered the Second World War in 1941, and demand still not up to 1929 levels, it did not achieve total recovery.

The criticisms of the right may be true, but the New Deal never set out to abide by right-wing economic ideas. The left-wing criticisms are fair points, but the New Deal was not a radical government: it did not try to reform US society, or change it. It set out to preserve it and restore it.

The New Deal should only be judged by its own aims. In these it was quite successful: probably as successful as possible in a worldwide depression. FDR's underlying intention was to give people back their optimism, their hope in the future, and in this he largely succeeded.

**Comments** The New Deal was not like Stalin's Five-Year Plans (see unit 6) or like Hitler's Germany (see unit 4).

That is, it was not calculated by the government to a blueprint. It was bunch of ideas, some of which worked and some of which did not: FDR expected some not to. It is not surprising that it was inconsistent.

Even more, it was democratic. FDR had to stand for election 4 times. People were not put in labour camps if they disagreed with it or did not fit in with it. It did preserve a lot of things in US society which were wrong: racial discrimination, low pay, sex discrimination, for example. But it also preserved a healthy democracy.

# Unit 8: International Relations, 1919–1939

## 1 The League of Nations (page 111)

**Q1** The League met in Geneva. This is because Geneva is in Switzerland, a country which was always neutral.

Comments It is important to realise that the League was set up with great popular idealism. Many ordinary people hoped it would succeed. Neutrality, not belonging to one side or the other, and acting on behalf of the League, not yourself, were an important part of this idealism.

**Q2** Britain, France, Japan, Italy plus other nations in rotation. The League had to combine the idealism of making all nations equal in the Assembly, with the realistic fact that some nations were much stronger than others. Putting these four nations on the Council recognised that the League could not do much without them anyway.

Comments The inclusion of these four nations on the Council also kept in being some of the criticisms of the League: they were the victors of 1918; three were white European imperial nations; when Germany and the USSR joined, should these powerful countries become permanent members of the Council?

## 2 The League in the 1920s (page 114)

**Q1** Very little. The Washington naval agreement stopped any new ships being built, but that is about all. It seemed impossible even to get a disarmament conference started. The Kellogg–Briand Act, 1928, did nothing to reduce arms, although nations promised not to use them.

Comments The nations which had been disarmed by the Treaties – Germany, Austria and Hungary – were very bitter about the failure of disarmament plans. They felt they had been forced to disarm and that the other nations were hypocrites. It increased their suspicion of the League.

**Q2** This statement is mostly true. There are examples, from the early 1920s, when the post-war determination to seek peaceful settlements was strong, of nations agreeing to accept the League's decisions even if they went against what they most wanted: Silesia, 1921 and Aalund Islands, 1921.

There are more important examples on the other hand: Mussolini was prepared to bully and threaten over the Corfu Incident, 1923, to get his own way. France and Belgium chose to invade the German Ruhr in 1923. Even more seriously, France made military alliances with Poland and Czechoslovakia.

Most of the serious diplomacy of these years went on outside the League: the Dawes Plan, 1924, the Locarno Pact, 1925, the Kellogg–Briand Pact, 1928. Clearly, most countries still preferred to do things the old way.

Comments This is a well-organised and well-balanced answer. It makes good use of factual information to support the points you want to make: it does not just tell the whole story of the 1920s from one end to the other. It has a point of view.

None of the criticisms you make of countries in the 1920s mattered much at the time: there were no serious crises, economies were improving and all seemed well. With hindsight, however, we can see that attitudes had not in fact changed: France still feared Germany; Germany still wanted revenge; Italy wanted glory; Britain wanted to keep clear; eastern European nations wanted security, and so on. Nearly all of these national aims were being met outside the League.

When things got serious in the 1930s the League had not established itself as the 'normal' way of doing things.

## 3 The League in the 1930s (page 118)

**Q1a** (i) Japan (ii) Italy

**Q1b** (i) Japan got away with it because the League took so long to report on the invasion that it was all over before they decided what action to take. Also sanctions could not work because Japan's main trading partners were in the League.

> **Comments** It was hard for the League to react to the Manchurian Crisis. China was in chaos; the civilian Japanese government had no control over what its army was doing in China. Further, Japan was a fellow Council member and Britain and France did not want to alienate the Japanese.

**Q1b** (ii) Italy got away with it because Britain and France were more worried about Hitler and did not want to drive the Italian dictator into an alliance with Hitler by imposing tough sanctions on Italy. Sanctions were imposed too little, too late.

> **Comments** Britain and France may have felt some guilt that they were imperialist powers trying to stop Italy building up its own Empire. In the end they got the worst of all worlds: Abyssinia was seized; the world's smaller nations despised them; and Italy and Germany made an alliance.

**Q2** Hitler would have learnt that if you were going to break the rules of international behaviour, the League would not stop you if you went ahead and took no notice. This was particularly the case if you were a strong nation.

> **Comments** Hitler could see that Britain and France – the only countries with the economic and military power to give the League some 'teeth' – usually did what they wanted, in a crisis, not what the League wanted.

**Q3** The cartoonist is critical of the League – he calls it a doormat. He shows the Japanese walking over the League's body into its building in Geneva. The diplomats try to save some of the reputation of the League with cosmetics.

> **Comments** Japan should really be shown walking out of the building because it merely left when the League criticised it. The cartoonist has shown the Japanese treading on the 'Honour of the League'.

## 4 Hitler and the causes of the Second World War (page 121)

**Q1** At (*a*), the Rhineland, he sent in soldiers in 1936. This was supposed to be a demilitarised zone.

At (*b*), he took over Austria in 1938, the Anschluss, by a mixture of threats and force.

> **Comments** Both these actions were against the terms of the Treaty of Versailles. Hitler had long condemned the Treaty and many Germans agreed with him.

**Q1b** Over the Rhineland, he was just showing that he was master of his own country. Over Austria, he was determined to unite the two German-speaking countries.

> **Comments** In both cases, he was serving notice that he was not going to observe the terms of the Treaty of Versailles. We might assume the joining of Austria and Germany in one state meant a lot to Hitler.
>
> He was, after all, born an Austrian. 1938 was his second attempt, following his threats in 1934 when he was forced to back down by Mussolini.
>
> It is worth noting just how weak Hitler felt in 1934 and 1936, before he had built up his armies. By 1939 he was prepared to take on the French army and regarded the Italian Army with contempt.

**Q1c** Over the Rhineland, he was clever in seizing the opportunity of other European countries being absorbed in the Abyssinia affair, and France being paralysed by being in the middle of a general election campaign.

Over Austria, he was much more calculated. After 1934 he knew he had to get Mussolini on his side. His armed forces were also stronger by four years' growth and he could now steamroller Schuschnigg when Schuschnigg tried to defy him.

**Comments** The re-occupation of the Rhineland was a huge risk – he would have looked very silly if anyone had kicked up a fuss. It was a calculated risk: he was clever in choosing his moment, but slightly lucky in getting away with it.

Over Austria we can see the results of clever planning: the Rome–Berlin Axis, the added strength of Germany's forces.

**Q2** Hitler was moving towards a war in Europe from the moment he came to power in 1933. But he was not solely to blame: there are other factors.

The League of Nations was supposed to keep the peace, and it was seriously undermined before Hitler even became Chancellor. Several nations, including the USA, share the blame for this.

Nor was Hitler to blame for the terms of the Treaty of Versailles, which led so many Germans to want revenge, a feeling Hitler was able to use.

**Comments** Britain and France failed to act to stop Hitler. They were torn between their duty to work within the League and their wish to follow their own interests. Their failure to work together to find a way of halting Hitler means they both have a share in causing the war. There is also the matter of appeasement (see revision session 5), which may have led Hitler into thinking that he could get away with aggressive actions without their leading to war.

## 5 Appeasement (page 124)

**Q1(i)** Hitler was trying to create an excuse for invading Czechoslovakia by stirring up trouble in the Sudetenland. Then Chamberlain asked for a meeting. Hitler was cooperative at first but then thought he might be able to force Chamberlain to let him have the Sudetenland without a war. Chamberlain agreed to this at Munich, provided Hitler signed a piece of paper promising not to go to war. Hitler signed, with no intention of keeping his promise.

**Comments** Remember that Hitler had no idea why Chamberlain wanted to meet him. Chamberlain was quite an old man; air travel was unusual. What did he want?

At Munich, Hitler was able to put on a show of anger, having to go to war to defend Germany's pride etc. He played on Chamberlain's fear of war and guilt over the terms of the Versailles Treaty brilliantly.

**Q1(ii)** Czechoslovakia was now severely weakened. It was easy to capture the country.

**Comments** This was a deep shock to Chamberlain: all he had worked for was in vain.

**Q1(iii)** Poland was next and Hitler needed breathing space to capture Poland. Britain and France would not lift a finger for Poland – after all they had done nothing over the re-occupation of the Rhineland, Mussolini's invasion of Abyssinia, the Anschluss. But it was necessary to square things with the USSR. They could agree to carve up Poland between them, hence the Nazi–Soviet Pact.

**Comments** The Nazi–Soviet Pact was the end of all the idealism of the inter-war years: here were two real enemies sinking their differences to carve up a weaker neighbour. They were just as bad as the pre-1914 nations.

**Q1(iv)** Poland was invaded, but, to Hitler's surprise, Britain and France declared war.

**Comments** This is the moment Hitler makes a miscalculation: he was going to have to fight in the west before invading Russia. But, thanks to the Nazi–Soviet Pact, he wasn't going to have to fight a two-front war, like the Kaiser's generals did in 1914.

**Q2** The reason Chamberlain gave for appeasement was that he wanted peace. Most British people felt the same and this is why Chamberlain was given a hero's welcome when he returned from Munich.

He also had information which could not be made public. The first was that war would bring huge casualties to the civilian population. Chamberlain was thus even less ready to consider war. The second was that Britain was simply not ready to fight a war.

Some people in Britain also thought that the real menace to Europe was Stalin and Communism. Some even approved of Hitler as a bulwark against Stalin. There was also an unwillingness to go to war for a distant country.

Comments The secret reasons are not unreasonable considerations and Chamberlain did start to make hurried preparations for war. You could argue he gained Britain 12 months. In fact, the experts were wrong and casualties were not that serious but Chamberlain could not have known that in 1938, of course.

Any judgement that puts Stalin or Hitler one above the other is at fault. There were plenty of people in Britain who apologised for Hitler, although Chamberlain himself was not one of them.

## UNIT 9: THE COLD WAR

### 1 The origins of the Cold War (page 128)

**Q1a** Only one party allowed, the Communist Party.

Comments The Communists still called this one-party system democracy. Elections were held, and debate took place inside the Communist Party rather than between parties. This confusion over the meaning of democracy was one of the key misunderstandings of the early days of the Cold War.

**Q1b** Capitalism. That is, all economic activity is owned and run by private individuals. They seek to make a profit from supplying what the public wants at a price the public will pay.

**Q1c** Communism. The state owns and runs all economic activity. Factories make what the state planners tell them to make, at a price fixed by the state.

Comments The description here applies to the USA (**A1b**) and the USSR (**A1c**). There are other forms of capitalism and Communism.

In several Western European countries, for example, capitalists are less free to do what they like and the state owns some businesses. Other Communist states are not so centralised as the USSR. It was the stifling of personal initiative and freedom which led to the failure of Soviet Communism.

**Q1d** More personal freedom. Owners of businesses – capitalists – have freedom to run their businesses how they like. People have freedom to travel. The press and TV criticise the government freely. There is less censorship.

Comments This freedom also includes the freedom to sack workers, to pay low wages and to make their people poor and homeless. State control of economic activity in Communist states prevented these things from happening.

### 2 The beginning of the Cold War (page 132)

**Q1** The USA, because it was by far the richest and had the atom bomb.

Comments It is clear, with hindsight, that this is right. The USSR was never really in the same league as the USA and the standard of living of its people was far below that of US citizens. However, it was not as clear as this in 1945. The huge Red Army had defeated the German army and lay across half of Europe. Its planes and tanks had proved superior. It is easy to see why they seemed more equal then.

**Q2** Western countries had tried to crush the Bolshevik government by helping Whites in 1918 in the Civil War. Western powers had refused to let the USSR join the League of Nations until 1934 and treated them as outcasts in the 1930s. Stalin thought some people in the West actually wanted Hitler to attack the USSR rather than Western Europe. Stalin thought the Western Allies had refused to open up a second front so that the USSR had borne the brunt of Hitler's invasion.

**Comments** All these were partly true: some leading figures in Britain openly preferred Hitler to Stalin, although it was never British government policy to nudge Hitler away from the West towards Russia: he always intended to invade Russia anyway.

**Q3** There were different people at Potsdam from Yalta: Attlee replaced Churchill; Truman replaced Roosevelt. Roosevelt had got on better with Stalin than Truman did.

Stalin was annoyed and worried by the US atom bomb test, partly because the USA had not shared their nuclear know-how and partly from fear of a US nuclear attack.

Truman was angry about the Soviet takeover of Eastern Europe, setting up puppet governments, ignoring the wishes of the people, and forcing communism on them.

**Comments** At Yalta, in February, the war was not over and the Allies still had to work together to defeat Germany. By July, at Potsdam, the war in Europe was over. The statesmen were more concerned to look forward to the peace and new rivalries emerged.

## 3 Truman Doctrine, containment and the Berlin Airlift (page 135)

**Q1** Armed minorities; outside pressure.

**Comments** Perhaps Truman had Greece in mind for the first, where armed Greek Communists were fighting to take over the country. Britain's inability to go on opposing them was the occasion for Truman making this speech. For 'outside pressure' he would have been thinking of all the countries of Eastern Europe, pressured by the USSR into setting up Communist-controlled governments.

**Q2** It was a helping hand to Europe, but that is not the whole story. It was also motivated by a fear that Communism flourished in conditions of poverty and desperation. A revived Europe would be able to resist Communism better.

**Comments** This answer is right as far as it goes. There was idealism, a 'helping hand'. There was also a real fear in the West at this time that Western Europe would soon join Eastern Europe in the Communist camp. However, US business did stand to gain, even if Stalin's complaint about the spread of worldwide capitalism was unjustified. They remembered the Wall Street Crash, caused mainly by over-production (see p101) and realised that the USA had to develop markets in other countries to avoid another depression.

**Q3** The Berlin Airlift is an example of Cold War because the USA and the Allies avoided direct confrontation with the USSR when they might have tried to bust through the Soviet blockade.

**Comments** The USSR also avoided direct confrontation by not attacking any of the planes in the airlift. They may have thought it was impossible to supply a big city by air, but they did not try to stop it.

## 4 Containment around the world: Korea (page 138)

**Q1** The victory of Mao Zedong and the Chinese Communists in 1949 affected US Cold War policy in several ways. It made the USA feel it was losing the fight against Communism. This was the climate in which McCarthyism was able to flourish. It made the USA realise that the Cold War was going to be worldwide, not confined to Europe. This led them into the Korean War and, later, into the Vietnam War.

**Comments** At first China just followed the Soviet line but after 1960, when they split from the USSR, Chinese Communism complicated the Cold War issues. It meant that there were now two types of Communism. The Chinese Communists had won the civil war and were undeniably popular. This ran counter to what Truman had said about Communism in his speech about the Truman Doctrine (see p133). It was hard for the USA to accept that some people could voluntarily want a Communist government.

**Q2** In the early 1950s it was a patriotic duty to oppose Communism. McCarthy posed as a great patriot, weeding out these foreign agents. It seemed unpatriotic to oppose him.

He got lots of favourable publicity. If you tried to oppose him, or question him, you got bad publicity. People were frightened to lose their jobs – this was especially true of Hollywood actors, producers and scriptwriters, who were looking for work. Film company bosses refused to hire those people McCarthy had named.

**Comments** McCarthy's accusations were lies and suggestions, not hard facts. It is easier to show that facts are untrue than to disprove a rumour. He was dealing with attitudes: was it 'Un-American' to be an admirer of the USSR? McCarthy was very popular from 1950–54. Many people made their name supporting him including a lawyer, Richard Nixon, and an anti-Communist actor, Ronald Reagan (both of whom later became Presidents).

**Q3** Truman and MacArthur disagreed over US war policy in Korea. MacArthur wanted to tackle the Chinese, who were helping North Korea. He wanted all-out war, perhaps including nuclear weapons, against China. MacArthur felt that there was a real opportunity for the USA to win the Cold War in the East.

Truman felt that to extend the war was going beyond simply containing Communism. The war was also a UN action, not just a US one. To go on to attack China was going far beyond what the UN had agreed.

**Comments** Here again we see leaders in the Cold War declaring a limit on how far they are prepared to go. Although the USA had the power, Truman was not prepared to use it aggressively. Note that MacArthur had tremendous support in the USA.

## 5 Containment around the world: the arms race (page 141)

**Q1a** The USA sees the USSR as a big Russian bear trying to seize the whole world.

**Comments** Remember to look hard at these cartoons: nothing is drawn by accident. Perhaps it is important that the bear is about to grab Africa in this cartoon. The bear has the star of the Soviet Army on its cap.

**Q1b** The USSR sees US military might as big and ugly, moving nearer to the USSR.

The airbases are all pointing at the USSR, threatening it.

The big cartoon soldier has dollars sticking out of his pocket. To the USSR, US loans, like Marshall Aid, were just another way of threatening the USSR.

The cartoon shows US politicians as just little creatures, talking away while the soldiers do what they like. Their words like 'Peace', etc. are meaningless.

**Comments** Note the date: in 1952 nuclear weapons were still being delivered to their targets by big bombers, so having bases near to the enemy was important. NATO is shown as just a way of getting US airbases nearer and nearer to the USSR. Everything in the cartoon is designed to show the USA as big, aggressive, rich, armed, moving ever closer to the USSR. It is saying that the USA says one thing but its armed forces do quite the opposite.

**Q1c** Both sides thought the other was trying to take over the world. Both sides claimed to be acting only peacefully, in their own defence. Both sides claimed the other was being aggressive.

**Comments** This answer is too closely based just on the cartoons. Note that the question asks you (i) to add some of your own knowledge, and (ii) to explain why the Cold War went on so long.

Under (i) you could mention the Soviet takeover of Eastern Europe in 1945–8, the growth of NATO, SEATO, CENTO, Korea, Berlin. Under (ii) the point to make is that both sides thought the other was hell-bent on destroying them. They dared not let up for fear of being defeated and so were locked in a spiral of aggression in which the arms race was a big part.

**Q2** Saving money was one of President Eisenhower's reasons for developing US nuclear weapons in the 1950s because they were cheaper than ordinary weapons.

Kennedy's claims of a 'missile gap' helped him win the 1960 presidential election; it was useful to him in making his opponent look as if he was not defending the USA properly.

Both the missile gap under Kennedy and the bomber gap under Eisenhower were mistakes; neither existed.

There were military reasons for each of the turning-points: the Soviet A-bomb meant the USA had to develop a more powerful bomb, the H-bomb; the change from bomber-aeroplane-delivered bombs to missile-delivered warheads were all military issues.

**Comments** Eisenhower's decision to build nuclear weapons is a rare example of trying to save money. Mostly, the arms race mopped up vast amounts of money. It was Eisenhower himself who complained about the power of the 'military-industrial complex'. Such vast amounts of money were involved that both the companies who built the planes, missiles and bombs, and the armed forces that ordered them and used them had a vested interest in the arms race continuing. Large numbers of jobs were involved too; an end to the arms race would mean huge adjustments to the US and Soviet economies.

It is open to debate whether the politicians really thought there were 'gaps' or whether they just used the idea as a stunt. It is possible that advisers from the armed forces persuaded the politicians there was a 'gap' in order to get them to spend more money on weapons.

## 6 Khrushchev, Kennedy and Cuba (page 145)

**Q1a** This picture was taken by a US spy-plane.

**Comments** The U2 was the same type of plane that was shot down over the USSR in 1960. It flew very high, over 15 km up, but could take accurate photographs, as you can see. Nowadays, satellites are used to do this kind of spying.

**Q1b** It alarmed Kennedy and his advisers because it showed that Soviet missile bases were being erected on Cuba. Soviet missiles launched from Cuba could hit almost every city in the USA.

**Comments** Soviet missiles on Cuba did not really make that much military difference: US cities were already within range of Soviet long-range missiles. However, they were a great propaganda advance for the USSR. Ever since the 1820s the USA had expected every country in both the Americas to be an ally. Cuba breached this policy, called the 'Monroe Doctrine'. The missiles just made it worse.

**Q2** Kennedy did very well out of the crisis because he forced Khrushchev to withdraw his missiles from Cuba.

Khrushchev did well because he got the USA to agree not to attack Cuba.

Kennedy could claim that he won because the Soviet missiles were withdrawn from Cuba. He discovered that the USSR was building missile sites on Cuba on 16 October 1962. The missiles were not yet in place, but some were already at sea in Soviet ships. He ordered US ships to impose a blockade on Cuba and told his armed forces to be ready for nuclear war. On 28 October Khrushchev agreed to send the missiles home and dismantle the sites.

However, he had not succeeded in removing the pro-Soviet government of Cuba, which stayed there as a permanent propaganda victory for Communism in the Americas. He had also taken the world to the brink of nuclear destruction, although he must share the blame for this with Khrushchev.

Khrushchev could claim that he won because he had kept Cuba as an ally in the Americas. He had made the USA promise not to attack Cuba and it now stood as an example of anti-capitalism to other American countries.

However, he had not succeeded in keeping his missiles in Cuba. If he had, he would have improved the Soviet position in the arms race. They were well behind in numbers of long-range missiles but the use of a base so close to US territory would have allowed the USSR to use short-range missiles, of which it had plenty.

My conclusion is that Kennedy made sure that the USA stayed ahead in the arms race, but that Khrushchev ensured the survival of Castro. The real gain was that both leaders made some moves towards avoiding such serious near-wars in the future by setting up the 'hotline' in 1963 between the White House and the Kremlin, and by banning some nuclear testing.

**Comments** You have written a good short essay here, by combining three stages: ideas + facts + a plan. All three of these elements are necessary for an effective essay-answer. You will have to do this for yourself in an exam, of course. Notice how the opening sentence of each paragraph, which you were given, helps you organise your answer, as you hang all the little points you want to make under it.

Khrushchev might receive more blame than you have given him for putting the missiles on Cuba in the first place. He did not try to hide them and he should have known it was bound to cause an angry American reaction. However, he might receive more credit for having the courage to back down on 28 October and pull back his missiles. It is easier to be tough than to give way in these situations. Kennedy got lots of praise in the West (which he refused to acknowledge, to his credit), for forcing Khrushchev to back down. However, he did take the world to the edge of nuclear annihilation in order to get his way.

## 7 Vietnam and the end of containment (page 150)

**Q1a** This American thinks that although North Vietnam sees the war as just a war to conquer South Vietnam, to China it was a war to take over both Vietnams and then all of South-East Asia.

**Q1b** The Domino Theory was an American idea that the little countries of South-East Asia would become Communist one by one. That is, a Communist victory in one would only lead them to move on to the next. Source I sees this expansion of Communism as all coming from China.

**Comments** This source is a brief outline of US motives for pouring so much money and so many US lives into Vietnam: it was the point where Communism was to stop in Asia, the Vietnam domino was not to be allowed to fall. In fact, North Vietnam got far more supplies from the USSR than from China. Relations between the two were never good and China invaded Vietnam briefly in 1979.

**Q2a** General Giap was the North Vietnamese commander. A genius at guerrilla warfare, he had defeated the French, the South Vietnamese and the Americans.

**Q2b** By a 'people's war', General Giap meant a war in which all the people are involved. This was essential for the kind of guerrilla warfare he was waging, because his soldiers depended on the support of the people to hide them, supply them, keep them informed, etc.

**Comments** Giap's kind of war was the same as Mao Zedong had fought in China from the 1930s until his eventual victory in 1949. Both were 'people's wars' and in both cases Communist forces defeated much stronger but conventional opposition armies because of their support from the people. In both cases this support was partly because of national feeling, partly because the Communists promised to give the peasants more land.

**Q3** The USA failed to win the 'hearts and minds' of the Vietnamese people because of how they carried out the war. Faced with opponents, the Vietcong, using guerrilla warfare, the US commanders used mass bombing, chemical warfare and destroyed villages. They were also supporting a corrupt government which did not have the support of the people.

**Comments** The war in Vietnam was really all about the hearts and minds of the Vietnamese people because it was supposed to be about beliefs and ideas, not power. The USA believed that their form of capitalist democracy was better than Communism and that people, given a real free choice, would choose it. Their failure in Vietnam was therefore not just a blow to US power but it undermined the basis of their Cold War ideology.

In Europe, in the 1940s, the USSR did take over countries and force Communism on them. This was the basis of the US sense of outrage at what the USSR was doing and the policy of 'containment'. By the 1960s, on the other side of the world, containment had simply come to mean resisting Communism wherever it cropped up, even if, unlike in Eastern Europe, it had popular support, and even if it meant supporting undemocratic, corrupt and unpopular governments.

## 8 Détente (page 153)

**Q1a** In source 1, Kennedy is committing the USA to unlimited intervention in the world. In source 2, Nixon is saying that there were limits on what the USA would do now.

**Comments** The two speeches are like mirror-images of each other. Probably Nixon had Kennedy's famous speech in mind when he made his own, deliberately opposite, speech.

**Q1b** The main thing that had happened was the Vietnam war. US intervention in this war, using massive amounts of resources and men arises from Kennedy's declaration in source 1. However, more commitment to 'pay any price, etc.' had not brought the USA victory. Not only had they been defeated, but their judgement of the situation had been wrong. In Vietnam, Communism was popular and the government the USA was fighting to prop up was undemocratic, corrupt and unpopular. Three hundred US soldiers were dying each week at the height of the war in 1968.

**Comments** In future, as Nixon says, the USA will not be so ready to assume that it should take the lead and jump in.

Whether you consider the cost, in money, or in lives, the atrocities, the defeat, the loss of 'moral high ground', Vietnam was very difficult for the USA to handle.

**Q2** The USA made an effort to make friends with China in the 1970s partly to drive a wedge between China and the USSR and prevent them making friends, partly also because China was a powerful influence in the Far East, where the USA had big interests.

**Comments** Another reason for friendship with China might be to open up trade opportunities with such a vast country. Further, China was very powerful, with the world's largest population and the world's biggest army. Some were arguing that it was a third superpower. It could not be ignored.

**Q3** There was some slowing down in the arms race: tension between the two sides lessened, so ordinary people may have felt less in danger of nuclear war.

**Comments** In fact, spending on arms continued to rise throughout the détente years. Apart from an improved mood of conciliation it is hard to see what all the effort put into détente achieved.

## 9 The USSR in Eastern Europe (page 157)

**Q1** The Hungarian revolt was about personal freedom; the Czech revolt was more about standards of living; while the Polish, Solidarity, protest was entirely economic.

**Comments** None of these was as clear-cut as this. The Hungarian revolt of 1956 was motivated by resentment over low standards of living, although their demands were mainly political. In Czechoslovakia the two elements were combined. The Solidarity protest seems purely economic, but lack of political freedom drove the protest to take the form it did.

**Q2** The Brezhnev Doctrine said that no Warsaw Pact member should have multi-party government or leave the Warsaw Pact. The 'Prague Spring' protest in Czechoslovakia did not demand either of these things.

**Comments** The Czech reformers indeed set out specifically to avoid breaking these two principles. The problem, for Brezhnev and the other hardline Communist leaders of Eastern Europe, was that their reforms looked as if they might lead eventually to more radical changes.

**Q3** The Czechs learned that they should not try to introduce multi-party democracy or try to leave the Warsaw Pact and become neutral. These were seen as the two factors which had led Khrushchev to send the tanks into Hungary in 1956. The Czechs emphasised that they were all loyal Communists and would remain so.

**Comments** The Poles carefully avoided making any political protest at all, trying to avoid the Czechs' problems.

What Brezhnev and his allies most feared was change and popular protest. Whatever they said, they were bound to see it as a threat and try to crush it. Solidarity lasted longest because its appeal was to the material well-being of the working classes – the very group the Communist Party was supposed to look after.

## 10 The end of the Cold War (page 161)

**Q1** The arms race ended in two arms reduction treaties following the Gorbachev/Reagan talks in Reykjavik in 1986. The INF Treaty, 1987, reduced medium-range missiles; START, 1991, reduced several kinds of missiles, including long-range missiles. In both cases Gorbachev offered more reductions than Reagan. This willingness on his part to make big concessions meant the treaties were quickly negotiated.

**Comments** The speed with which Reagan and Gorbachev reached agreement contrasts with the long drawn out SALT negotiations of the détente period in the 1970s. At that time, both sides may have wanted arms reduction, but neither was willing to see a deal that gave any advantage to the other side.

In the INF Treaty, the USSR gave up 3,000 warheads, the USA 800. In START, the USSR gave up 5,000 warheads and the USA 3,500. These were big concessions on Gorbachev's part, but he thought it was worth it because if the Cold War came to an end he would have more money to spend on changes in the USSR.

**Q2** Perestroika was restructuring. This meant dismantling the whole apparatus of state control of the Soviet economy that Stalin had set up with the Five-Year Plans. He wanted a free market economy, in which production levels and prices (both of which had been set by the government before) would be decided simply by what goods factories could make at a price the customers would pay.

In order that this economic freedom could flourish, there had to be political freedom, openness – glasnost. This meant free elections, free speech and a free press.

**Comments** The fact that Communism was dismantling itself and choosing to turn the USSR into a capitalist state was seen by many as the West having 'won' the Cold War.

The idea of a free society, with a free market, like in the West, may have been a good one. The problem was getting from a highly-controlled state economy to a free market one, with a population which had no experience of it. The problems of the change are still making life in Russia very difficult. Not surprisingly, many people in the late 1990s now look back on the Communist era with some affection.

**Q3** The end of the Cold War was popular in the West as it removed the threat of another major war which had been hanging over people's lives since 1945. Gorbachev was seen as a hero who had rejected the USSR's past and was trying to give it a Western system.

**Comments** In Eastern Europe, which had never really accepted Communism, the changes were also popular. It was the hero's welcome that Gorbachev received in East Germany in 1989 which led them to realise that the old system was on the way out.

# UNIT 10: HOW TO ANSWER EXAM QUESTIONS

## (Questions to try)

**Q5** This picture shows how deeply the Depression affected the USA. In just one part of New York several dozen people are queueing for bread handouts. It shows that charities were ready to help the unemployed by handing out free bread and it reminds us that there was no dole or welfare system in the USA, so people who lost their job were utterly dependent on what they had saved, if anything, and on charity.

### WHAT MAKES THIS A *GOOD* ANSWER?

- *This answer relates the visible evidence of the source to the wider issue quite well. It points out that there are large numbers of people queueing, so the Depression was widespread. It notes that charities were providing the assistance that was given by the state in other countries.*
- *It could have mentioned that the queue is orderly, showing that the people of the USA accepted their fate. However, with only 4 marks available, examiners are not looking for every possible point to be made.*

**Q6** This poster tells the German people that only Hitler can help them now. The people on the poster look desperate, poor and worried and the Nazis are claiming to be the only ones with a solution to their problems. The Depression and unemployment following the Wall Street Crash in 1929 was serious in Germany, whose economy relied on loans from the USA. By 1932, the date of this poster, there were 6 million unemployed. Before the Depression, support for the Nazis was low and no one seemed to be interested in their remedies. Hitler took advantage of Germany's desperate situation. He told the German people that the Weimar system was bound to fail and only he could solve their problems. He came a good second in the Presidential elections of 1932 and nearly doubled the number of Nazis in the Reichstag.

### WHAT MAKES THIS A *GOOD* ANSWER?

- *The writer analyses the poster well, commenting on its mood as well as its words.*
- *It only offers recalled information on the Depression and Germany and how Hitler used the situation. This has been well selected and shows accurate knowledge of the chronology.*
- *It relates both the poster and the information to how and why Hitler gained support.*

**Q9** Source A shows boys lined up in uniform. One boy is giving the Nazi salute as he swears an oath and holds the flag. It is a propaganda photo, but may be quite an accurate record of what happened. It is therefore quite reliable and shows a bit of the ceremony.

Source B is an adult's comment on the Hitler Youth. It is hard to judge its reliability: perhaps she thought this all along, perhaps she only said this in 1945, either just before or just after the end of the war, when Nazism was discredited. If it was not just designed to give an impression of anti-Nazism then it is quite useful as evidence of the propaganda nature of the Hitler Youth.

I think Source A is more useful: it shows that the Hitler Youth went in for ritual, tried to make everyone look alike and be utterly loyal to the Nazis, but Source B does help us understand that some Germans had doubts about it all.

### WHAT MAKES THIS A *GOOD* ANSWER?

- *Both sources are commented on fully.*
- *A judgement is made ('Source A is more useful'), with some reasoning behind it.*
- *The last paragraph really concentrates on use. It gets to the heart of the question and doesn't waste time simply telling the examiner what is in the sources.*

**Q11** Source A describes the situation in Petrograd. Rodzianko describes food and fuel shortages leading to riots. The troops were unreliable. There was a feeling that a new government was needed. Source A shows Tsar Nicholas' reply, ignoring Source A and showing his contempt for Rodzianko. Nicholas disliked the Duma and all it stood for, even though it was far from fully democratic.

In fact, Rodzianko was right: within days there was a revolution. Nicholas was deposed and a Provisional Government set up.

Nicholas has brought this on himself, not only by his ignoring good advice in 1917, but ever since he had become Tsar in 1896. He was out of touch with his people, so had little idea of the hardships of the workers, the difficulties of the peasants. He despised democracy and used his power to weaken the Duma set up after the 1917 revolution. His secret police suppressed all opposition.

It is therefore largely true that Nicholas was responsible for his own downfall. However, it was the First World War that pushed Russia over the edge. Nicholas must take the blame for the defeats and the problems that it caused in Russia which led to the revolution, but he was not responsible for the war.

### WHAT MAKES THIS A *GOOD* ANSWER?

- *This answer is very clearly planned. It moves from the sources to recalled information about Nicholas, selected around the issue of whether he was to blame for his own downfall, and deployed accurately.*
- *The conclusion doesn't fall in with the statement and agree that Nicholas was responsible for his own downfall, it offers some explanation of factors beyond his control.*

### Other possible points to include

*There was not much Nicholas could have done, given the system of rule in Russia before 1914. Everyone around him was opposed to democracy and Russian society was backward. For more on this, see unit 5.*

**Q12** British and French policy towards Hitler went through a complete change between September 1938 and September 1939, as this question suggests. In order to understand why this happened we need to look at why the agreement was made in 1938 and what happened afterwards.

Czechoslovakia had been set up in 1919, with a large German-speaking minority, in the area bordering Germany and Austria called the Sudetenland. Hitler had always said he resented the fact that there were Germans living outside Germany and that he intended to re-unite them with the 'Fatherland', as he called it. He probably knew that this could involve Germany in war sooner or later and had made preparations for a war by re-arming his country ever since he came to power in 1933. In 1938 Nazis in the Sudetenland began to stir up trouble, probably asked to do so by Hitler. He could then pose as the protector of his fellow-Germans and threatened to invade the Sudetenland. Czechoslovakia prepared for war.

The leaders of Britain and France viewed these events with horror. The policy of the British Prime Minister, Neville Chamberlain, was called appeasement. In his view the Treaty of Versailles had caused lots of problems by making Germans like Hitler look for revenge. Britain had already allowed Hitler to break the terms of the Treaty in several ways: by marching into the Rhineland in 1936, by the Anschluss with Austria in 1938, and by re-arming. It was Chamberlain's belief that Hitler had genuine grievances but that once these were settled by giving him what he asked for ('appeased'), peace would follow. France at that time was weak and disunited, so Chamberlain took the initiative.

As war over Czechoslovakia threatened, Chamberlain took the unusual step – at that time, and for a man of his age (he was 70) – of flying to meet Hitler. To many British people like Chamberlain the memory of the First World War was still strong and this led them to look for peace at almost any cost. Hitler could see that he might be able to bluff his way to getting the Sudetenland without fighting, so stepped up his demands. Chamberlain flew to a meeting at Munich in September 1938. The Czech government did not take part and Britain, France, Italy and Germany agreed that Hitler could take over the Sudetenland. Czechoslovakia was left virtually defenceless.

In return for the Sudetenland, Hitler promised that he had 'no more territorial demands to make in Europe'. Chamberlain regarded this as a triumph for his appeasement policy, claiming it was 'peace in our time'. So the agreement of September 1938, referred to in the question, was reached.

Obviously Chamberlain totally misunderstood Hitler. To Chamberlain a promise was a promise; to Hitler it was just a step on his path to what he wanted. In March 1939, only 6 months later, Hitler sent troops into most of the rest of Czechoslovakia, including the capital city Prague. Chamberlain's hopes for peace were in ruins.

However, Hitler also misunderstood Chamberlain. Hitler now thought that Britain would never go to war to stop him. He prepared to take over his next victim, Poland. Chamberlain could see that Poland would be next and made an agreement to go to war if it was invaded. Hitler's main concern in taking over Poland was not Britain, but the USSR, which was much nearer. In fact, the USSR was also interested in taking Polish territory. So, in August 1939, although they were bitter enemies and Hitler had always stated his hatred for Communism and his intention of invading Russia, the Nazi–Soviet Pact was signed. In September 1939 German troops invaded Poland. Chamberlain stuck to the terms of his agreement with Poland and, to Hitler's surprise, declared war in Germany.

At the time, Chamberlain swung from huge popularity in 1938, when he seemed to have avoided war, to ridicule and contempt when he was seen to have been completely taken in by Hitler. However, he did stick by his agreement with Poland and the Munich agreement did gain Britain 12 months of valuable extra preparation time for war.

## WHAT MAKES THIS A *GOOD* ANSWER?

- *The third paragraph gets to the heart of the double explanation: appeasement and determination to avoid war.*
- *The whole essay hangs together: it all contributes to an answer to the question, with nothing irrelevant, or just there to show you know all the dates and facts. The dates and facts are deployed to fit the plan, not the other way round.*

Published by HarperCollins*Publishers* Ltd
77-85 Fulham Palace Road
London W6 8JB

www.CollinsEducation.com
On-line support for schools and colleges



First published 2003

ISBN 0 00 720902 9



**British Library Cataloguing in Publication Data**
A catalogue record for this book is available from the British Library.

Edited by Steve Attmore
Production by Jack Murphy
Design by Sally Boothroyd
Printed and bound by Printing Express, Hong Kong

**Acknowledgements**
The Author and Publishers are grateful to the following for permission to reproduce photographs (T = Top, B = Bottom, C = Centre, L = Left, R = Right):
Bettman/Corbis 92
Bildarchiv Preussischer Kulturbesitz 44, 51, 60, 169
Deutsches Historisches Museum 34
Mary Evans Picture Library 6T
Hulton Archive/Getty Images 1B, 6B, 25L, 25C, 25R, 49, 62, 70, 72, 99, 100, 110, 129, 143
The Trustees of the Imperial War Museum, London 11, 16, 17, 18L, 18C, 18R, 24, 31, 41, 48, 122, 125, 155
David King 63T, 63B, 66, 73, 86, 89
Peter Newark's Pictures 94, 97
Novosti 64, 78, 170, 172
Novosti/Gamma/Katz 160
Popperfoto 55, 152, 162
Rex Features 71
The Royal Archives © Her Majesty Queen Elizabeth II 1T
Süddeutscher Verlag 32, 52
TimePix 79
Topham Picturepoint 106, 121, 168
Wiener Library 174

**Illustrations**
Gecko Ltd: pp. 8, 11, 14, 37, 61, 137, 175
Jerry Fowler: pp. 40, 41, 56, 101, 110, 112, 127, 151
Jillian Luff: pp. 9, 13, 27, 75, 76, 83, 115, 117, 119, 130, 134, 143, 146, 167
Julia Osorno: p. 147

Every effort has been made to contact the holders of copyright material, but if any have been inadvertently overlooked, the Publishers will be pleased to make the necessary arrangements at the first opportunity.